Buddhism in America

The Columbia Contemporary American Religion Series

Columbia Contemporary American Religion Series

The United States is the birthplace of religious pluralism, and the spiritual landscape of contemporary America is as varied and complex as that of any country in the world. The books in this new series, written by leading scholars for students and general readers alike, fall into two categories: some of these well-crafted, thought-provoking portraits of the country's major religious groups describe and explain particular religious practices and rituals, beliefs, and major challenges facing a given community today. Others explore current themes and topics in American religion that cut across denominational lines. The texts are supplemented with carefully selected photographs and artwork, annotated bibliographies, concise profiles of important individuals, and chronologies of major events.

—

Roman Catholicism in America
CHESTER GILLIS

Islam in America
JANE I. SMITH

BUDDHISM

in America

Richard Hughes Seager

COLUMBIA UNIVERSITY PRESS

NEW YORK

COLUMBIA UNIVERSITY PRESS
Publishers Since 1893
New York   Chichester, West Sussex

Copyright © 1999 Columbia University Press
Library of Congress Cataloging-in-Publication Data
Seager, Richard Hughes.
    Buddhism in America / Richard Hughes Seager.
        p.   cm. — (Columbia contemporary American religion series)
    Includes bibliographical references and index.
    ISBN 0-231-10868-0
    1. Buddhism—United States. I. Title. II. Series.
BQ732.S43   1999
294.3'0973—dc21   98-52755

⊗

Casebound editions of Columbia University Press books are
printed on permanent and durable acid-free paper.
Printed in the United States of America
c 10 9 8 7 6 5 4 3 2 1

For Ann

CONTENTS

INTRODUCTION

This work is no exception to the general rule that all books are shaped by the experience, interest, and training of their authors. In a book for general readership, there is no call for extensive reflection on methodology or a lengthy examination of the contributions of earlier scholars. But brief attention to how the study of American Buddhism has developed in the last few decades helps to set in perspective the basic historical and interpretive questions that run throughout this book.

Two decades ago, as a graduate student in the study of religion, I became interested in the history of the encounter between the religious traditions of East and West, after having studied Hinduism and Buddhism for several years. To pursue this interest, I entered a new Ph.D. program at Harvard University devoted to the study of religion in the modern West, with an emphasis on American religious history. There were a number of us in the program in its first few years with an interest in eastern religions, particularly Buddhism, but we soon found that there was very little scholarship devoted to its history in America, a topic that was only then beginning to emerge as significant.

Early on, we relied on a few new interpretive works such as Robert S. Ellwood's *Alternative Altars: Unconventional and Eastern Spirituality in America* (1979), which focuses largely on selected developments in the counterculture, and Tetsuden Kashima's *Buddhism in America* (1977), which treats the history of the Jodo Shinshu tradition of old-line Japanese immigrants. More inclusive treatments of the contemporary Buddhist scene could be found in Emma Layman's *Buddhism in America* (1976) and Charles Prebish's *American Buddhism* (1979).

A great deal changed with the publication of Rick Fields's *How the Swans Came to the Lake* in 1981. *Swans* combined well-understood developments in the East-West encounter in the nineteenth century, such as the interest of the Transcendentalists in Asian spirituality and the emergence of popular movements like Theosophy, with new research on pioneering Zen teachers in the early and mid-twentieth century. Fields linked these and other developments with the burgeoning interest in Buddhism in the 1960s counterculture to develop a plausible, and highly readable, historical narrative. I can still recall the excitement that the publication of *Swans* generated among the small clutch of Americanists who were interested in these matters. And I know for a fact that we repeatedly scoured it for new data and hints as to how to proceed with our own studies, even though we knew that, as a general readership book published by a commercial press, it did not quite meet the formal academic standards demanded by the American Historical Association.

Within several years, however, important shortcomings of Fields's book became apparent. In particular, Fields developed his entire discussion to account for how a generation of cultural revolutionaries in search of alternative spirituality found their way to Buddhism. In effect, he gave countercultural Buddhists a sense of their own indigenous Buddhist lineage. But by the mid-1980s, the importance of changes in immigration law made in 1965 became clear to all observers as immigration from Asia soared and a wide range of Buddhist traditions began to take root in new immigrant communities. Despite revisions in subsequent editions, Fields's story of American Buddhism never satisfactorily factored in the arrival of this new, complex Buddhist cohort.

At that stage of the game, intellectuals within countercultural Buddhist communities and scholars trained in Asian Buddhist history, many of them practicing Buddhists, more or less picked up the ball as commentators on American Buddhism. During the 1980s and into the '90s, they explored a range of questions first raised by Prebish: What kind of commitment does it entail to call oneself an American Buddhist? What kinds of change ought to be made to Asian Buddhist traditions to adapt them to this country? Are there two American Buddhisms, one found among European Americans and another among immigrants? During these years, a number of new books were published that focused sustained attention on selected developments primarily associated with contemporary European American Buddhism, among them Jane Hurst's *Nichiren Shoshu Buddhism and the Soka Gakkai in America: The Ethos of a New Religious Movement* (1992) and Helen Tworkov's *Zen in*

America (1989). At the same time, popular religious publishing on Buddhism flourished, with more than a hundred titles produced in quick succession, reflecting the growing interest of Americans in Buddhism.

While these developments were taking place in and around contemporary Buddhism, those of us trained as Americanists published new works on Buddhism-related topics in the more established field of American religious history, focusing primarily on the nineteenth century. For instance, Thomas Tweed published *The American Encounter with Buddhism, 1844–1912* in 1992, answering important questions about how Americans at that time regarded philosophical Buddhism. I published two books on the World's Parliament of Religions of 1893, a much acclaimed but little studied event in the history of the East-West encounter in this country, one book in 1993, the other in 1995. Stephen Prothero published *The White Buddhist: The Asian Odyssey of Henry Steel Olcott* in 1996, the first critical study of the attitudes toward and contributions to Buddhism by a key figure in an earlier era during which Americans were fascinated with Asia. The first book-length study of current Buddhist immigration by a scholar trained in American religious history, *Old Wisdom in the New World: Americanization in Two Immigrant Theravada Buddhist Temples*, was published by Paul Numrich in the same year.

All this is to say that American Buddhism has grown immensely over the last few decades and critical reflection on it has grown as well, but in a very uneven fashion. At this writing, there is a good deal of scholarly commentary on European American Buddhism, particularly on Zen and Soka Gakkai International, but little on Tibetan Buddhism in America and on a range of Pacific Rim immigrant traditions. There are no wholly reliable statistics on how many Buddhists are in America. Most issues have been defined by European Americans who have been engaged in running debates over the future of American Buddhism since the early 1980s. But these debates are largely framed in terms derived from the politics of the 1960s and are carried on with little reference to immigrant Buddhists, who clearly comprise the largest part of the community. This gives the debates an unreal quality at times, as important issues such as gender equity and the role of monastics and laity become swept up into programmatic agendas that are both ideological and visionary. Many of these questions have yet to be examined systematically by dispassionate observers.

To some degree, this situation is about to change, as a series of new studies are published at the same time that many American Buddhist communities have achieved a degree of stability. Tweed and Prothero are publishing

Asian Religions in America: A Documentary History, an anthology of texts drawn from sources from the antebellum era to the present. This will help to correct the chronology developed by Rick Fields by setting the current burgeoning of Buddhism within a more complex American historical context. Prebish is publishing two new books. One is *The Faces of Buddhism in America* with Kenneth Tanaka, an edited collection of essays by a number of authors that survey a wide range of Buddhist traditions in this country. The other, *Luminous Passage: The Practice and Study of Buddhism in America*, is Prebish's own interpretation of major developments in American Buddhism in the last three decades. The latter is framed by the kind of questions asked by scholars in Buddhist Studies and will further efforts to understand how an American tradition of Buddhism is taking shape and place it in a comparative Buddhist perspective. Chris Queen, a scholar with a publishing record in modern Asian Buddhism, and Duncan Williams, a younger Buddhist scholar, have coedited *American Buddhism: Methods and Findings in Recent Scholarship*. These essays offer the kind of fine-grained studies of selected developments that are sorely needed to add depth and complexity to the study of American Buddhism.

These and other new works promise to advance the study of American Buddhism considerably. A reader who examines them together, however, will find them often running at cross-purposes because they come out of different disciplines and lack a set of clearly defined, common questions. But they mark an important step in the emergence of American Buddhism as a new field of academic study, one at the intersection of American religious history and the global history of Buddhism. The emergence of this new field mirrors in many respects the growth of American Buddhism as a vital and vibrant part of the multicultural and religiously pluralistic United States, at a time when the economic, political, and religious consequences of globalization have seized the attention of numerous scholars and commentators.

Several years ago, I was commissioned to write this book with a mandate to design it for the general reader, a task I have found alternatively rewarding, challenging, and frustrating. My primary goal has been to fashion an engaging and informative text to introduce interested people to the fascinating world created by Buddhists in the United States in the last half century. I have come to think of it as a road map to the American Buddhist landscape, in which histories, communities, institutions, and individuals are set in meaningful relationship to each other in order to make sense of developments that are often baffling in their complexity. To develop a richly textured discussion, I have drawn upon documentary films, newspaper articles, academic sources, contemporary commentary, and the vast amount of information bearing on contemporary Buddhism that is now found on the World Wide Web.

In an effort to sweep many disparate parts into a reasonably coherent whole, I have emphasized large-scale developments such as immigration, exile, conversion, and schism that have structured the introduction of Buddhism to this country. This has required that I include pertinent historical background information on modern Buddhism in Asia. Most Buddhists tend to express their religious convictions with reference to general ideas about liberation, enlightenment, or realization; the importance of transcending egotism; the cultivation of nonattachment; and the importance of compassion. One major way to bring out the substantial differences among them is to look at how they practice Buddhism, so I have also attended closely to the practice vocabulary taken for granted in most communities.

I have not taken up philosophical questions under debate in American Buddhism or explored the very important question of the relationship between Buddhism and psychotherapy, except in occasional and descriptive ways. Nor have I taken sides with one or another party in the multifaceted discussion about how Americanization ought to proceed. Due to the unique circumstances of Buddhism in Hawaii, I have more or less restricted my observations to developments in the continental United States. There are a number of topics I originally hoped to address but have not, such as Buddhism in popular culture; in literature, painting, and sculpture; and in the martial arts. As my research progressed, I found that it was challenging enough to develop a sustained discussion of America's many practice communities.

The discussion is structured to bring out the dynamic tension between tradition and innovation that is expressed in many different ways in America's Buddhist communities. But the general idea I develop throughout the book is that there are so many forms of Buddhism and so many different roads to Americanization that it is too early to announce the emergence of a distinct form that can be said to be typically American. Some forms of Buddhism have been overtly retailored to fit with one or another American ideal, often in very pronounced ways. But this in itself is not evidence that they are more authentically American or are more likely to become permanent parts of the long-term development of Buddhism in the United States.

Part 1 deals with background material related to Asian and American religious history. Chapter 1 is a brief introduction to a few of the general contours of the American Buddhist landscape—an opportunity to get one's feet wet before plunging into the subject at a greater depth. Chapter 2 and 3 are brief sketches of key ideas and historical developments in Buddhist history. Their chief purpose is to orient readers to the basic vocabulary and general geography of Buddhism in Asia, a grasp of which is essential to any understanding of Buddhism in the United States. At various points I draw analogies to Christianity, not to suggest that Buddhism and Christianity are reducible to each other, but as aids to the reader. Chapter 4 outlines major developments in the early history of the transmission of Buddhism to this country, to set its burgeoning in the last half century in historical perspective. It includes a few reflections on how immigration has functioned in American religious history in the past as a way to begin to think about the current Buddhist immigration and its possible long-term impact.

Part 2, the heart of the book, consists of six chapters that are interpretive accounts of selected forms of Buddhism and some of the unique forces at work in their introduction to this country. The first three chapters are devoted to traditions from Japan, and they all deal, to varying degrees, with background considerations related to modern Japanese Buddhist history. But I have placed an emphasis on key developments that shaped each tradition in this country. Chapter 5 is devoted to the Jodo Shinshu tradition of the Buddhist Churches of America and the way it became a part of the fabric of American religion through dynamics at work in immigration. Chapter 6 deals with the Nichiren tradition, most particularly with Soka Gakkai International and its emergence as an independent, lay-based form of humanistic Buddhism quite in tune with the values and ethos of the American mainstream. Chapter 7 addresses the development of Zen, one of the most highly differentiated forms of American Buddhism. I have emphasized how Zen was introduced as a set of ideas divorced from institutions in the 1950s and '60s, but subsequently developed a range of institutional forms that give it the adaptability and flexibility that have helped it to become the most popular form of Buddhism in this country.

The next three chapters examine selected developments in a number of other Asian traditions. Chapter 8 deals with Tibetan Buddhism in the United States and how its introduction and reception here have been informed not only by the Chinese occupation of Tibet and the creation of a community in exile but also by political concerns, efforts to preserve Tibetan culture and religion, and support from America's popular culture and entertainment industry. Chapter 9 deals with the uniquely complex landscape of the Theravada Buddhist traditions of south and southeast Asia. More than any other form of Buddhism, Theravada is being reshaped by both conversion and immigration. I have highlighted a spectrum of developments within that community that run from highly traditional to self-consciously innovative. Chapter 10 is devoted to developments related to Chinese, Korean, and Vietnamese immigration, most of which occurred only in the last three decades. In order to give a sense of how these traditions are undergoing Americanization, these developments are set in the context of adaptive patterns related to immigration. But I have also indicated ways in which selected leaders and teachers in each tradition have made an impact within the broader American Buddhist community.

Part 3 takes up Americanization more thematically by looking at the ways in which three important developments have played themselves out in recent decades. To a large degree, the focus of this discussion is on European American Buddhists, who emerged from the '60s with a fairly clear set of political ideals that have informed the process of Americanization since the 1980s. Regrettably, I have not been able to give adequate attention to comparable developments among immigrants, largely due to my lack of Asian language skills and the absence of secondary literature that addresses these issues across a range of immigrant communities. Chapter 11 describes how the ideal of gender equity has gained expression in American Buddhism in a way that parallels developments in liberal Judaism and Christianity. Chapter 12 deals with how a number of prominent people and organizations have been attempting to create forms of American Buddhism devoted to progressive social change. Chapter 13 describes current intra-Buddhist and interreligious dialogues in the American Buddhist community. The concluding chapter contains a general assessment of the state of American Buddhism at the end of the 1990s, together with a few suggestions about what might be expected in the coming century.

A Note on Historical Perspective

There is a great deal of cooperation among American Buddhists in different traditions, but there is also much controversy about issues that range from the future of monasticism in the West to appropriate forms of sexual expression for American Buddhist laity. Some commentators in the convert communities talk as if these questions had been answered and American Buddhism were now more or less a known entity. Others stress the degree to which distinctly American forms of Buddhism are now only in the making. But most Buddhists have hardly begun to express their hopes and aspirations publicly in the English language, a fact that suggests it may be premature to assume too much about what Buddhism is and is going to become in this country.

How one thinks about Americanization has a great deal to do with how one frames the question in a historical perspective. Rick Fields's book, *How the Swans Came to the Lake*, played an important role in opening American Buddhism up to historical inquiry. In an early edition of *Swans*, Fields recounted a conversation he had in the course of his research with Professor Mas Nagatomi at Harvard University, to whom he turned for advice and assistance. Fields recalled Nagatomi saying he doubted there were sufficient documents available for a critical history of American Buddhism, which Fields must have found disheartening. Surely much to his relief, he went on to discover many pertinent documents, some of them related to developments between 1930 and 1950, which at the time was uncharted territory in American Buddhist history.

Having studied under Nagatomi and with a long-standing interest in the history of the East-West encounter, I have thought about that story many times, particularly once I began research for this book and found myself immersed in reams of material about the current American Buddhist scene. In the course of my reflection, I have come to wonder if Nagatomi's remarks were not more about a lack of historical perspective on Buddhism in this country than about a lack of documents per se.

Nagatomi used to teach a two-semester sequence on the history of Buddhism in Asia. It was a brilliant course in which he took students from the teachings of the Buddha through their development in India to Sri Lanka, Tibet, China, Japan, and Korea. He managed to place in historical context the way Buddhist philosophy and practice developed over centuries, attending closely at every turn to both innovations and long-term continuities. He was extremely skilled at what I thought of at the time as "playing the pipe organ of Asian Buddhist history." Students came away from the two semesters with a dizzying but indelible impression of how Buddhism began, evolved, differentiated, and was recast over and over again as it moved from region to region during more than two thousand years of Asian history.

I now think Nagatomi may have been saying to Fields that there was not yet enough American Buddhist history to create the kind of magisterial interpretation that was his stock-in-trade, a situation I think is still more or less the case. Buddhism has been in this country for over a century, but only in the past few decades has it blossomed into what might be called a mass movement, expressed in a wide range of American institutions. There are now a great many things to study, but it is premature, even if one were talented enough to give it a try, to write the kind of history Nagatomi used to teach. It is possible to talk about many developments in contemporary American Buddhism, but impossible to assess which of these "has legs" and will pass the tests of time required to become a living Buddhist tradition in the United States. It is my conviction, however, that in the future both Buddhists and historians of Buddhism will look back to the last half century and find the origins of uniquely American forms of Buddhism that will bear comparison with the great traditions of Asia.

Numerous individuals have helped me develop this book, only some of whom I am able to thank here. Charles Prebish, Chris Queen, Paul Numrich, and Stephen Prothero gave me invaluable assistance by prodding me to see issues from the perspective of their expertise and disciplines. Others have also read portions of it and offered helpful criticism; they include Kenneth Tanaka, Rob Eppsteiner, John Daido Loori, Judith Simmer-Brown, Peter Gregory, and Arnold Kottler. After an afternoon's conversation with Helen Tworkov, I first began to see issues in a way that enabled me to put pen to paper and get started on the manuscript. People at The Pluralism Project at Harvard University have assisted by providing me with access to their archive, photo collection, and student research, of which that of Stuart Chandler was particularly helpful. Thanks also go to Thanissaro Bhikkhu, who as a host, critic, and friend has been especially patient in helping me balance the need to confront substantive issues with the unique demands of writing a survey for a general readership.

A number of individuals in the Buddhist publishing world, in Tibet support groups, and in various Buddhist communities have provided me with a great deal of information in the course of lengthy phone conversations. Among them are Larry Gerstein, Ron Kidd, Virginia Strauss, Asayo Horibe, Dennis Genpo Merzel, Nicolee Jikyo Miller, and Therese Fitzgerald. Others have generously given of their time in the course of my visits to their communities, including Masao Kodani in Los Angeles; Joanna Fagin at Shambhala Rocky Mountain Center; Mark Elliott in Crestone, Colorado; Seisen and Tenshin in Mountain View, California; Marty Verhoeven and Bhikkhu Heng Sure in the San Francisco area; Sarah Smith in Woodstock, New York; and Al Albergate and others at SGI-USA's Santa Monica headquarters. Thanks also go to Dave Nyogen of the Vietnamese Chamber of Commerce, who proved to be a very informative guide to many Buddhist sites across Orange Country, California. I am also indebted to Julia Hardy, Wendy Kapner, and Pamela Montgomery for their support and assistance.

I also thank Hamilton College and the Emerson Foundation, whose support for research and travel was substantial. I owe deep gratitude to Hamilton students who, over the course of three years, have waded with me through the material in this book and have contributed a great deal to its development. In particular, I want to thank Jaime Tackett and Matthew Berman. At Columbia University Press, James Warren has been both enthusiastic and sane with his suggestions, Leslie Kriesel keenly insightful with her editorial assistance, and Elyse Rieder creative in her role as photo researcher. My wife, Ann Castle, deserves a great deal of credit not only for her patience but also for her many contributions: reading the manuscript in progress, offering advice and comments, and clipping articles from numerous publications to keep me abreast of fast-breaking developments in the world of Buddhism.

Buddhism in America

Part One

BACKGROUND

CHAPTER ONE

The American Buddhist Landscape

Mid-Sunday morning in Los Angeles, drumbeats and the ringing of a bell open a service in a temple of the Buddhist Churches of America (BCA), the oldest institutional form of Buddhism in the United States. Despite the drum and bell, commentators have often observed that BCA services, with their hymn singing and sermons, resemble those of American Protestantism, which is taken to be evidence of the assimilation of the BCA into mainstream American society. To a great degree this is true. After more than a century in the United States, the Japanese Americans who compose the bulk of the BCA membership have wrestled in many ways with the Americanization issues faced by racial and religious minorities. But even the most casual observer will note substantial differences between the temple and a Protestant church, the most conspicuous being the altar, with its centrally located, burnished image of Amida Buddha.

Close attention to elements of the service that are familiar—readings from scripture, remembrances for deceased members of the congregation, and birthday congratulations for children—reveals some further, more important differences of a philosophical or, as a Christian might say, theological nature. Most conspicuously, the first of three congregational chants, which are led by the priest and followed by the people sitting in the pews in soft, monotone chant, is called the Three Respectful Invitations:

> We respectfully call upon Tathagatha Amida to enter this dojo.
> We respectfully call upon Shakyamuni to enter this dojo.

Among the most venerable of the buddhas and bodhisattvas, Amida Buddha is central to the Pure Land tradition of which the Buddhist Churches of America is a part. This Amida image and altar are found in the Midwest Buddhist Temple in Chicago, Illinois, one of a network of temples established by Japanese Americans since the end of the nineteenth century. PAUL NUMRICH

> We respectfully call upon the Tathagathas of the ten directions to
> enter this dojo.[1]

This is followed by additional recitations, including the phrase *Namo Amida Butsu*, a key element in BCA practice, referred to as the *Nembutsu*.

Rituals are seen by scholars of religion as windows into the larger religious worldview of a community. This ritual is a glimpse into the landscape of Buddhism in America, but only into one of its many traditions, Jodo Shinshu, the True Pure Land school, founded by the religious reformer Shinran in the thirteenth century. There are many forms of American Buddhism and many different Buddhist rituals, most of which have their origins in Asia but are being transplanted and adapted to the United States.

Later that Sunday night, in the living room of an apartment in Los Angeles's Wilshire district, a group of about twenty people, mostly Anglos but also several Latinos and African Americans, sit cross-legged with their shoes off on the living-room floor. They are grouped before an altar that appears to be a small version of the altar in the BCA temple. But instead of a statue of Amida Buddha, this altar contains a scroll called a *gohonzon* inscribed with

Japanese characters. These people are members of Soka Gakkai International, a group of lay Buddhist practitioners in the Nichiren tradition of Japan, which has flourished in this country since the 1960s.

No priest leads the chant, but the woman hosting the meeting begins by ringing a small bell and intoning the phrase *Nam-Myoho-Renge-Kyo* while facing the gohonzon. A moment later, those assembled join in and the entire group bursts into a rapid, highly energetic recitation of passages from the *Lotus Sutra*, one of the most important texts of the Mahayana Buddhist tradition in east Asia. After about a half hour of chanting, one member leads the rest in studying an aspect of Nichiren's philosophy, much of which is contained in his letters, or *Gosho*. Afterward, a number of members make informal testimonies about how Nichiren practice has transformed their lives.

Whether they take place in a public temple or before a home altar, rituals such as these are basic expressions of the Buddha *dharma*, the teachings of the Buddha, and have been for many centuries. Many Buddhists refer to them as their *practice*, a term that conveys both their repetitive character and, more important, that these techniques are practiced, often for many hours and on a daily basis. This is particularly the case with sitting meditation practice, which is used to cultivate a state of awakening many Buddhists call Buddha mind or Buddha nature.

Sitting meditation is central to all Buddhist traditions that have a strong monastic component, such as Zen, Tibetan Vajrayana, and the Theravada tradition of southeast Asia. But if one were to observe Buddhists from each of these traditions meditating side by side, there would be few differences to note, aside from small details like the color and shape or presence or absence of their meditation cushions. Meditation practices are designed to transform consciousness, and most of them are based on close attention to the intake and outflow of breath. All are used to cultivate the state of consciousness the Buddha attained some 2,500 years ago in India. All look more or less the same from the outside, but significant matters of technique and style differentiate them.

Millions of Americans who know little about Buddhism are familiar with Zen and the idea of Zen meditation, if only in a very general sense. Like Jodo Shinshu and Nichiren Buddhism, Zen is a Japanese tradition, and it shares with these other traditions many details of liturgy—altars, images, bells, and chanting. But the tenor of Zen is quite different. For most of its history in Asia, Zen meditation was practiced primarily by monastics, while the practices of Jodo Shinshu and Nichiren Buddhism have been more associated with the religious life of the laity. Only in the past century have *zazen* and other monastic meditative practices been widely taken up by laypeople in Asia, Europe, and the United States.

Many Americans think that Zen is a Buddhist tradition without formal ritual, which is not really the case. Zen was first introduced into this country in books that led many Americans to think of it as a philosophy rather than a religious tradition. People also tend not to think of Zen sitting meditation, or zazen, when a practitioner might face a wall or sit with downcast eyes for hours, as ritual activity. But daily or even twice-daily stints of Zen sitting meditation, during which a practitioner notes the movement of his or her mind, help to structure the lives of many American Buddhists, one of the primary functions of ritual. Zazen is also embedded in other, smaller rituals such as *gassho*, or bowing, and the making of offerings of water, food, or incense to an image of the Buddha.

Zen meditation also takes other forms such as *oryoki*, in which contemplation is combined with communal eating in a ritual form that requires the skillful use of wooden utensils, nested bowls, and carefully folded napkins. To do oryoki well requires practice. Note the bemused discomfort expressed by Lawrence Shainberg, a long-time American Zen practitioner, when he first encountered eating oryoki-style at an American monastery in the Catskill Mountains outside New York City. "Clumsy with my bowls, I make more noise, it seems to me, than everyone else in the room combined. I have completely forgotten the elaborate methods of folding, unfolding, unstacking and stacking. . . . The harder I try, the clumsier I get. Rational it may be, but the ritual seems a nightmare now, one more example of Zen's infinite capacity to complicate the ordinary."[2]

In contrast, many Tibetan Vajrayana meditative practices are based on visualizations, which is a very different meditation technique. During a visualization, a practitioner, who to an observer might appear to be simply watching the breath, is engaged in conforming his or her body, speech, and mind to an image of one of the many buddhas found in the Tibetan tradition. Visualizing a buddha entails sustained concentration, whether it is done in a richly decorated dharma center in Vermont, a simple retreat hut in the Rocky Mountains, a rented conference room in a hotel in Atlanta, or at home. But in any case, a Tibetan visualization is a rigorous form of meditation that may take a number of years to do well, which is one of the reasons Buddhists call it a practice.

Theravada meditation techniques are also practiced by many American Buddhists. In the excerpt below, Mahasi Sayadaw, an Asian teacher who taught a number of Americans *vipassana* or insight meditation, describes

how to develop insight using a technique often called noting, naming, or la-
beling, a basic practice in dharma centers across the United States. The point
of this meditation is to heighten one's insight into mental processes such as
thinking, intending, and knowing and into unconscious physical movement,
in an effort to cultivate detachment from the mind's incessant activity and
bodily instincts. Sayadaw is describing how a practitioner, thirsty after many
hours of sitting, can continue to develop insight even as he or she gets up to
take a drink.

> When you look at the water faucet, or water pot, on arriving at the
> place where you are to take a drink, be sure to make a mental note
> *looking, seeing.*
> When you stop walking, *stopping.*
> When you stretch the hand, *stretching.*
> When the hand touches the cup, *touching.*
> When the hand takes the cup, *taking.*
> When the hand brings the cup to the lips, *bringing.*
> When the cup touches the lips, *touching.*
> Should you feel cold at the touch, *cold.*
> When you swallow, *swallowing.*
> When returning the cup, *returning.*[3]

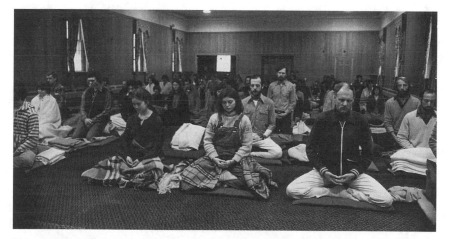

Sitting meditation is a central ritual in many Buddhist traditions and is of particular
importance among converts in the United States. At the Insight Meditation Society in Barre,
Massachusetts in the 1970s, a group of Americans are engaged in vipassana meditation, a
form most closely associated with the Theravada tradition of south and southeast Asia.
INSIGHT MEDITATION SOCIETY

In an effort to Americanize the dharma, some converts advocate divorcing meditation from other rituals that play a part in Buddhism in Asia, viewing them as unnecessary elements of Asian culture. Others, however, maintain and adapt them to American settings. In a monastery in California, a small group of people, both Asian immigrants and Anglo converts, can be found most mornings re-creating a ritual whose origins date from the earliest days of Buddhism. Just after sunrise, they bustle about in a small, informal kitchen preparing breakfast for the monks of the monastery. As laypeople, they have little intention of taking up monastic discipline, but express their devotion to the dharma by providing support for monks who have chosen to devote their lives to study, teaching, and meditation. A half hour or so later, four men, one American and three Asians, file down from their retreats to the kitchen, dressed in the ochre robes of Theravada monks of southeast Asia. There the laity serve them a few spoonfuls of rice, a symbol of the meal and a form of religious offering. Shortly thereafter, the monks eat the breakfast prepared for them in the temple up on the hill. Afterward, the laypeople and monks may gather together for chanting or to engage in consultations, after which the laity consume the remainder of the meal.

This kind of activity can often be observed in many Buddhist temples in most major American cities. Such rituals play a particularly important role among Asian American Buddhist immigrants, who are re-creating their received religious traditions in immigrant communities. Ritual acts such as making prostrations, doing Buddha *puja*, celebrating Vesak, and taking refuge (all of which will be discussed in the following chapters) are the bread and butter of the religious life of many American Buddhists, as familiar to them as baptism and Sunday churchgoing are to American Christians. But there are also new rituals only now taking form here as the result of religious experimentation. Some Buddhists, both European American and Asian American, are beginning to mix elements of practice drawn from the different traditions of Asia that are now found in this country. Others, primarily European American, are experimenting with creating new Buddhist rituals by adding elements to dharma practice drawn from other religions, be these wicca (western witchcraft), ancient goddess spirituality, the shamanic practices of Native Americans, Judaism, or Christianity.

All these rituals, whether chanting the Nembutsu, sitting zazen, or feeding monks, provide the observer with glimpses into the landscape of American Buddhism. By many Americans' standards, it is an exotic terrain of unfamiliar religious convictions and foreign practices, but it is all a part of

America's multicultural and religiously pluralistic society in the making. From a historical perspective, American Buddhism is also an epoch-making undertaking. One of the great religious traditions of Asia is moving west. For about four hundred years, western missionaries, explorers, scholars, and seekers probed Asia, wondered about Buddhism, and studied it. A few even practiced it. The groundwork for the transmission of the dharma to the West was prepared by many people over many years, but the emergence of the dharma as an important element in American religion is a development that by comparison occurred only very recently.

What is American Buddhism? During the 1980s and '90s, many Americans were debating among themselves what Buddhism was in this country and what they wanted it to be. They came up with many different ideas about how to create American forms of the dharma, so there is not a single answer to that question, nor is there likely ever to be. There is not one American Buddhism, any more than there is one American Judaism, Islam, or Christianity.

Who are American Buddhists? That question can be answered, but only quite generally. On the one hand, there is no Buddhist "type" in America. Buddhists come from a wide range of racial and ethnic backgrounds, and there are white collar Buddhists; Buddhist cab drivers, mechanics, and chefs; and Buddhist artists and musicians. Some Americans are highly self-conscious about being Buddhist, while others take the fact that they are Buddhist for granted. At the outset, it should be assumed that there are many different kinds of Americans who, in one way or another, identify themselves as Buddhist.

On the other hand, there are at least three broadly defined groups within American Buddhism. One group consists of a mixed bag of native-born Americans who, over the course of the last fifty or so years, have embraced the teachings of the Buddha. They are part of a broad movement that had its origins in the 1940s and '50s, took off in the 1960s, and then continued to gain momentum through the end of the century. They are often referred to as western or European American Buddhists, but they include Asian, African, and Native Americans. I will generally refer to them as convert Buddhists to distinguish them from other Americans, mostly from Asian backgrounds, who were raised and educated in Buddhist communities. By *convert* I mean not so much a person who has embraced an entire religious system, but, in keeping with the original meaning of the term, someone who has turned their heart and mind toward a set of religious teachings, in this case the teachings of the Buddha.

A second group is composed of immigrant and refugee Buddhists from a range of Asian nations who are in the process of transplanting and adapting their received traditions to this country. This development is also linked to the 1960s; legislative reforms passed in Washington in 1965 made possible a dramatic increase in the number of immigrants arriving from Asia. Most American Buddhists are in the nation's Asian communities, and they are generally referred to as immigrant or ethnic Buddhists to distinguish them from converts. But for well over fifty years, Buddhist immigrants taught native-born Americans, and many of the founders of convert Buddhist communities were Asian immigrants.

A third group is composed of Asian Americans, primarily from Chinese and Japanese backgrounds, who have practiced Buddhism in this country for four or five generations. The most well-known institutional form of religion in this group is the Buddhist Churches of America, Japanese Jodo Shinshu Buddhism. As a group, BCA Buddhists do not share with converts the heady sense that comes from having discovered the teachings of the Buddha only recently. Nor are they preoccupied with building the foundations of their community, as are recent immigrants and refugees. They are America's oldline Buddhists who, in the landscape of late twentieth-century Buddhism, were neither fish nor fowl, neither convert nor immigrant.

During the last decades of the twentieth century, converts and immigrants have held center stage in American Buddhism, and they have given the dharma in this country much of its vibrancy and complexity. But their approaches to adapting Asian traditions differ radically due to the nature of their relationship to Buddhism and their location in American society. Many converts first discovered Buddhism in books. Some then traveled to Asia to learn more about it, while others set out to find Buddhist teachers in America, something that only three or four decades ago was not easy to do. By the 1980s, convert Buddhists began to speak in their own voices when a generation of native-born Americans moved into prominence as scholars, dharma teachers, and community leaders. At about that time, converts began to explore in earnest ways to create indigenous forms of the dharma suited to those born and bred in the cultural mainstream of the United States.

During these same years, immigrant Buddhists were also creating forms of the dharma suited to America, but out of a different social location. Like Jews and Catholics a century or two before, they approached developing forms of American Buddhism as part of the immigrant experience, in which questions about adapting religion to America were intimately related to a broad range of economic, cultural, and linguistic issues. The first generation needed to find work, re-create their traditional religious life, and explain their religion to their rapidly Americanizing children. The long-term contribution of immigrants to Buddhism in America is very hard to assess, because the nature of the immigrant experience is such that adaptation occurs only over the course of several generations.

A few statistics on American Buddhism are available, but they vary considerably. One source put the total number of practicing Buddhists at a round one million in 1990, but another at 5 or 6 million only a few years later. A more recent estimate must be considered rough, but appears to be the best available. Martin Baumann of Germany suggested in 1997 that there were 3 or 4 million Buddhists in the United States, the most in any western country. In contrast, he estimated that there were 650,000 Buddhists in France and 180,000 Buddhists in Great Britain. His estimates also suggest that converts consistently are outnumbered by immigrants. In the same year, France had roughly 150,000 converts and 500,000 immigrants, Great Britain 50,000 and 130,000 respectively. In the United States, he estimated there were 800,000 converts and between 2.2 and 3.2 million Buddhists in immigrant communities.[4]

These figures, however, need to be treated with caution. In the same year, 1997, *Time* magazine suggested there were "some 100,000" American Buddhist converts. It did not even venture to estimate the number of Buddhist immigrants.[5] As a result, we must proceed without definite information regarding the actual number of American Buddhists. Suffice it to say, there are a great many and, more important, they are engaged in practicing the dharma in a wide variety of fascinating ways.

CHAPTER TWO

Very Basic Buddhism

The transmission of Buddhism to America is an epoch-making undertaking. For 2,500 years, Buddhism has played a central role in the religious life of Asia. Its philosophical schools, institutions, rituals, and art have informed the lives of countless people from the Iranian plateau to Japan and from Tibet to Indonesia. Throughout many centuries, it has taken on fascinatingly different shapes as it has adapted to many different cultures and regions, a process that is repeating itself as Buddhism moves west and into the United States. Essential in understanding this process is a grasp of the most elementary teachings of the Buddha and some of the vocabulary used within American Buddhist communities.

Teachings of the Buddha

Siddhartha Gautama, the historical Buddha, was born in the sixth century B.C.E. in what is today Nepal. According to tradition, he was heir to his father's throne as head of the Shakya clan, but instead chose at the age of twenty-nine to depart from the comfortable life of the palace, renounce his inheritance, leave his family, and retire to the wilderness in search of a way to end human suffering. Siddhartha set out on his quest at a time of great spiritual ferment in India, when ascetic philosophers and wandering sages were debating fundamental questions that remained central to the Indian religious traditions through subsequent centuries. What is the nature of human action, or *karma*? What role does karma play in shaping one's life and fate? Is there rebirth after death? Assuming there is rebirth, is it possible to escape *samsara*, the endless wandering through round after round of death and rebirth? Siddhartha's answers to these questions informed the development of Buddhism throughout Asia and continue to do so in the United States today.

For six years after leaving home, Siddhartha studied and practiced harsh ascetic disciplines taught to him by teachers he encountered on his journey. But at the age of about thirty-five, he discovered his own path during a long night of meditation sitting under a pipal tree. According to tradition, he entered a state of deep mental absorption, or *dhyana*, during which he observed the unfolding of his own many past lives, thus answering questions about death and rebirth. He also saw how karma influenced the shaping of events both in the present moment and in the future, not only in this life but in many lives to come. Most important, Siddhartha analyzed how karma worked to trap human beings in samsara, and he discovered a path or method to follow to gain liberation, an experience generally referred to as *nirvana*.

The term *nirvana* was originally borrowed from the physics of ancient India and meant the extinguishing of a fire. It literally means "unbinding," reflecting the idea that fire was thought to be trapped in its fuel while burning but freed or unbound when it went out. The freedom and coolness connoted by the term reflect Siddhartha's understanding that the path of liberation entails quenching passionate attachments to illusions that keep human beings trapped in suffering. He saw his path as "the middle way," a point of balance between the sensual indulgence he engaged in as a youth in his father's home and his teachers' severe austerities.

As a result of his discoveries, Siddhartha became known as the *Buddha*, "the awakened one" or "enlightened one." Many who subsequently followed his path also became awakened and, according to some traditions of Buddhism, there have been many buddhas. He is also called *Shakyamuni*, or sage of the Shakya clan, and *Tathagatha*, which means "thus come" or "thus gone" and signifies that the man who was Gautama achieved total liberation. Shortly after his awakening, he began to teach what he called the *dharma*, which means "doctrine" or "natural law." He also formulated a discipline, or *vinaya*, for his most devoted followers.

The Buddha was not a Buddhist. That term came into usage only many centuries later when western observers used it to refer to the many traditions that had grown out of his teachings. The Buddha called his path the *dharma-vinaya*, the doctrine and discipline, and he taught it to numerous disciples over the course of the next forty-five years.

A great many scriptures or *sutra*s are thought to contain the Buddha's manifold teachings. Many were written by later Buddhists who, having attained awakening, claimed to speak with the Buddha's authority. The dharma, after all, was not the Buddha's personal property but was open to all who practiced the middle way and were awakened through it. According to tradition, however, Shakyamuni Buddha first delivered the essence of his teachings in the form of a sermon in Deer Park at Sarnath, several miles outside the city of Varanasi. The most fundamental of these teachings is known

According to tradition, the Buddha first began his work as a teacher at Sarnath in India, where he presented the essence of his awakening in the form of the Four Noble Truths. This image is from a sequence of paintings devoted to major events in the life of the Buddha at Wat Dhammaram, one of the major Thai temples in Chicago, Illinois.
FROM *THE LIFE OF THE BUDDHA ACCORDING TO THE WALL PAINTINGS AT WAT DHAMMARAM*, (C) 1997, WAT DHAMMARAM, THE THAI BUDDHIST TEMPLE OF CHICAGO

as the Four Noble Truths, which he offered to his listeners both as a diagnosis of the human condition and as a form of medicine or cure. Like Jesus' teaching in the Sermon on the Mount in the Christian tradition, the Four Noble Truths have been the subject of a great deal of subsequent commentary in Asian Buddhism and remain a touchstone for most practitioners in the American Buddhist community.

1. The First Noble Truth is that life is characterized by *dukkha*, a term translated as suffering, unsatisfactoriness, stress, or more colloquially, "being out of joint." Dukkha conveys the essential quality of life in samsara. It means personal physical and mental pain; grief, despair, and distress; the anguish of loss and separation; and the frustration associated with thwarted desires. At its most subtle level, dukkha denotes the suffering people endure in clinging to things that are subject to disease, old age, and death, or to change and flux in general. Even one's self, the most enduring thing one knows in life, has no fixed quality but is subject to dukkha. Buddhists consider this focus on suffering to be neither tragic nor pessimistic but a realistic and correct diagnosis of the central problem in human life.

2. The Second Noble Truth is that craving, or *tanha*, is the cause of dukkha. The Buddha pointed out that, at the most basic level, people always want what they do not have and cling to what they have in fear of losing it. This is a fundamental cause of suffering. On a more complex level, he taught that craving is rooted in ignorance, a misunderstanding of the transient nature of reality that leads people to seek lasting happiness in things that are subject to change.

3. The Third Noble Truth is that the cessation of dukkha comes when craving is abandoned. For many decades, western commentators emphasized the first two Noble Truths and saw the Buddha's teachings as negative and contrary to the western humanistic spirit. Buddhists, however, place the emphasis on the truth that suffering can cease and that quietude, equanimity, joy, and even liberation from the wheel of samsara can actually be achieved.

4. The Fourth Noble Truth is the Eightfold Path, a prescription for how to engage in action or karma that will lead beyond samsara to nirvana, beyond suffering to liberation. Stated succinctly, it sounds much like a laundry list of good behaviors. But it contains the essence of the Buddha's middle way and forms the foundation for Buddhist wisdom traditions, ethical teachings, and meditative disciplines.

The first two steps on the Eightfold Path—right view and right resolve—are forms of wisdom. Right view begins with the conviction that good and bad, healthy and unhealthy actions have real consequences. People shape their own destiny because they choose to act in ways that create good and bad karma. More specifically, right view means seeing life in terms of the Four Noble Truths. Right resolve builds on this understanding with the decision to abandon mental attitudes, such as ill will, harmfulness, and sensual desire, that stand in the way of liberation.

The next three steps—right speech, right action, and right livelihood—bear on ethics. Right speech is the recognition of the power of language to harm both oneself and other beings. Divisive and harsh speech, idle chatter, and untruthfulness are destructive, create bad karma, and thus should be avoided. Right action entails avoiding behaviors such as killing, stealing, and profligate or harmful sexual activity. Right livelihood requires that a Buddhist earn a living in a way that is honest, nonexploitative, and fair.

The last three steps—right effort, right mindfulness, and right concentration—are more directly related to meditative practices. Right effort is the patient, persevering cultivation of good mental states. Right mindfulness requires attention to body, feelings, mind, and mental states in the course of meditation and maintaining presence of mind in daily living. Right concentration means the inward focusing of the mind and heart in states of mental absorption that lead to the kind of liberating insight the Buddha experienced in his own meditation.

In contemporary America, the Four Noble Truths are frequently interpreted in a modern, humanistic, and often secular spirit. But throughout Asian history, they have operated within a complex worldview that, for lack of better terms, might be called traditional or prescientific. The Buddha himself, and certainly later Buddhists, understood these and other teachings as operating on both personal and cosmological levels. Samsara is seen as a personal fact of existence and a cosmic process. Karma is not simply a part of human psychology but a force operating in the natural world. Rebirth is thought to take place among all forms of sentient life, and the worlds into which beings can be reborn include a range of heavens and hells. Impermanence is not simply a truth that has a bearing on ideas of selfhood and personal fulfillment but is a fundamental characteristic of the natural order of the universe.

As a result, Buddhism in Asia developed an immensely rich philosophical, cosmological, and mythological tradition that flourished up to and into the modern period. Just as many modern Christians have little trouble balancing faith in God, the divinity of Jesus, and belief in miracles and angels with a secular or scientific point of view, so too many modern Buddhists maintain strong convictions rooted in a traditional religious worldview. Some modern Buddhists understand the inhabitants of heavens and hells in metaphorical terms, but for others they are actual beings. Ideas such as samsara, karma, and rebirth may or may not continue to play an important role in their religious imagination. The Four Noble Truths and other basic Buddhist teachings may be fused with a secular and humanist outlook, but they may also be considered as directly related to a more traditional cosmology and worldview.

All this is to say that the introduction of Buddhism to America and the West entails more than importing a neat set of religious propositions or an ethical system. There are a wide range of spiritual, cosmological, and mythological dimensions that are often assumed to be a part of the Buddhist worldview. Some of the debate over what American Buddhism should be is rooted in questions about if, how, and to what degree traditional ideas and convictions should be reshaped to suit the very different ethos of contemporary America.

The Formation of the Sangha or Community

Shortly after the Buddha preached at Sarnath, his followers began to form the first Buddhist community or *sangha*. From the outset, many of his disciples sought to follow his example by leaving their settled lives behind, taking up the dharma and vinaya, living as mendicants, and practicing meditation. These monks (*bhikkhus*) and nuns (*bhikkhunis*) formed the basis of what would later become the Buddhist monastic community. The importance of Buddha's example as teacher was perpetuated in the monastic tradition, where the relationship between teacher and student became institutionalized in lineages. These lineages played an important role in the transmission of the dharma throughout Asia in subsequent centuries and continue to be important today in many communities in the United States.

At about the same time, roles began to develop for the laity. Some people who held the Buddha and his dedicated followers in highest regard had no expectation of imitating their extraordinary undertaking. These men (*upasakas*) and women (*upasikas*) contributed money and goods for the support of monks and nuns, becoming a model for later Buddhist laity. The complementary roles played by monastics and laypeople became a pattern that was

repeated as Buddhism later spread throughout Asia. Bhikkhus and bhikkhunis pursued the extraordinary religious goal of attaining liberation, while
upasakas and upasikas provided them with support and sustenance, an act
that was considered to be meritorious. Such merit-making was understood
as a way to earn good karma for oneself or a loved one and was itself seen
as an important religious practice.

Within the first century after the death of Shakyamuni, patterns of Buddhist practice began to emerge for both monastics and laity. The first Buddhist ritual was taking refuge, an act still repeated in ordination ceremonies,
daily meditation sessions, and as a before-meal prayer in Buddhist communities throughout Asia and the United States. It consists of the simple formula "I take refuge in the Buddha. I take refuge in the dharma. I take refuge
in the sangha." The simplicity of what Buddhists call the *triratana*, the Triple
Jewel or Gem, however, can be misleading. Over the centuries, *Buddha*,
dharma, and *sangha* have taken on a wide range of different meanings. *Buddha* might refer to Shakyamuni or to another enlightened being. The dharma has been subjected to a great deal of philosophical and sectarian interpretation over the centuries. In some forms of Buddhism, *sangha* refers
specifically to the monastic community. In others, it refers to a Buddhist
priesthood. In still others it is taken to be a broadly inclusive term that refers
to all Buddhists. In the United States, *sangha* may mean an informal group
meditating together, a particular community who share the same tradition or
teacher, or the entire American Buddhist community. The *cyber-sangha*, the
sum of all those Buddhists who are part of the virtual community sustained
by websites, Buddhist list servers, and dharma chat groups, has become a
significant element in American Buddhism.

From early on, all Buddhists were expected to follow the five basic precepts, the *panca sila*—to refrain from killing, stealing, engaging in sexual
misconduct, lying, and taking intoxicants. Monks and nuns, however, soon
developed a far more rigorous and extensive code, found in the canonical
Buddhist texts, that forms the heart of the monastic vinaya. The vinaya contains a wide range of rules concerning the food, dress, and dwellings appropriate to monks and nuns, their personal comportment, and ways to ensure
the peaceful running of the community. Until the modern period, Buddhist
monastics were routinely expected to practice celibacy, an area of discipline
that has been loosened in some communities but rigorously adhered to in
others. There are more than two hundred rules that govern traditional
monastics, all of which are considered to be natural extensions of the Buddha's original teachings.

Devotional forms of Buddhism soon emerged that were used by both monks and laity. Buddhists gathered together under pipal trees to recall the night of the Buddha's enlightenment. These trees became known as *bodhi* trees, trees of awakening, and continue to be a major element in Buddhist iconography. *Stupas*, mounds containing relics of the Buddha, became major cult sites in Asian Buddhism. There are now many Buddhist stupas, perhaps as many as fifty of significant size, in the United States. The Buddha is also symbolized by an empty throne or footprints, images signifying that although the dharma remains on earth, Shakyamuni himself attained ultimate liberation. The lotus, a beautiful flower with roots planted firmly in mud, is a reminder that while nirvana is a transcendent goal, it is attained from within the realm of human suffering. By the first century B.C.E., the human image of the Buddha, which is found in virtually all forms of Buddhism today, came into widespread use. Standing, sitting, and reclining figures of Shakyamuni or another buddha are often complex symbols in which colors, hand gestures, and adornments all have esoteric meanings.

The general pattern for monastics and laypeople that emerged in Buddhism was not unlike that in the West during the Middle Ages. Monks and nuns formed a religious elite. They were the intellectuals, philosophers, teachers, poets, and religious practitioners at the formal core of the community, performing their roles sometimes brilliantly and at other times carelessly. Some monastics took on secular roles as diplomats and advisers at court. The laity, whether humble rank-and-file or royal patrons, deferred to them, although relations between the two camps were often fraught with tension and complexity. In one major way, however, these relations differed from those in the West. Many Asian schools of Buddhism developed traditions of temporary ordination, in which laypeople can take on the monastic role for a time and then return to their former way of life, with an ease not found in most forms of monastic Christianity.

The use of the term *ordination* in reference to Buddhism is, moreover, a source of further confusion. In the West, the common understanding is that ordination occurs after the completion of an educational process and marks the formal entrance into a religious profession as a priest, monk, nun, rabbi, or minister. In the Buddhist context, however, ordination often denotes a formal entrance into a protracted period of study and practice, one that may or may not lead a practitioner to take a "higher ordination," to become a "fully ordained" monk, nun, or other type of advanced practitioner. As the monastic tradition moves to the West, where most Buddhists remain laypeople, there is a great deal of variation and ambiguity in the use of this language.

Within four or five centuries of Shakyamuni's death, a highly complex Buddhist tradition had taken shape in India. Both monastic institutions and lay Buddhism prospered. The oral tradition that had grown up around the teachings of the Buddha was transformed into a written canon and schools of Buddhist philosophy flourished. Ritual, iconography, and musical expressions of Buddhist piety became highly articulated. Most developments in Buddhist history can be traced in whole or in part back to origins on the Indian subcontinent, even though Buddhism largely vanished from India after the twelfth century C.E., in large part as a result of the Muslim invasions. For this reason, the teachings of the Buddha that are now being transplanted to the West have been reshaped by centuries of adaptation to other Asian cultures from Sri Lanka to Korea.

CHAPTER THREE

Three Vehicles

The foundations of American Buddhism rest on a variety of national, regional, and sectarian traditions of Asian Buddhism. There are a great many forms of Buddhism in Asia, but three broad traditions have structured Buddhist thought and practice for many centuries. A comparable development is found in the West, where the teachings of Jesus are generally seen as expressed in Orthodox, Catholic, and Protestant traditions of Christianity. In order to understand American Buddhism, it is important to have a general grasp of the leading principles of these traditions and their general place in Asian history and geography.

These three traditions are often called *yanas*, or vehicles that convey people from samsara to nirvana. They are also likened to rafts that carry people from one shore of a river to the other, from suffering to liberation. In this sense, the three major yanas share a common purpose, but differ due to their historical evolution in different parts of Asia. All three traditions are currently flourishing in America, but communication among them is limited both by ethnic and sectarian differences inherited from Asia and by the gulf that tends to separate Buddhist converts and immigrants. Many American Buddhists hope and expect that the presence of these many different traditions in the United States will provide an opportunity for greater mutual understanding among all of them, and for the emergence of new forms of Buddhism suited to the needs of Americans and American society.

Theravada, the Way of the Elders

Theravada is the most traditional and orthodox of the three vehicles. Many centuries ago, *Theravada*, which means "the way of the elders," was one among a number of early schools of Buddhism. In about the second century of the common era, these schools were collectively referred to by their detractors as *Hinayana*, or "little vehicle," a pejorative term coined to contrast their traditionalism with the more expansive and innovative spirit of a second great tradition, *Mahayana*, which means "great vehicle." All of the older Hinayana schools have long since died out, except for Theravada. While ancient tensions between Theravada and Mahayana have abated in recent centuries, the contrast between the two remains; it is an important way to highlight different religious emphases in the Buddhist tradition.

Theravada Buddhism is based on the canon of Buddhist scripture written down in Pali, an ancient Indian language, some two thousand years ago. Many scholars regard the Pali canon as the textual source closest to the teachings of Shakyamuni, although there are also very early texts in Sanskrit, another Indian language of great antiquity. In translation, references to Buddhist concepts are often made in either language, which are themselves related. For instance, *dharma* is expressed as *dhamma* in Pali, and *nirvana* as *nibbana*. For many centuries, Theravada monks and nuns have closely imitated the life of the historical Buddha and have attempted to maintain his dharma and vinaya as preserved in the Pali canon. They consider the Eightfold Path and the monastic codes as strictly authoritative. Deviations were and are considered delusory and hindrances on the path to liberation.

Theravada scripture contains a great deal of sophisticated reflection on the dharma, vinaya, cosmology, and human psychology, but the monastic path that took shape in the tradition many centuries ago was relatively direct and simple. Family life, sensuality, and worldly attachments were seen as obstacles to liberation. In time, a succession of stages to enlightenment were recognized within the monastic community. There were "stream-winners" who had gained the path and "once-returners" whose level of attainment assured them not more than one rebirth. The central and most venerable figure in the tradition, however, was the *arhat*, or "worthy one," who possessed the certainty that delusory and egotistic grasping had been extinguished. Arhats suffered no attachments in this life and expected no rebirth. Monastic Theravada Buddhism remains more or less oriented to these same ideas today.

In Theravada Buddhism, the monastic community is identified with the sangha while laity play a complementary, if somewhat secondary, role. Lay Buddhism is largely devoted to ritual practices, devotional expressions, and temporary ordinations that often serve as rites of passage, all of which are understood to be occasions for merit-making. The idea behind the relationship between monastics and laypeople has its own compelling logic. If one is moved to become a monk or nun and pursue liberation, this is caused by good karma in past lives. If one pursues the more ordinary goals of household and family, this too is a result of karma. Gaining merit is an important religious activity because it is thought to secure a better rebirth in which the exalted goal of nirvana might be pursued. In one sense, the Theravada tradition is marked by clerical elitism, but in another, lay Theravada Buddhists are comparable to churchgoing Christians who may be deeply pious and highly spiritual but are quite willing to forego the obligations of the clerical life of nuns, priests, and ministers.

Elements derived from the old Hinayana schools are found throughout Asia, but the Theravada tradition is today the dominant form of Buddhism in Sri Lanka, Thailand, Burma, Cambodia, and most other countries in southeast Asia. They all share a strong family resemblance in their ritual life, aesthetics, and institutional arrangements. They vary because Theravada has absorbed regional animistic religious traditions that remain important in rural south and southeast Asian villages, and has been reshaped by regional politics and history. There has not been a women's monastic order in the Theravada tradition since the tenth century c.e., when the bhikkhuni lineages were wiped out in the course of warfare, but more informally organized women pursue monastic practice in a number of countries. The questions of if and how these lineages are to be reestablished are a major source of controversy in the Theravada world today.

Theravada Buddhism seems to have a very bright future in the United States. It is one of the major forms of Buddhism in the Asian American immigrant communities, and the meditation techniques of the Theravada traditions are among the most popular forms of lay practice in the convert community.

Mahayana, or the Great Vehicle

Mahayana Buddhism began to emerge around 100 c.e. as a set of distinct emphases in the interpretation of the Buddha's teachings. For centuries, older and more traditional Buddhists and Mahayanists studied and practiced

together in monasteries on the Indian subcontinent. The gulf that eventually opened up between them is largely a product of geography, because the
innovations central to Mahayana later became dominant in China, Vietnam,
Japan, and Korea. The tradition took the name Great Vehicle because its
proponents saw the orthodoxy of the way of the elders as too narrow. Its development into a distinct tradition also gained momentum as Indian Mahayana Buddhists incorporated philosophies and devotional practices they
borrowed from Hinduism, which remained the dominant tradition of India,
into the dharma. As Mahayana spread outside the Indian subcontinent, it
further incorporated elements drawn from Taoism, Confucianism, Shintoism, and other indigenous traditions found in the civilizations of northern
and eastern Asia. Many American Buddhists, whether converts, immigrants,
or old-line ethnics, are part of the Mahayana tradition.

The contrast between the arhat and the *bodhisattva* is one of the chief
ways of differentiating between Theravada and Mahayana Buddhism. In the
early centuries of the common era, some Buddhists in India began to develop a critique of the arhat as the ideal practitioner of the dharma and vinaya.
They viewed the pursuit of personal liberation by individual monks and
nuns as fundamentally selfish. Mahayana philosophers began to give prominence to a different ideal, the bodhisattva who aspired to Buddhahood—the
attainment of wisdom or supreme enlightenment infused with a compassionate concern for all beings. On the level of practice, this emphasis gave
rise to the bodhisattva vow, a pledge that a person on the path, whether
monastic or lay, would forego ultimate liberation until such time as all people became free of suffering. On a more exalted level, this fostered the emergence of cosmic bodhisattvas, great mythological figures such as Manjusri,
Avalokiteshvara, and Kuan Yin, who were thought to reincarnate through
numerous lifetimes, always foregoing nirvana in order to teach wisdom,
compassion, and the liberation of all sentient beings. The ideal of the bodhisattva is central to Mahayana thought and practice and plays an important
role in its iconography and art.

This shift in understanding the dharma was also expressed in new
schools of philosophy whose consequences were far-reaching. Mahayana
Buddhists rejected the contrast between samsara and nirvana, seeing the two
as interpenetrating rather than as distinct modes of being. They expressed
this unified view of reality in terms of *nonduality*. There was neither nirvana
nor samsara, this world or another; all such distinctions rested on concepts,
ideas, and discriminations considered illusory. Philosophers expressed this
nondualism in terms of *shunyata* or emptiness, the idea that everything in the

universe is devoid of fixity and permanence. But emptiness also conveys the idea that beyond illusory distinctions is the blissful clarity of universal wisdom and compassion. Mahayana Buddhism is universalistic in the largest sense of the term. In some schools of philosophy, all sentient beings are thought to have the potential to realize awakened Buddha mind. Everything is ultimately thought to partake of Buddha nature. In analogous Christian terms, it is as if Mahayana philosophers argued in highly refined dialectics that heaven is earth, that eternity and the present are the same, and that the beatific vision of God is seen in all of creation. As a result of these shifts in interpretation, Mahayana Buddhists tend to speak of realizing Buddha mind or Buddha nature rather than attaining total liberation.

The Mahayana worldview was articulated in new scriptures such as the Diamond, Heart, Avatamsaka, and Pure Land sutras. Given Mahayana views about the universality of Buddha nature, the teachings in some of these, such as the *Lotus Sutra*, were readily attributed to Shakyamuni Buddha. But there are in Mahayana literature many buddhas and bodhisattvas. Some, such as Amida and Maitreya, are seen as saviors and play important roles in devotional Buddhism. Others are wise and compassionate teachers and brilliant preachers. Mahayana sutras also delight in depicting a universe vast in both time and space, infused by the energy of cosmic buddhas and bodhisattvas and sectored into many buddha lands and buddha fields.

Within this expanded cosmic view, Mahayana gave prominence to ideas inherited from earlier Buddhism about the interdependence of all beings, but with a new twist. For older schools of Buddhism, the interdependent nature of samsara was inescapably tied to impermanence, clinging, and suffering. In light of Mahayana nondualism, however, interdependence was more positively interpreted as interconnectedness or interrelatedness and, as such, something to be celebrated. With no interest in speculative questions about who or what created the universe, Mahayana Buddhists developed a vision of it as an endless cascade of causes and effects, driven throughout by moral purpose. Mahayana Buddhists often describe the interdependence of all beings as Indra's net. Indra was an ancient god of India, and his net became a metaphor for the interconnected universe in which each point of life was a jewel of Buddha nature, a node of potential enlightenment, sensitive to any movement toward enlightenment that occurred at any time and in any sector of the universe. The point of Buddhist practice was to realize this. Many American Buddhists are now applying Mahayana ideas about the interdependence of all beings to environmental and social concerns and see in these beliefs a spiritual complement to modern scientific theories about ecology and astrophysics.

Mahayana is a major influence in the United States, but within the tradition there are many distinct lineages, sects, and movements, a few of which are playing particularly important roles in the creation of indigenous forms of American Buddhism. In Chinese Mahayana Buddhism, there are many philosophical systems and regional traditions. But both monastic and lay Buddhism tends to be eclectic in approach to practice and philosophy, drawing together elements that in Japan and Korea later took shape as sectarian movements. As a consequence, Chinese Buddhism in this country, which flourishes primarily in Chinese immigrant and ethnic communities, is known for its diversity and complexity of expression. Chinese influence is also strong in the Vietnamese American Buddhist community.

Korean and Japanese Buddhism were originally imported from China. Over the course of centuries, however, they absorbed many elements of the indigenous traditions of their two countries and tended to reshape elements of Chinese Buddhism into particular sects and movements. Lay Korean Buddhism is practiced primarily in Korean American immigrant Buddhist temples, while the monastic tradition has been established in America in several thriving centers in the convert community.

Three Mahayana traditions of Japan are of particular importance in the United States; their distinctiveness is such that each requires a brief description here that will be further developed in later chapters. To a large degree, all three emerged as separate forms of Japanese Buddhism around the thirteenth century, and as protests against corruption in the monastic sangha. The founders of two of them, Shinran and Nichiren, emphasized devotional elements of Buddhist practice to suit lay practitioners in an age they saw as marked by the degeneration of the dharma. The third, Dogen, was more concerned with revitalizing the meditative disciplines practiced within the monastic community.

Shin Buddhism

Shin Buddhism is in the Pure Land tradition, a broad current in east Asian Buddhism that centers on the Amida Buddha and his paradise or Pure Land. Shinran, a monk in the powerful monastic establishment of Japan, was among the most influential founders of Shin Buddhism. Convinced that common people could not attain liberation in a degenerate age, he abandoned his monastic vows, married, and established himself as a married Buddhist cleric, a move that at the time was considered revolutionary. The doctrine he promulgated gave a unique emphasis to an ancient tradition of

Pure Land Buddhism. In a way quite consistent with Mahayana doctrines about universal Buddha nature, he taught that all people were guaranteed access to the Pure Land through the grace and mercy of Amida. The practice he taught was chanting the name of Amida out of a sense of respect, reverence, and gratitude. Shin Buddhism, which eventually split into a number of sects, became a highly popular and influential form of Buddhism in Japan. In the nineteenth century, one branch, the Jodo Shin-shu sect, was brought by Japanese immigrants to the United States, where it is today the oldest institutionalized form of American Buddhism.

Nichiren Buddhism

Like Shinran, Nichiren left the monastic establishment to become a religious reformer. His passionate conviction that the dharma was degenerate in Japan and the political importance he saw in this development have led many commentators to liken him to Martin Luther. Unlike Shinran, who tended to see other forms of Buddhism as partial and incomplete, Nichiren saw them as false and deluded. Like Shinran, Nichiren promulgated chanting as the most efficacious form of practice, but he focused his devotion on the *Lotus Sutra*, which many consider the most important text in Mahayana Buddhism, rather than on Amida Buddha and the Pure Land. Nichiren was a zealous missionary who envisioned Japan as the center from which his doctrine would spread throughout the world. Although he died in obscurity, his movement flourished, eventually developing a variety of sectarian traditions. There are a number of schools of Nichiren Buddhism in the United States, but the most prominent are Nichiren Shoshu Temple and Soka Gakkai International, both of which trace their American roots to the mid-twentieth century. They have the distinction of being the major form of lay devotional Buddhism with a substantial following in the American convert community.

Soto and Rinzai Zen

Zen Buddhism is a Japanese form of what in China was the Ch'an lineage of Mahayana Buddhism. Dogen was among Japan's most important Zen teachers. He traveled to China in about 1220 C.E. and returned to renew Zen in Japan; he is remembered as the founder of the Zen Soto school. The words *Ch'an* (Chinese) and *Zen* (Japanese) are related to the term *dhyana*, which in India meant "mental absorption." This origin points to

In all three vehicles or traditions, monastic institutions have played a critical role in the transmission of the dharma and in the creation of Buddhist philosophy, literature, architecture, and art. Eiheji, shown here, is the head monastery of the Soto school of Zen in Japan, one of the most prominent forms of Buddhism to have taken root in the United States.
DON FARBER

the emphasis this tradition places on meditation, whose chief form in Japan is called *za?en*, or "sitting in absorption." Soto Buddhists emphasize *shikanta?a*, "just sitting," a method of meditation in which the mind rests in a state of brightly alert attention, free of all thoughts and directed to no particular object of contemplation. But the Soto school became very popular in Japan because its monks also performed rituals for the laity, creating a relationship between monks and laypeople not unlike that in Theravada Buddhism.

Another school of Zen, Rinzai, also took on a distinct shape in Japan at about this time. Rinzai is often characterized as less formal and ritualistic than Soto Zen. This school also emphasized the systematic study and contemplation of *koans*—brief stories or fables whose enigmatic quality is meant to drive the mind toward enlightenment. Rinzai Zen has been important in American Buddhism since the early twentieth century, but the Soto school began to move into prominence in the 1960s. Many American Zen practitioners currently use elements drawn from both the Soto and Rinzai schools.

Vajrayana, the Diamond Vehicle

Some see Vajrayana as an extension of Mahayana, but others see it as a distinct Buddhist vehicle. It derives its inspiration from texts called *tantras*; thus it is also called Tantric Buddhism. Vajrayana arose in northern India and became important in the eclectic Buddhist mix in China and in Japanese Buddhist history. But Vajrayana became most thoroughly developed in Tibet and the surrounding regions of central Asia, where it fused centuries ago with indigenous shamanic religions. Vajrayana Buddhism was long dismissed by scholars and other observers as a corruption of the dharma. But in the last few decades, it has come to be seen as a brilliant expression of the teachings of the Buddha that developed in a unique setting. Much of this change in evaluation can be traced to the work of scholars, both Tibetan and American, in the United States.

Vajrayana draws upon the teachings and meditation techniques of the older, Hinayana schools, Mahayana cosmology, and forms of ritual practice adapted from Hinduism. *Vajra* means "diamond" or "adamantine" and is meant to describe the clear and immutable experience of the luminous void that is thought to be the essence of the universe. But Vajrayana practitioners also understand it to be the most complete form of the dharma, which if practiced assiduously can lead to total liberation in a single lifetime. In the last three decades, the tradition has come to play an increasingly important role in the Buddhist community in the United States, where the terms *Vajrayana*, *Tantra*, and *Tibetan Buddhism* are often used synonymously.

Vajrayana consists in part of visualization methods used to infuse the body, speech, and mind of the practitioner with the body, speech, and mind of enlightened beings. *Mudras* are ritual gestures used to express the qualities of particular bodhisattvas and buddhas whom a practitioner is visualizing. *Mantras*, chanted syllables or phrases, are used to harness speech to the path of liberation. *Mandalas*, symbolic representations of the forces of the universe in the form of divine beings, are used as aids to visualization. In early Tantra, sexual practices also played a role in harnessing the body to spiritual transformation. In Tibetan Buddhism today, this kind of practice is primarily expressed in art and iconography. Male figures represent compassion, females wisdom. When joined together in sexual union or *yab-yum*, which literally means "father-mother," they represent the unity of the two, which is understood to be the essence of the universe.

Mudras, mantras, and mandalas are used in the visualization methods of meditation in Tibetan, or Vajrayana, Buddhism. This sand mandala was constructed in the home of a television producer in Hollywood. Many in the entertainment community of the 1990s became outspoken supporters of the Tibetan struggle for religious and cultural independence.
DON FARBER

Tibetan Buddhist leaders are called *lamas* or teachers. Those who have completed a long course of study are often given the honorific title *rinpoche*, or "precious one." Many of them are also considered *tulkus*, reincarnations of prominent and highly evolved lamas. Tibet's major religious institutions are organized into four schools or orders, the Sakya, Gelugpa, Kagyu, and Nyingma. Within these schools are many lineages and sublineages, all of which have distinctive traditions and practices inspired by the examples of heroic founders and teachers. Each is associated with different buddhas, bodhisattvas, demon protectors, and guardian spirits. Tibetan Buddhists, however, also teach more austere meditative techniques that resemble Zen. One of these is *Mahamudra*, or "the great seal," which is considered the highest form of practice among the Kagyus. A similar practice in the Nyingma tradition is called *Dzogchen*, "the great perfection," which its practitioners consider the definitive, secret teaching of Shakyamuni Buddha. Formal monastic institutions play an important role in Tibetan Buddhism, but there is also a lively and influential tradition of married clergy. The power of these and other institutions in Tibet remained immense into the middle of the twentieth century.

All these traditions and institutions share strong resemblances that point to their origins in a shared national history. Tibetans also share a number of national figures, such as Gesar of Ling, a great warrior, king, and dharma hero celebrated in epic and song, and Padmasambhava, "the lotus-born," who is credited with taming the demons of Tibet and bringing them into the service of Buddhism. Tibetans consider Padmasambhava a second Buddha. Since the seventeenth century, the Dalai Lama, who is the head of the Gelugpa school, has also been the Tibetan head of state. All these traditions have been placed in serious peril as a result of the Chinese invasion of Tibet in the 1950s, an event that helped precipitate the transmission of the dharma of Tibet to the West. The fact that Tibetans are a community in exile has given a distinct shape to the processes by which it is being adapted in the United States.

In the last century or two, the teachings of the Buddha as expressed in all three vehicles have been further transformed in response to developments from European imperialism to industrialization, urbanization, secularism, and World Wars I and II. These and other developments have shaped an Asian Buddhist landscape that varies from country to country and region to region. The overall impact of modernity on Asian Buddhism, however, resembles more familiar effects in the West. In general, the great monastic traditions that flourished in medieval Asia have declined in influence over the past several centuries. There has been a parallel trend toward laicization, encouraged by the emergence of Asian democracies. New religious movements have also flourished in many countries, most noticeably in Japan, all of which owe a great deal to the past but are distinctly modern in their tone and emphases. Despite all these changes, Buddhism's basic vocabulary and many traditions remain inextricably rooted in history, as is the case in modern Judaism and Christianity. Despite the Anglicization of Buddhist philosophy and practice in the United States, this vocabulary remains essential to any discussion of the American Buddhist landscape today.

CHAPTER FOUR

The American Setting

The path of liberation taught by the Buddha was reshaped time and again as it spread throughout Asia, and new, indigenous forms of it are taking shape today in the vibrant Buddhist communities of the United States. The process of adapting the dharma to a new culture is highly complicated, involving the adaptation of religious practices to a new environment, the association of formerly unrelated ideas, and the recasting of received values into new ethical language. It takes many centuries for the dharma to become fully indigenized in a new setting because the immense work of cross-cultural translation requires the creativity of individuals but is at the same time essentially a collective undertaking. Buddhism has become a significant religious presence in this country only in the last few decades, so it makes more sense, strictly speaking, to talk in terms of there being many Buddhisms in America now rather than an American Buddhism per se.

However, two broad developments shed light on the current Buddhist landscape and suggest some of the forces at work in the creation of American forms of the dharma. The first development involves specific people and events that played integral roles in the introduction of Buddhism to this country. They not only helped to shape some important forms of American Buddhism but also provided convert Buddhists with both a history and a kind of indigenous spiritual lineage.

The second development sheds light on American Buddhism more indirectly. Immigration has played a powerful role in American religious history. Over the long term, it has reshaped entire communities and their religious traditions and has in the process altered the American ethnic, political, and spiritual landscape. A grasp of how immigration operated in the past provides some insight into how immigrant Buddhism may adapt to this country, even if it is too early to assess adequately how these adaptations will contribute to American forms of the dharma in the twenty-first century.

Early American Buddhist History

Many convert Buddhists see themselves as part of an alternative religious or spiritual tradition in this country that can be traced back to the decades before the Civil War. The historical accuracy of this claim is less important than the fact that it has created for converts a series of precedents and a sense of having an indigenous lineage. More generally, it also connects them to the nation's culture and history, which enables converts to select elements from America's past in forging new forms of the dharma. From a more strictly historical point of view, this lineage provides a glimpse of Americans' understanding of Buddhism as it evolved from romantic, often uninformed, simplicity to the complexity found in the community today.

The source of this lineage is often traced back to the Transcendentalists and America's early romantics such as Ralph Waldo Emerson, Walt Whitman, and Henry David Thoreau. Like romantics in Europe, they became fascinated with the religions of Asia, and their enthusiasm helped to shape the popular reception of those religions by Americans in subsequent decades. These men were among the first generation of western writers and intellectuals to have at their disposal the Hindu and Buddhist texts that scholars had been at work translating for several generations. The romantics' exposure to Buddhism was often very limited, but what they lacked in knowledge they compensated for with ardor and creativity.

It is easy to overestimate the importance of Asian religion to Emerson, Thoreau, Whitman, and others in their generation. Their example as creative writers and alternative religious thinkers inspired by the East is what really places them at the head of this lineage. Their importance to American Buddhism rests primarily in the fact that they inspired another generation of American seekers about a century later, the poets and writers of the Beat generation such as Jack Kerouac, Gary Snyder, Allen Ginsberg, Anne Waldman, and others. The Beat poets played critical roles by drawing Americans' attention to Buddhism and creatively appropriating the dharma in ways that inspired many in the convert community. The Transcendentalists, Beats, and a range of other writers are responsible for helping to indigenize the dharma through literary means. Buddhist images and ideas are finding expression in a wide range of fine and popular arts today, but Buddhism, particularly Zen, has had a substantial impact on American literature, particularly poetry, for several generations.

The Theosophical Society, which was founded in New York City in the 1870s, is another important development in this American lineage. Its founders, Henry Steel Olcott, a disaffected Presbyterian, and Helena Petrovna Blavatsky, a naturalized Russian immigrant, were probably America's first convert Buddhists. They took refuge in the Buddha, dharma, and sangha in Sri Lanka after moving to south Asia from New York. Olcott later became prominent when he helped Buddhist leaders in Sri Lanka defend themselves against Christian missionaries. He also worked to create a united front among Theravada and Mahayana Buddhist leaders in south, southeast, and northern Asia in an effort to resist the encroachment of Christianity in the age of European imperialism. Olcott is now regarded as a Sri Lankan national hero. Blavatsky and Annie Besant, Blavatsky's successor as head of the Theosophical Society, are remembered today as innovative spiritual leaders and as great sympathizers with the religious traditions of Asia.

Theosophy is a characteristically nineteenth-century and Victorian development in this American Buddhist lineage, insofar as it was a kind of fusion between East and West at a time when there was little real communication between the two. The Theosophical Society became one of the most important points of contact and continued to function in this way for many decades. Many Theosophists claim Theosophy is a form of Buddhism, but it is best understood as a hybrid modern spirituality that draws upon occultism, scientific thought, elements of Christianity and Judaism, and both Hinduism and Buddhism. Many features of Theosophy can be found today in New Age religious movements that are quite distinct from Buddhism. Some older convert Buddhists were Theosophists before embracing more orthodox, Asian forms of Buddhism.

The World's Parliament of Religions held in Chicago in 1893 is generally seen as a pivotal moment for this lineage. The Parliament was convened in conjunction with the World's Columbian Exposition, and was hailed at the time as the most comprehensive interreligious gathering in history, with delegates from around the globe representing ten different religious traditions. In many respects, the Parliament was most important as a domestic American religious event. It marked the emergence of Jews and Catholics as coequals with Protestants in the American religious mainstream and the coming of age of the first wave of American religious feminists. The glory

of the Parliament, however, is usually recalled in terms of its contributions
to the history of the encounter between East and West, which is somewhat
ironic because most Jews and Christians in attendance displayed attitudes toward the religions of Asia that were at best ill-informed and condescending.
The Parliament did, however, mark the formal debut of Asian religions,
particularly Hinduism, Buddhism, and Islam, in the United States. It was of
sufficient importance that a larger, more complex assembly was convened in
Chicago in 1993 to celebrate its centennial.

Although Buddhism played a somewhat secondary role at the original
Parliament, there are at least four reasons why it is a significant event in
American Buddhist history. First of all, Asian Buddhists presented Theravada, Zen, Nichiren, and other forms of Buddhism before a largely sympathetic audience, so that some Americans began to see Buddhism as a highly
variegated complex of traditions, rather than as a monolithic entity. The
Parliament also marked a point at which Buddhism was beginning to be understood within the context of modernity. Representatives such as Anagarika Dharmapala, a Theravada Buddhist and protégé of Olcott, and Shaku
Soyen, a Rinzai Zen monk and priest, were important leaders of modern
Asian Buddhism. They presented the dharma as a fully up-to-date, living
tradition at a time when most westerners still thought of Buddhism as a mys-

Held in Chicago, Illinois in 1893, the World's Parliament of Religions was a pivotal event in
the early history of the transmission of the dharma to the United States. Delegates from
the Nichiren, Zen, and Theravada traditions of Asia, seen to the right of the speaker,
received an enthusiastic reception from the American audience.
ORIGINALLY PUBLISHED IN JOHN HENRY BARROWS, THE WORLD'S PARLIAMENT OF RELIGIONS (CHICAGO: PARLIAMENT
PUBLISHING CO., 1893).

terious form of mysticism, exotic and hoary with antiquity. These Asian leaders also asserted that Buddhism, with its nontheistic and essentially psychological orientation, could better address the growing schism between science and religion than Christianity, a point that continues to be emphasized by many Buddhists today.

The Parliament is also seen as the beginning of the modern interreligious dialogue movement. A number of organizations devoted to cultivating understanding among the religions of the world date their origins from the Parliament. Such dialogue came to play an important role in the twentieth century, as globalization and intimate contacts among people of various religions increased decade by decade. Dialogue is also an essential element of the contemporary American Buddhist landscape, where converts and immigrants from a wide variety of traditions are engaged in conversation about how they differ and what they share. Dialogue among Buddhists, Christians, and Jews is also fostering greater understanding, aiding Buddhists' efforts to enter the American religious mainstream.

Above all else, however, the Parliament is a historic landmark because it set in motion the first Buddhist missions to the United States. After the Parliament, Dharmapala made a number of American tours, during which he encountered many earnest and intelligent people interested in Buddhism, although he grew weary of the self-indulgent quest for easy mysticism he also found among American seekers. Shaku Soyen made a number of tours as well, but more important, several of his Japanese colleagues and students, among them Sokei-an, Nyogen Senzaki, and D. T. Suzuki, followed in his footsteps. Their work in the first decades of this century effectively laid the foundations for American Zen Buddhism. Soyen also inspired Paul Carus, a scientific naturalist from Illinois, to become America's first major promoter and publisher of Buddhist scripture.

At around the turn of the century, a small number of Americans, at the most a thousand or two, were engaged in a conversation, largely carried on in print, about the demands of the American environment and the viability of Buddhism in it. They asked the kind of fundamental questions that had to be posed before a conscious process of translating the dharma into an American idiom could really begin. Could the teachings of the Buddha about the nonexistence of the self be reconciled with American individualism? Could a tradition emphasizing contemplation thrive in a culture known for its extroversion and activism? Would Americans embrace a nontheistic tradition? Wasn't a religion based on the premise that human life is characterized by suffering too negative and world-renouncing to appeal to a nation known for its optimism?

Eighty years later, these questions still elicit a wide range of answers among American converts and within the Buddhist immigrant community.

The character of the lineage and the quality of Americans' opportunities to encounter Buddhism changed significantly in the early decades of the twentieth century, when the Rinzai Zen colleagues and students of Shaku Soyen arrived in this country from Japan. Sokei-an was Soyen's dharma brother, which meant they shared the same teacher. He arrived in the United States in 1906, eventually taking up residence in New York City, but he returned to Japan for a time to complete his Zen training and, in 1929, was authorized to teach. He was later ordained a Zen priest. After returning to New York, he founded the Buddhist Society of America in 1931, later renamed the First Zen Institute, which was among the first Buddhist institutions established to serve native-born Americans. Ruth Fuller was among the leading lights of the Buddhist Society. She later married Sokei-an, eventually studied in a monastery in Japan, and is now celebrated as one of America's pioneering Buddhist women.

During this same period, Nyogen Senzaki, a student of Soyen, arrived on the West Coast. On the order of Soyen, he made no attempt to teach Buddhism in the United States for seventeen years, but spent this time familiarizing himself with American norms and mores. He worked for a time as a houseboy and tried his hand at farming and at the hotel business in San Francisco. In 1922, after he had fulfilled his vow to his teacher, he opened an informal group for Buddhist study and practice, which he called "the floating *zendo*" because it had no fixed headquarters. He first located it in San Francisco and then in Los Angeles, where he taught Zen meditation and Japanese culture to both Japanese Americans and European Americans. His poetry, such as this piece composed in 1945 on the anniversary of the death of Soyen, poignantly reflects his experience as an early immigrant Buddhist teacher.

> *For forty years, I have not seen*
> *My teacher Soyen Shaku, in person.*
> *I have carried his Zen in my empty fist,*
> *Wandering ever since in this strange land.*
> . . . .
> *The cold rain purifies everything on the earth*
> *In the great city of Los Angeles, today.*
> *I open my fist and spread the fingers*
> *At the street corner in the evening rush hour.*[1]

The fledgling Zen organizations founded by Sokei-an and Nyogen Senzaki became pioneering outposts for the few Americans who expressed an interest in the dharma in the early decades of this century. The approach to teaching they shared also anticipated a pattern that recurred later in the convert community. Both Sokei-an and Senzaki were trained in the rigorous regime of Zen monasticism, but they shared a critical attitude toward its institutional forms. They were also both attracted to the adventure of teaching the dharma and its practices to American laity, who were wholly oblivious to the traditionalism of Zen and its long institutional history. This combination of monastically trained Japanese teachers and American students with lay status and lifestyle was to become common in convert Buddhism in this country, even as Americans became much more sophisticated in their understanding of Japanese history and traditions.

Most American converts today have not, in any formal and traditional sense of the term, become Buddhist monastics. By and large, they have not been willing to submit themselves to the kind of institutional rigor found in Asian monasteries. Most are not celibate and need to balance practice with the demands of the nuclear family. But most have also not adopted the Asian lay role of providing support for monastics as a form of religious activity. As a result, most convert Buddhists are not quite monks and nuns and yet not quite typical laypeople, and convert Buddhism has yet to develop a strong, traditional monastic community. Many converts today applaud the absence of a Buddhist monastic tradition in this country and see mostly positive results from reshaping Buddhist practice to suit the needs of laypeople. Others, however, express concern that over the long term the lack of a strong American monastic tradition will hamper the growth of the dharma and undermine the integrity of the Buddha's teachings.

The issue was anticipated by a third figure during this early period, a native-born American named Dwight Goddard, a Protestant missionary first drawn to the dharma in the 1920s, when he lived and practiced for a time in a Kyoto monastery. Goddard was convinced the lay approach was inadequate for forging an American dharma. "The weakness of this method seems to be that coming under the influence of Buddhism for only two or three hours a week," he wrote, "and then returning to the cares and distractions of the worldly life, they [laity] fall back into the conventional life of the world."[2] Goddard sought to remedy this by founding the Followers of Buddha in 1934, which he intended to be an American monastic movement. He envisioned two monasteries, one in Vermont and another in California, to serve as homes for celibate renunciates who would devote their lives to the dharma with the support of American lay Buddhists. Goddard's vision did not materialize, but in 1932 he published *The Buddhist Bible*, an anthology of Theravada and Mahayana material, which several decades later introduced Jack Kerouac and others in the Beat generation to important Buddhist sutras.

The "Zen boom" of the 1950s is considered a major watershed in this American Buddhist history and lineage. Two individuals, D. T. Suzuki, a lay student of Shaku Soyen, and Alan Watts, an Episcopalian priest and popularizer of eastern religions, were instrumental in introducing Buddhism, and the Zen tradition in particular, to the United States. Together with the Beats, they helped to thrust Buddhism into the American mainstream. Prior to and through the 1950s, the dharma had remained more or less confined to bohemian quarters and was the preoccupation of a small handful of spiritual seekers. In the course of the next decade, however, Buddhism began to turn into something that resembled a mass religious movement.

D. T. Suzuki first came to the United States in 1897 as a young man, and for eleven years worked as a translator of Buddhist material for Open Court Publishing, a press run by Paul Carus. In the early decades of the twentieth century, Suzuki moved between Japan and the Sokei-an circle in New York. During the 1950s, however, he taught Buddhism for six years at Columbia University, where his lectures caught the attention of many literary and academic figures, as well as younger New York poets and bohemians at the core of the Beat movement. Suzuki's Columbia lectures also caught the attention of publications such as *Vogue* and *Time* magazine, which helped to move Zen toward the mainstream. The Columbia lectures, *Time* reported, "are drawing a wide variety as well as a large number of students since the war. Painters and psychiatrists seem especially interested in Zen, he finds. Psychoanalysts, says Dr. Suzuki, his tiny eyes twinkling under wing-like eyebrows, have a lot to learn from Zen."[3] Suzuki became the outstanding figure in American Buddhism at mid-century. He also helped to inaugurate a dialogue between psychotherapy and Buddhism, which has played an increasingly important, sometimes controversial, role in the Americanization of the dharma.

Four years later, in 1958, *Time* charted the Zen boom by devoting an article to Alan Watts, noting that "Zen Buddhism is growing more chic by the minute."[4] Watts, an Englishman, had explored Buddhism for years, first in England, then in New York, and later in California. In the 1950s and early '60s, he became a widely read author on Buddhism, Christian mysticism, psychotherapy, and spirituality. His book *Beat Zen, Square Zen, and Zen*, published in 1959, remains a valuable glimpse into American Buddhism on the eve of the 1960s. Watts tended to dismiss Beat Buddhists like Jack Kerouac as self-indulgent dabblers. He was only slightly less critical of Square Zen, by which he meant the Buddhism of Japanese immigrants and of monastic establishments of Japan and their small circle of American followers. However, Watts praised what he saw as the true spirit of Zen, which he presented as a kind of free-form, humanistic spirituality infused with creative potential. His effort to popularize the dharma was immensely successful. The individualistic, upbeat, and humanistic quality of his version of Buddhism and its emphasis on creative self-expression fit well with the expansive idealism of the early 1960s.

The Beat movement also played an important, and at times highly controversial, role in the popularization of Buddhism. Early Beats such as Kerouac, Ginsberg, and Gary Snyder helped to Americanize the dharma through their creative use of Buddhism in poetry and other literature. Kerouac became the archetypal spiritual rebel; Ginsberg, the ecstatic and ironic holy man. Gary Snyder, who served as the inspiration for Japhy Ryder, a central

The publication of Jack Kerouac's *The Dharma Bums* in 1958 marked the emergence of Beat Zen, one important development during the Zen boom of the 1950s. The book subsequently played a key role in introducing Americanized ideas about Buddhism to the generation that came of age in the 1960s, and continues to interest young people in the dharma.
VIKING PRESS

character in Kerouac's seminal novel, *The Dharma Bums*, is now the most highly regarded of all of them. Unlike many others in the Beat generation, Snyder made an early decision to cultivate Zen in a sustained way, and he spent much of the 1960s practicing in a Japanese monastery. While in Japan, he also married and began to raise a family, and published his first two books of poetry. In his later poetry and essays, Snyder was a pioneer in linking Buddhism to broadly American themes such as Native American myths, nature, and ecology.

The Beats selectively identified themselves with the Transcendentalist generation and, as with their role models, much of their writing was the expression of a spiritual revolt with political overtones. To the degree that they cast this revolt in Buddhist terms, they paved the way for identifying the dharma with social and political criticism, a trend that would become more pronounced in some quarters in the following decades. For instance, Kerouac, who was by and large not a political thinker, saw Buddhism as a vehicle to protest conformity, as when he wrote around 1954:

> *Self be your lantern/self be your guide—*
> *Thus Spake Tathagata*
> *Warning of radios*
> *That would come*
> *Some day*
> *And make people*
> *Listen to automatic*
> *Words of others.*[5]

Snyder was more outspoken, libertarian, and utopian in some of his writing about the social implications of the dharma moving West. "The mercy of the West has been social revolution; the mercy of the East has been the individual insight into the basic self/void. We need both," he wrote in 1961. For Snyder, Buddhist morality implied

> supporting any cultural and economic revolution that moves clearly toward a free, international, classless world. It means using such means as civil disobedience, outspoken criticism, protest, pacifism, voluntary poverty and even gentle violence if it comes to a matter of restraining some impetuous redneck. It means affirming the widest possible spectrum of non-harmful individual behavior—defending the right of individuals to smoke hemp, eat peyote, be polygynous, polyandrous or ho-

mosexual. Worlds of behavior and custom long banned by the Judeo-Capitalist-Christian-Marxist West.[6]

As Snyder's remarks suggest, the Beats also forged a link between the pursuit of enlightenment and the use of drugs, an association not wholly without Asian precedents that became widespread in the counterculture in the 1960s. This left an indelible impression on many, but by no means all, who are now in the older generation in the convert community. *Tricycle*, a highly regarded Buddhist review associated with a Beat-hip strand in convert Buddhism, conducted a poll among its readers in 1996 regarding the relationship between Buddhism and the use of psychedelics. Of 1,454 people who replied, 89 percent stated they engaged in Buddhist practice, and 83 percent said they had also taken psychedelics. Over 40 percent said that their interest in Buddhism had been sparked by taking LSD or mescaline. While statistics indicated that most respondents no longer took drugs, 71 percent believed that "psychedelics are not a path but they can provide a glimpse of reality to which Buddhist practice points"; 51 percent saw no fundamental conflict between Buddhism and psychedelics, while 49 percent expressed the conviction that drug use and Buddhism do not mix.[7]

Suzuki, Watts, and the Beats helped to create a distinctive American approach to Buddhism, which many regard in hindsight as both highly creative and deeply problematic. But it influenced many converts in the baby-boom generation. Their introduction to the dharma was largely through books, and they easily drew from them the conclusion that the pursuit of enlightenment could be highly individualized and personalized, filtered through humanistic psychology, augmented through the use of mind-altering substances, pursued without sustained discipline, and divorced from institutions. Many Americans who became involved in Buddhism in the 1960s had little idea what they were getting themselves into. Most who stayed and developed deep commitments to Buddhist practice eventually distanced themselves from the more extreme expressions of free-form spirit promoted in the 1950s.

"The Sixties," a phrase that generally refers to a period from about 1963 to the mid-'70s, are likely to be looked back upon for some time as the most important turning point in American Buddhist history. At around that time, convert Buddhism in this country grew from a small community of seekers preoccupied primarily with Zen to a far larger and more differentiated community, as people in the burgeoning counterculture went in search of spiritual alternatives and found them in Zen, Nichiren, Tibetan, Theravada, and other kinds of Buddhism, whose teachers they discovered among immigrants to this country and overseas. The thin line of historical precedents that ran from the antebellum period to the 1950s dramatically broadened in the course of those years, creating the foundation for what is today the vibrant complexity of American convert Buddhism.

The '60s also had a dramatic impact on immigrant Buddhism, because migration from Asia soared after changes in immigration law in 1965, a result not apparent to most observers until the 1980s. Immigration had helped to shape American Buddhism in the past, when Chinese and Japanese Buddhists arrived on the West Coast as early as the 1840s. But the far larger post-1965 wave of Asian immigration introduced a wide range of traditions into American Buddhism, with a long-term impact that is undeniable but is at present extremely difficult to gauge.

A Note on Immigration

The importance of immigration to American Buddhism cannot be overstated. America's first Zen teachers, Sokei-an and Nyogen Senzaki, were immigrants, as were a good many of the Theravada bhikkhus, Zen masters, and Tibetan lamas who taught some of the most prominent leaders in the convert community today. In most Buddhist quarters in this country, there are lively channels of exchange between the United States and Asia maintained by immigrants, refugees, and exiles and by teachers and practitioners within the convert communities. Buddhist immigrants from Asia, both teachers and the rank and file, continue to arrive in this country, adding fresh blood and ideas. To put the impact of immigration on American Buddhism into perspective, it is helpful to have a sense of how immigration influenced other American religions in the past.

Immigration is not always a mass phenomenon with dramatic consequences. It sometimes entails just a handful of newcomers having only a subtle effect on the religious lives of a limited number of individuals. For instance, the Catholic community in the late colonial period was relatively small and confined, more or less, to Maryland. These English Catholics maintained a low religious profile due to legal and religious restrictions imposed by Protestants. Mass was often said at home, and Catholics cultivated forms of piety that were unadorned and simple. They practiced their religion in a style informed by the rationalism of the British Enlightenment and the aristocratic character of their English-speaking community. This began to change in the 1790s, when a number of priests arrived fleeing the chaos of the revolution in France. Once in this country, they taught American Catholics different, more baroque forms of continental observance. This did not result in American Catholics building baroque churches or taking up French Catholicism as a whole, but it did subtly reshape their religious lives. As a result, an Anglo-French form of piety became prominent in American Catholicism in the early decades of the nineteenth century, one that virtually disappeared only when a much larger wave of Catholic migration began from Ireland and Germany in subsequent decades.

Immigration is having this kind of small-scale effect throughout the American Buddhist community, where Chinese, Tibetans, Thai, Japanese, and practitioners of other national forms of Buddhism are influencing Americans' and each other's modes of practice in numerous ways. For instance, several years ago, in a Zen center in the mountains of southern California, young students asked their American teachers to allow them to construct a weight room and fitness center, expressing their need for more strenuous activities than sitting zazen or doing t'ai chi, a form of martial art. After due consideration, the teachers turned down their request, thinking that StairMasters and Nautilus machines were not appropriate to a contemplative setting. Shortly thereafter, however, the center was visited by a group of young Korean monks who had recently arrived in this country. They spent an hour or more each morning engaged in a rigorous practice regime that involved the repeated performance of full-body prostrations. Their prostration regime was soon incorporated by the Zen students into their daily practice as a way to vent energy and get physical stimulation while cultivating discipline. This kind of cross-fertilization between Buddhist traditions is at work across the country, even if commentators have not yet given it sustained attention because it is often difficult to see. In time, however, this mixing of traditions is likely to lead to the emergence of new forms of practice that are distinctly American.

Mass immigration also has had very dramatic effects on American religious history. It has reshaped the religious contours of entire communities, as in the case of American Judaism. Throughout the nineteenth century, the liberal Reform movement was on the rise among German American Jews, who at the time formed the bulk of the nation's Jewish community. While its origins were in Germany, the Reform movement became particularly strong in America as its leaders dropped many traditional forms of piety and practice in an effort to give Judaism a religious style resembling that of the Protestant mainstream. Rabbis adopted hymn singing and began to give sermons. Some moved their services from Friday night to Sunday morning. Many leaders

soft-pedaled the traditional idea that Jews had a special relationship with God
and abandoned their hope of being able to return to Israel.

This kind of innovation was called into question around the turn of the
century, when a vast new wave of Jewish immigrants, more traditionally religious than Reform, began to arrive in this country from Russia and eastern
Europe. For several decades, there was acute tension between the two communities, not unlike that which today separates convert and immigrant Buddhists. In the early twentieth century, however, these tensions began to abate
as the two communities mingled and began to influence each other. Eventually, American Judaism was reshaped into the Reform, Orthodox, Conservative, and Reconstructionist traditions that accommodated the religious
and political differences within a greatly enlarged Jewish community.

This kind of large-scale reshaping has already occurred in American
Buddhism in the case of the Jodo Shinshu tradition, where ongoing migration from Japan has continually introduced traditional elements into an
Americanized group. But it is likely to recur as further waves of immigration
influence both particular ethnic and national groups and the entire American
Buddhist community. This process is observable, however, only in the long
term, and it is difficult to discern at present how such large-scale processes
are shaping indigenous forms of the dharma. But barring any curtailing of
Asian immigration, a constant stream of newly arriving Buddhists is certain
to have an impact on the first generation of immigrants and their highly
Americanized children.

Immigration has also changed America in ways that can only suggest
how Buddhism might one day have a powerful impact on the entire nation.
Over the course of a century or more, both Jews and Catholics, representing a wide range of ethnic and national groups, moved from the margins of
American society into its mainstream. The many legal, political, and cultural developments resulting from this process are the substance of a great deal
of American religious history. Most of the consequences are today largely
taken for granted. But one need only think about the complex role played by
the papacy in American Catholicism, or by Israel in American Judaism, or
by ethnic identity in both groups to grasp how immigration forges living
links between the United States and communities overseas.

This kind of link is being forged in American Buddhism both in convert
and in immigrant communities, although they tend to operate quite differently. While there is a good deal of interaction among and between converts,
most take their primary inspiration from a single tradition, whether Theravada, Zen, Nichiren, Vajrayana, or another. These traditions tend to operate

as points of contact with Asia in what can be called "communities of discourse." All Buddhist traditions have unique literary and philosophical heritages, distinct ways of practicing the dharma, and different Asian vocabularies. They have been introduced into this country in different ways, which have in turn affected the histories, institutional expressions, and ongoing relations to Asia of particular groups in a wide variety of ways. In contrast, immigrant (and refugee) Buddhists are forging these links to Asia within "diaspora communities," nationally, culturally, and religiously distinct groups in this country that maintain ties to their homelands including familial relations, religious institutions, political convictions, and an enduring sense of cultural and ethnic identity. As in the case of Catholics and Jews, the strength of these ties may wax and wane over generations but they are rarely entirely severed, even when groups have been thoroughly Americanized.

The next six chapters explore historical and contemporary developments within selected American Buddhist communities. Each chapter is meant to stand alone and is shaped somewhat differently because there have been unique developments and issues in each community. While it is my intention to provide a kind of road map for American Buddhism, readers should understand at the outset that this account is far from comprehensive. There are numerous Buddhist traditions and groups in this country that do not appear in this book. But my hope is that this account is sufficiently rich to enable readers to grasp some of the drama and complexity of a momentous event going on all around them—the transmission of the dharma from Asia to the United States.

Part Two

MAJOR TRADITIONS

CHAPTER FIVE

Jodo Shinshu:
America's Old-Line Buddhists

The Buddhist Churches of America (BCA) is the oldest major institutional form of Buddhism in the United States. Its Japanese American members are among the nation's Buddhist pioneers, who have the most experience with the challenges involved in creating American forms of the dharma. For over a century, BCA Buddhists followed classic patterns of religious adaptation by immigrants. They brought received philosophies, institutions, ritual practices, and customs to the New World, where they selectively retained, abandoned, and adjusted them to make them work in a new culture. As was the case among Catholics and Jews, their course was determined largely by trial and error and was driven by perennial forces such as Anglicization, generational change, and the gradual movement up from the margins of society into the middle-class mainstream.

However, there have been important variables at work in their version of the immigrant saga, related to Buddhist history in Japan, Americans' preoccupation with race, and long-standing tensions in Japanese-American international relations. The name Buddhist Churches of America was suggested during World War II by Japanese Americans in an internment camp in Topaz, Utah. It was adopted shortly thereafter at a conference in Salt Lake City, in an effort to blunt associations with America's wartime enemy across the Pacific and to emphasize the institution's Americanness. There was no Buddhist vogue in this country during World War II; that would only come later. Nor was there much of a precedent for being both Buddhist and American.

The Buddhism of the BCA is part of a broad stream of Pure Land doctrine and practice that runs from India throughout China, Vietnam, and

As the oldest major institutionalized form of American Buddhism, the BCA has been a pioneer in transplanting and adapting the dharma to the culture and society of the United States. This stupa, a devotional reliquary mound, is located on the roof of BCA headquarters in San Francisco and is reputed to be the oldest of the many stupas now found in America. THE PLURALISM PROJECT AT HARVARD UNIVERSITY

Korea to Japan, where it is called Shin Buddhism. There it became a discrete movement in the thirteenth century, and subsequently one of the most popular forms of Japanese Buddhism. The BCA is in a specific school of Pure Land founded by Shinran and known as Jodo Shinshu, the True Pure Land School. More particularly, it is a branch of Nishi Hongwanji, the Western School of the Original Vow, a form of Jodo Shinshu that was prevalent in the region of Japan from which many Japanese Americans originally migrated. For about fifty years it was called the Buddhist Mission to North America (BMNA), a name that reflected both its status as subordinate to its headquarters in Kyoto and its original missionary character.

The members of the BCA are America's old-line, ethnic Buddhists, but they do not comprise a large community. One estimate placed BCA membership at roughly 20,000 adults in 1996. Nor do they wield a great deal of influence in the broader American Buddhist community. They are, however, seasoned veterans of the American experience and have negotiated many of the pitfalls in the process of assimilation for over a century. They not only have paid a high price for being Japanese but also have had to articulate and defend their distinct brand of Pure Land Buddhism, which has been easily and often confused with Christian theism. In the current landscape of American Buddhism, they are in between categories, neither convert nor immigrant. But their sensitivity to the issues involved in the Americanization of the dharma may, in the long term, enable them to help broker relations between the two much larger groups that currently dominate discussions about the future of Buddhism in the United States.

A Century of Adaptation

The history of the BCA has been largely shaped by a long-term conflict between Japanese and American national interests. The origins of American Jodo Shinshu can be traced to the 1870s, when Japanese began to arrive on the West Coast, where they often worked as agricultural laborers. At this early date, most immigrants assumed they would return to Japan, so transplanting their religious and cultural traditions was not an issue. But by 1900, the community had grown to over 24,000, a substantial enough number to warrant establishing the Buddhist Mission to North America. At about this time, Pure Land, Nichiren, and Zen Buddhism were also being introduced to the United States at the World's Parliament of Religions in Chicago. The two developments are not wholly unrelated; both Japanese immigration and the Parliament were a part of a larger sequence of events as Japan and the United States explored each other and their political, economic, and military interests in the Pacific basin. Eventually, American Jodo Shinshu Buddhists would be caught between the two countries.

Hindsight reveals perennial tensions in BCA history, dating back to small events of the first year it began to set down roots in this country. The first missionary priests arrived in San Francisco to serve the Japanese community in 1898, the same year the United States went to war with Spain and annexed Puerto Rico, Guam, and the Philippines, an inauspicious conjunction of events that would lead to a wartime disaster for the community in the middle of the next century. There was also a hint of how religious innovation and traditionalism would both come to play a role in the community. During their brief stay, these priests founded a Bukkyo Seinen Kai, a Young Men's Buddhist Association (YMBA), an innovative form of lay Buddhist organization inspired by Christian institutions in Japan. The following year, the first Hanamatsuri and Gotan-E ceremonies, honoring the birthdays of the Buddha and Shinran respectively, were held in the community. YMBA members soon sent a formal petition to the Kyoto headquarters of Nishi

Hongwanji to request the posting of a permanent missionary in America, a move the Japanese consul to the United States disapproved of as politically imprudent and potentially inflammatory.

The formal history of the BCA is usually dated from 1899 and the arrival of the first permanent Jodo Shinshu missionaries, Shuye Sonoda and Kakuryo Nishijima. The following decades were marked by the kind of institution building normally undertaken by the pioneering generation in an immigrant community. Young Men's Buddhist Associations and temples were founded along the West Coast from Seattle to San Diego. A newsletter was established to facilitate communications between isolated communities, many of which were located in rural, agricultural areas. The Fujinkai, or Buddhist Women's Association, was established, and would subsequently play an important role in the development of Jodo Shinshu. Throughout this period, BMNA religious activities were conducted primarily in Japanese.

In the early 1900s, the first anti-Japanese agitation gripped the West Coast, resulting in attacks on Japanese businesses and buildings and the formation of the Asiatic Exclusion League, based in San Francisco, in 1905. This agitation resulted in the Gentleman's Agreement of 1907, legislation that restricted immigration to the wives and children of Japanese men already residing in this country. On one hand, this limited the growth of the BMNA. On the other, it fostered the emergence of stable, family-oriented Japanese communities in which the Jodo Shinshu temples came to play an increasingly important part. Unlike in Japan, temples in America became the site of a wide range of religious and social functions—bazaars, dance parties, baseball games, and movies; funerals, weddings, memorial ceremonies, and Sunday services. In rural areas, temples became especially strong because they had a virtual monopoly on the social life of the community.

During this period, relations were also normalized with the Nishi Hongwanji temple in Kyoto. The leader of the BMNA was first called a *kantoku*, or director, but in 1918 was elevated to *socho*, a chancellor or bishop, and headquartered in the San Francisco temple. By 1914, the BMNA had constructed a new building from which the socho directed an institution with about twenty-five branches and temples. Until World War II, these North American institutions remained under the spiritual direction of the Monshu, the abbot of Nishi Hongwanji, who by tradition was always selected from among the direct descendants of Shinran. The more routine management was carried out by various Kyoto legislative and administrative bodies. Despite continuing anti-Asian sentiments, the BMNA was sufficiently confident to host a World Buddhist Conference in 1915 at the Panama Canal Exposition in San Francisco, during which BMNA leaders decided to create missionary programs for youth and to open Sunday schools, and began to draft a formal constitution.

The BMNA entered another phase around 1920, which continued up to the start of World War II. It was marked by increasing anti-Japanese and anti-Buddhist pressure from the dominant society and, with the coming of age of Japanese American youth, the emergence of second-generation issues.

State and national legal initiatives began to effectively isolate Japanese Americans several decades before their wartime internment. In the early 1920s, with increased concerns about the influence of Japan in the Pacific, a number of western states passed alien land laws aimed at limiting Japanese ownership of property. In 1922, the Supreme Court reviewed a long-standing case that bore on naturalization, ruling that American citizenship was a privilege reserved for "free white Americans" and people of African descent. The Oriental Exclusion Act was passed in 1924. It included a provision that no Japanese who were not already citizens or who had not been born in the United States would be granted citizenship. Immigration quotas were subsequently set that overwhelmingly favored Europeans.

As a consequence of these legal initiatives, Japanese often encountered difficulty securing land for new temples. Sometimes Caucasian Christians aided them, but at other times blocked them by whipping up local anti-Japanese sentiments. In the 1920s, a number of Japanese religious groups in Los Angeles, both Buddhist and Christian, were prevented from founding new temples and churches.

The unjust nature of this legislation actually helped to increase the number of American Buddhists. Many Japanese Americans had been hesitant to identify themselves as Buddhist, but exclusion encouraged them to band together for welfare and security. As a result, the temple also became increasingly important, as the headquarters for a range of social and cultural services from Japanese-language schools to rotating credit systems, and as a center in which continuity with Japanese culture could be maintained. Many Caucasians viewed this inward turn on the part of the Japanese as evidence of chauvinism, but the temples actually served as vehicles for Americanization by sponsoring athletic leagues, Boy Scout troops, and American-style dances. This double function of the religious center—providing both cultural and religious continuity and mechanisms for adaptation and change—is a phenomenon also found in Jewish and Catholic immigration history.

This period also marked the beginning of a rift between the first, immigrant generation, the *Issei*, and the second, American-born generation, the

Nisei, a type of generation gap unique to immigrant communities. Anglicization is a primary second-generation issue, and the way in which it is resolved has a long-term impact on the religious life of a community. The Japanese language was used by the Issei and BMNA ministers, and it structured the religious life of the entire community well into the 1920s. Questions about how to translate Jodo Shinshu doctrine and practice into English surfaced in 1926, when the BMNA began to train Nisei as instructors for its Sunday schools. As the numbers and importance of the Nisei grew over the next decades, it became necessary to selectively retain, translate, and abandon religious language that had long played a central role in defining the community. In the short term, changes made in religious language posed a threat of unintended Christianization. In the long term, however, they helped to create a fluid vocabulary, part Japanese, part English, that continues today to give a distinct ethnic and religious character to the Jodo Shinshu community.

Anglicization gave what some have seen as a Protestant cast to the Jodo Shinshu religious worldview. *Socho* became "bishop," *gatha* "hymn," and *kaikyoshi* or *jushoku*, "minister." *Bukkyokai* and *otera* were translated as "church" or "temple," *dana* as "gift," and *sangha* as "brotherhood of Buddhists." Countervailing trends also emerged. Terms associated with religious service—*shoko*, the offering of incense; *juzu* or *nenju*, rosarylike beads; and *koromo*, the robe worn by the priest—were retained. Complex abstract and historical terms—*karma*, *nirvana*, *Mahayana*, and *Hinayana*—gained expression in Anglicized forms of ancient Indian Sanskrit. At the same time, other ancient south Asian terminology that began to come into vogue among early convert Buddhists, such as the use of *bhikkhus* and *bhikkhunis* to describe individuals committed to the dharma, were rejected as alien to the religious spirit of a Japanese lay community.

More fundamental institutional shifts underway also were expressed in the shifting use of language. There were varied ministerial ranks in the Nishi Hongwanji sect in Japan—*tokudo, soryo, jushoku, kyoshi, fukyoshi*, and others—that reflected degrees of formal education, residential status, and level of ordination and certification. All the nuances of office conveyed by such terms vanished when translated into rough English equivalents, "priest," "minister," or "reverend." Similar shifts had consequences on a highly practical level. Most Jodo Shinshu temples in Japan are owned by families and are passed on to eldest sons on a hereditary basis. In contrast, Jodo Shinshu ministers in the United States became personnel hired by the BMNA to serve congregations.

Despite the BMNA's strong move toward Americanization, many Nisei began to drift away from Buddhism, without necessarily converting to Christianity. At the same time, Issei began to recognize the permanent character of their stay in the United States. The older generation did not necessarily feel at home or at ease in America, which had often given them little reason to do so. But their commitment to the new country had become manifest in their work, their emotional ties with other Japanese Americans, and in the lives of their Nisei children who had become thoroughly American.

This situation was radically altered at the onset of World War II. The bombing of Pearl Harbor on December 7, 1941 resulted in an immediate roundup of Issei businessmen, religious and community leaders, and martial-arts teachers. Despite formal statements of loyalty issued by BMNA leadership, the Federal Bureau of Investigation began to investigate all Japanese Americans, but especially those in the Buddhist community. For most of the summer of 1942, the community was under suspicion, which led many BMNA members to burn sutras and conceal family altars. In February of 1942, President Franklin Roosevelt signed Executive Order 9066, which designated the West Coast as a military district from which all alien Germans, Italians, and persons of Japanese ancestry were to be removed. Subsequently, 111,170 Japanese Buddhist, Catholic, and Protestant—were interned in about a dozen camps located in several states across the nation. Of these, 61,719 were Buddhist, the majority of them Jodo Shinshu.

The internment camps accelerated both the processes of Anglicization and Americanization and the emergence of the Nisei as the leaders of the Jodo Shinshu community. For a time, religious services in the camps were required to be in English, which marked the beginning of the use of the English language in worship. People from a range of Buddhist traditions also found themselves interned together, which fostered the growth of an ecumenical dimension within the larger Japanese American Buddhist community. Nyogen Senzaki, the Zen pioneer who led his floating zendos in San Francisco and Los Angeles, left a poetic record of this defining moment in American Buddhist history. "Thus I have heard," begins one poem written in 1942, echoing the opening lines of many a Mahayana sutra, "The army ordered / All Japanese faces to be evacuated / from the city of Los Angeles." Other poems convey a sense of the collective religious life of Buddhists in camps such as Heart Mountain, Wyoming, where Senzaki was interned.

An evacuee artist carved the statue of baby Buddha.
Each of us pours the perfumed warm water

Over the head of the newly born Buddha.
The cold spell may come to an end after this.
A few grasses try to raise their heads in the tardy spring,
While the mountain peaks put on and off
Their veils of white cloud.

Or again:

Sons and daughters of the Sun are interned
In a desert plateau, an outskirt of Heart Mountain,
Which they rendered the Mountain of Compassion or Loving-Kindness.
They made paper flowers to celebrate Vesak, the birthday of the Buddha.[1]

Internment also pushed Nisei ministers, of whom there were only four at the time, to the forefront of the community, due to their ability to negotiate with authorities in English. Nisei also rose to prominence as a result of a questionnaire issued by the War Relocation Authority in 1943 in an attempt to determine Japanese American loyalties. Two questions in particular served to drive a wedge between the Issei and Nisei, one about the willingness of those interned to serve in the United States armed forces, the other about renouncing all allegiances to Japan. These questions posed few problems for Nisei, who were native-born, English-speaking, American citizens. But for Issei, who were legally excluded from citizenship, they proved more problematic. Those Issei who answered no were considered high risk by the government. They were isolated together in a camp at Tule Lake, California. Those who answered yes to both questions were moved elsewhere and eventually granted early release if they did not return to the West Coast, a development that led to the establishment of temples in the east.

The camps also played a decisive role in reshaping and Americanizing the Jodo Shinshu institutions. Ministers met in February of 1944 at the camp in Topaz, Utah, where Ryotai Matsukage, the current socho, was interned. There they first proposed to change their name to Buddhist Churches of America. Later the same year, they voted to reincorporate as the BCA, repudiate all ties to Japan, redefine their relation to Nishi Hongwanji in Kyoto, and redesign the organizational structure of the BCA to shift more power to the Nisei. They also made the position of BCA bishop an elective office.

The history of the BCA after the war is a Japanese American and Buddhist version of the return to normalcy. Temples that had been closed during the war needed to be reopened. Businesses had to be rebuilt and wartime financial reversals overcome. New temples in the east founded by those released early from the camps had to be integrated into the institutional life of the BCA. Soon the *Sansei*, or third generation, began to come of age in postwar America.

This period of reconstruction came to an end in 1966 with the founding of the Institute of Buddhist Studies (IBS) in Berkeley, California, an event that is often cited as the symbolic culmination of earlier Americanizing tendencies. BCA ministerial candidates, who previously had gone to Kyoto for Japanese language-based religious education, were now able to receive English-language education in their native land. New Issei candidates, who continued to play an important role in the BCA, were expected to arrive in this country with English fluency and to attend IBS for intensive study and training. In 1968, a Canadian-born Nisei was selected as bishop and, for the first time in the history of American Jodo Shinshu, the inaugural ceremony was held not at Nishi Hongwanji in Kyoto but in the United States.

Mainstreaming Jodo Shinshu

Despite the trauma and humiliation of internment, the Japanese Americans in the BCA emerged in the 1960s as a small, ethnically and religiously distinct minority group that was part of the broader American middle class. With renewed confidence, they began to play a role in political and religious debates in the secular arena. The BCA was influential in California debates over public-school curricula during the 1980s and '90s, which tested the strength of the nation's commitment to multicultural education.

The BCA Ministerial Research Committee also helped to successfully challenge the use of a grade-school textbook that contained racial stereotypes about Japanese Americans and displayed a pro-Christian, anti-Buddhist bias. The BCA publicly adopted a strong "wall of separation" position against the teaching of creationism and prayer in the public schools and thus joined in a long tradition of appeals to the Constitution by ethnic and religious minorities. Its position, however, contains a Buddhist twist, as evidenced in several key paragraphs in a document entitled "BCA Resolution Opposing the School Prayer Amendment."

Whereas, Prayer, the key religion component [of the amendment], is not applicable in Jodo Shin Buddhism which does not prescribe to a

Supreme Being or God (as defined in the Judeo-Christian tradition) to petition or solicit; and

Whereas, Allowing any form of prayer in schools and public institutions would create a state sanction of a type of religion which believes in prayer and "The Supreme Being," would have the effect of establishing a national religion and, therefore, would be an assault of religious freedom of Buddhists;

Resolved, That the Buddhist Churches of America and its members strongly oppose any form of organized prayer or other religious observances in public schools and public institutions, which are organized, supervised, or sanctioned by any public entity, except as permitted by the current constitutional law.[2]

These efforts reflect the sensitivity of the leaders of the BCA to the kind of pressures they had experienced in this country over the course of a century as both a racial and a religious minority group. Minority immigrant communities face special challenges because the ideas, customary modes of thought, and even sentiments of the dominant group take on a normative character in any society and exert a great deal of pressure, both subtle and gross, on all immigrants. The ways in which they both conform and resist conformity give a unique dynamism to the religious life of the community.

Some outside pressures brought to bear upon Japanese Americans in the BCA have been extraordinary—racism, the rising competition between the United States and Japan, World War II, and the internment camps. But much subtler forces have also been at work in the past and still are today, from norms of decorum to the theistic religious ideas presumed by most Americans.

Two examples illustrate the intimate ways in which the sensibilities of the dominant culture affected Jodo Shinshu Buddhists in subtle but concrete ways. The first is drawn from an interview conducted with an Issei kaikyoshi (a distinct type of Japanese missionary minister) in the early 1970s, reproduced here with the definitions and clarification of the interviewer.[3]

INT: What is the difference between Issei Buddhism and Nisei Buddhism, and then Sansei Buddhism?

RESP: That definition would be based on majority membership, and so, of course, [on the] accompanying psychological or other cultural differences.

INT: But are they all Buddhists?

RESP: All Buddhists, yes.

INT: Now, is Jodo Shinshu Buddhism different between the Issei, Nisei, and Sansei?

RESP: I don't think so, and the doctrine, of course, never changes. Buddhism you know consists of the triple jewels: [the Buddha], the teachings of the Buddha, and the Sangha [brotherhood of Buddhists]. . . . The Sangha may be changing. Even the vocabularies must be carefully used. This is a funny example, but the lady's breast is a symbol of mother's love in Japan. So we often refer to Ochichi o nomaseru [literally: to allow someone to drink from the breast], but some Issei ministers came to this country and explained [this concept] pointing [to the breast region] causing laughter among the [non-Japanese speaking] audience. So we have to adapt ourselves to this particular situation even linguistically. So from that standpoint, maybe our way of presentation must be changed.

INT: But not the doctrine.

RESP: Not the doctrine.

A second example comes from "The Point of Being Buddhist, Christian or Whatever in America," an article by Evelyn Yoshimura first published in 1995 in *Rafu Shimpo*, the oldest and largest Japanese American daily newspaper in the United States.[4] But it soon found its way into *Hou-o: Dharma Rain*, the online community newsletter of the Vista Buddhist Temple in southern California. The article is about how peer pressure from Christian friends can have an impact on teenage Buddhists.

One part is devoted to recounting events that took place at a local Baptist church sponsoring Friday-night socials for area youth. Buddhist teenagers in attendance found themselves confronted with an inspirational talk that reiterated simplistic and, for many people in Christian circles, old-fashioned ideas about Buddhism. Christianity was promoted as the only true religion, while Buddhism was characterized as the " 'worship of suffering' and the quick ticket to hell." Some Baptist children later began to aggressively evangelize Buddhist students at school. This religious zeal, Yoshimura noted, was experienced by Buddhists as "the pressure to 'fit in.' " Some Buddhist teenagers reportedly converted to Protestantism. A second part of the story was about a Buddhist girl who had hosted a party at her home, where she was cornered by Christian students who urged her to convert. She was so angry and upset that she left her own party.

The upshot of all this, however, was that a number of Buddhist children began to explore the Buddhist tradition more deeply. As Yoshimura recounts it:

> The Buddhist kids began talking to each other and their parents and other temple adults about this pressure they were feeling. And during the course of these discussion, they realized that Buddhism is harder to explain than Christianity because there's a lot of ambiguity, and it's not based on "belief." Rather, it focused on seeking the "truth" and trying to be honest with others and especially yourself. There is no supreme being. No soul. Only actions [karma] and what remains from them. Hard to explain in 25 words-or-less.

Yoshimura went on to report that teenagers from temples in other areas in southern California subsequently participated in a Saturday-night Buddhist discussion group.

The temples of the BCA have long served both as religious organizations and as cultural centers in which traditional language and folkways can be maintained as a vital part of community life. Taiko, a form of ceremonial drumming, is practiced by young people in many Jodo Shinshu temples, as at Senshin Buddhist temple in Los Angeles, pictured here.
THE PLURALISM PROJECT AT HARVARD UNIVERSITY

Given its century of experience, the BCA now approaches such pressures with both confidence and self-consciousness. Renewed attention is being paid to the priorities and sensibilities of the youngest generations, those who are now the third, fourth (*Yonsei*), or even the fifth (*Gosei*) in line from the founding one. Sectarian doctrine and traditionalism remain important in American Jodo Shinshu, but the BCA is by no means monolithic. BCA leaders advocate renewal of a dharma-centered church, temple, or sangha, in a range of conservative and progressive modes. Others emphasize the cultural dimensions of the life of the temple and the importance of the Japanese language to the maintenance of religious sentiments and ethnic identity.

As is often the case in the histories of American immigrant communities, there is a movement in the third and subsequent generations to return to tradition. Masao Kodani, a prominent Sansei minister in Los Angeles, wrote in the mid-1990s that a "renewed emphasis on traditional ritual allowed many Jodo Shinshu Buddhist temples to remove many of the Congregational Christian elements of service worship that found their way into the Sunday service, while maintaining the 'Sunday go to meeting' custom of American religion."[5] This also meant that temple-sponsored basketball leagues, an important element in contemporary temple life, flourished side by side with Japanese cultural traditions such as *taiko* (folk drumming), *Bon Odori* (an annual ceremonial dance), and *Mochi-tsuki* (the making of rice cakes).

There was, however, a downside to the mainstreaming of the BCA. Like the mainstream Protestant churches, it has problems such as institutional inertia, financial shortfalls, and declining membership. Like ethnic Jews and Catholics, BCA members discovered that their arrival in the mainstream often resulted in the loss of ethnic and religious identity. Declining membership, together with a high rate of outmarriage, has encouraged renewed attention to adult education and to developing international exchanges with Japanese Jodo Shinshu and other Pure Land groups. At the same time, some temples and study groups have attracted more non-Japanese, who despite their long presence as both members and ministers in the BCA have always formed a very small percentage of the total community. One minister has included zazen groups in the temples he leads, a move that conservatives consider controversial for doctrinal reasons that will be considered shortly. A number of Jodo Shinshu leaders have also worked to set up lines of communication among converts and new immigrants within the broader American Buddhist community.

American Jodo Shinshu Practice and Worldview

Most American convert Buddhists identify the dharma with sitting meditation, tend to dismiss Jodo Shinshu as a form of lay devotional Buddhism, and have little understanding of its traditions. But over the course of four or five generations, Jodo Shinshu has been Anglicized, modernized, and adapted to the culture of the United States. Despite its minority status in the Buddhist community today, the BCA is in the forefront of Americanization. Pure Land Buddhism is, moreover, one of the most popular dharma traditions in Japan and it is of major importance in other Asian American Buddhist communities, most prominently the Vietnamese and Chinese. Thus, while the BCA is itself a small and distinctive sect outside the ken of most converts, its philosophy, doctrine, and practice resonate with the traditions of other immigrant communities.

The Pure Land

Jodo Shinshu means literally the "True" (*Shin*) "School" (*shu*) of the "Pure Land" (*Jodo*). For many centuries, Pure Land practice in east Asia took the form of chants, visualizations, and vows, many of which are still used in Chinese Buddhism. They have been used to gain a temporary rebirth in the Pure Land, which is thought to provide an ideal environment in which to prepare for the attainment of enlightenment in another life. Ancient sutra literature describes the Pure Land in lavish language meant to convey its transcendental nature—golden trees, jeweled terraces, delightful music, scented winds, and beautiful birds whose singing calls to mind the Buddha, dharma, and sangha. The Pure Land is an environment wholly designed to foster one's ability to ultimately achieve liberation.

Over the centuries, many Buddhists have thought of the Pure Land as a distinct, otherworldly location, and many westerners have likened it to popular ideas of Christian heaven. But other interpreters have long understood the Pure Land to be more a transcendent state of being than a location. Ancient sutras portray the Buddha as passing into *samadhi*, a deep trance state, before he preached on the Pure Land, which suggests it is best understood as a reflection of his awakened consciousness. His descriptions of the Pure Land are often considered an expression of the Buddha's skill in using symbols to communicate with unenlightened beings. Today some Jodo Shinshu Buddhists describe the Pure Land as a liberating realm into which one passes after death, later returning to the world of samsara to carry on the bodhisattva's task of helping all beings achieve enlightenment. Others talk of it more as a sense of joy, peace, and delight experienced within the conflicts and contradictions of this life.

Amida

Amida Buddha has often been understood by non-Buddhists to be a direct parallel to the western idea of a personal God. Some American Jodo Shin-shu Buddhists have been known to equate the two—one result of the linguistic pitfalls that have come with Anglicization. In some forms of Buddhism there are many gods, but Amida is not one of them. He is rather among the greatest of the cosmic buddhas of the Mahayana tradition.

As told in the sutra literature, Amida was originally a man named Dharmakara who renounced the world and set out to attain enlightenment. After meditating for many ages, he announced his intention to create the most perfect Pure Land, the character of which he described in forty-eight vows. By fulfilling these vows through rigorous devotion and practice, he eventually became a fully realized buddha. From the great storehouse of merit he accumulated, he created the Pure Land, where he took up residence as Amida. *Amida* means infinite life and light, and connotes the boundless wisdom and compassion of all the buddhas and bodhisattvas.

This story has inspired philosophical reflection and undergone doctrinal elaboration over the centuries. Since the time of Shinran, the Jodo Shinshu tradition has emphasized Dharmakara's vows, particularly the eighteenth. In this vow, Dharmakara stated that he would forego total liberation if rebirth into his Pure Land lay beyond the reach of people "who sincerely and joyfully entrust themselves to me, desire to be born in my land, and contemplate on my name even as many as ten times."[6] Because Dharmakara eventually gained liberation and took up residence in the Pure Land, this vow is taken to mean that all can enter there by calling on Amida.

Amida is somewhat like the Christian God insofar as they are both considered to be other than mere humans. God and Amida are also both considered the source of love and mercy. Jodo Shinshu is a *tariki* or "other power" path, in contrast to paths characterized by the term *jiriki*, which means "one's own efforts." In this context, "other power" means that realization comes through the power and grace of Amida. Practices such as zazen are considered to be jiriki, and it is a point of Jodo Shinshu doctrine that all such paths are fruitless activities. Unlike the Christian God, however, Amida is not understood to be an omnipotent creator, judge, and law-giver. Nor is Amida considered a being distinct from the created universe. He is rather a manifestation of "oneness" or "suchness," terms used in the Mahayana tradition to denote the Buddha nature (or mind) innate in the universe.

Shinjin

Shinjin is often translated as "faith," but is also used without translation, such as in the phrase "shinjin consciousness." It refers to a spiritual transformation that takes place within this life, which simultaneously involves understanding, awareness, and insight. It is an awakening to an entirely new mode of being in the world, becoming aware of one's own limited human nature and the oneness of all being. This transformation is brought about not by self-initiated acts such as rituals or zazen, but through the grace and compassion, the other power, of Amida. Shinran equated shinjin with the initial state of enlightenment referred to by Theravada Buddhists as that of "the stream-winner," who has not overcome all defilements but can be assured of eventually attaining total liberation. Shinjin also implies insight into Mahayana teachings about the interdependence and interconnectedness of all things in the universe. Jodo Shinshu Buddhists understand the transformative power of shinjin as resting on the merit of the vows fulfilled by Dharmakara and bestowed on people by Amida.

Nembutsu

The term *Nembutsu* refers to the phrase *Namo Amida Butsu*, or "Name of Amida Buddha," which plays a particularly important role in Jodo Shinshu Buddhism. As a chant or recitation, the phrase has a long history of use in Pure Land Buddhist traditions, but it was elevated to its central position in Japanese Pure Land schools in about the twelfth century. One Japanese reformer, Honen, emphasized the oral repetition of the Nembutsu as a way to attain rebirth in the Pure Land. Shinran, who was his disciple, recast his understanding of the phrase in a small but important way. He taught that the Nembutsu should be chanted not to attain the Pure Land, but out of thanks to Amida for already having granted one entrance into it. By doing this, Shinran moved the other power of Amida into the foreground of Pure Land philosophy.

In Jodo Shinshu, the Nembutsu is understood to be an expression of joy and gratitude to Amida, a call to him naturally arising from shinjin consciousness. On a more modern and colloquial level, chanting the Nembutsu is a way to entrust oneself to Amida, who will buoy one up in the face of inner and outer turmoil and confusion. Jodo Shinshu Buddhists do not consider the Nembutsu a mantra to be used to evoke awakening or to invoke Amida, as a Vajrayana Buddhist might. Chanting mantras, like doing zazen, is a jiriki practice that Jodo Shinshu Buddhists consider ineffectual.

The importance of fine doctrinal considerations such as these should not obscure the fact that the religious life of the BCA is also rich in traditional ritual and ceremony—Hanamatsuri, the commemoration of Gautama's birth; Gotan-E, Shinran's birthday; and Jodo-E, the celebration of Buddha's enlightenment. Home altars, which are used both to call Amida to mind and to honor ancestors, have long played an important role in Jodo Shinshu piety and still do today. Funerary rites and periodic memorial services for ancestors remain an integral part of BCA religious life, inherited from the many centuries in Japan during which Buddhism became associated with death and the next life. Forms of temple etiquette—gassho, a small bow made with hands pressed together as a sign of respect; the carrying of the juzu, a rosarylike string of beads used in chanting; the precise ways in which to burn incense on different occasions; the reception of a *homyo*, or dharma name—continue to influence Jodo Shinshu identity, sensibilities, and piety.

But despite the importance of tradition, doctrine, and ceremony, America's Jodo Shinshu Buddhists are in many ways much like parish Christians. There are "bazaar Buddhists" who are rarely seen at temple services, but turn out to work at annual socials that are big events in the communal life of the BCA. There are "board Buddhists," whose chief contribution to religious life is helping to administer the temple. There are also Buddhist "basketball moms," who devote a good deal of their time to shuttling children in minivans from one temple activity to the next. The Fujinkai, or Buddhist Women's Association, has been a mainstay of Jodo Shinshu since its earliest days, and in the past few decades women have also joined the ministerial ranks of the BCA.

However much Jodo Shinshu Buddhists may resemble many middle-class Christians in these and other regards, there are noteworthy differences. The BCA community has over its relatively long history in the United States negotiated ways to live in two worlds—a Buddhist world rooted in east Asia and a European American world shaped largely by western Christianity. In one of his writings, Masao Kodani of the Los Angeles Senshin temple notes that "the way in which we absorbed these two seemingly incompatible traditions, the Far Eastern and American, is what makes us unique. We are not Japanese as in Japan, we are not American as in apple pie, nor are we the best of both." Most times BCA Buddhists move easily between these overlapping worlds "but with periodic moments of anguish when we try to resolve the contradictions."[7]

Some of the anguished moments to which Kodani refers are undoubtedly related to religion. BCA Buddhists often criticize themselves for what they see as their passivity, their unwillingness to identify the pursuit of happiness as success, and their reluctance to engage in extroverted, American-style positive thinking. But Kodani sees these same traits as an introspective Buddhist value orientation that is to be cultivated and cherished. "The truth about ourselves is more important than positive self-image and positive-thinking. The joy of the dharma is because one has been moved to the truth of oneself, not because one get what he wants. Getting what one wants is happiness, being guided to what is true is Joy. Happiness and Joy in this context are two unrelated words."[8]

Kodani further developed this line of Buddhist religious thinking in *Becoming the Buddha in L.A.*, a 1993 documentary produced by Boston's WGBH Educational Foundation.[9] His remarks reflect the confidence and collective wisdom of a religious and racial minority community that, over the course of a number of generations, negotiated its way from the margins to the American mainstream. "If you came from western Europe, you share a tradition," Kodani told the interviewer, Diana Eck of Harvard University.

> Ours is very much different. It is based on a very different view, that you do not press upon somebody else what fundamentally may not be real anyway—yourself, or your idea of who you are. If you come from a Buddhist tradition, a mature person is someone who learns to be quiet, not to speak out. Which is quite different from an American tradition. If you come from a Buddhist tradition, someone who says he knows who he is is rather suspect. A mature person is someone who says that he doesn't know who he is.

Referring to an idea central to traditional Christianity and implicit in many Americans' ideas about themselves, Kodani added that "our religion says that there is no such thing as a soul. Not only that, the impulse to believe in one is what causes suffering. This is fairly, radically different, I think, and it affects how you look at everything."

In his view, however, such fundamental divergence of religious beliefs need not be a source of antagonism and conflict. "We need to understand, I think, that unity does not mean unanimity," Kodani noted.

The Buddhist experience is based on this. Oneness does not mean agreement. It means everybody is different and that is the reason why we can get along. . . . I don't think that it is true you have to agree—on pretty much anything—to get along. I mean if you don't believe that there's no such thing as a soul that doesn't impinge on me. It doesn't ruin my day, you know. Why should my insistence on a nonsoul ruin yours? Right? That position is very important for America because more than any other country, the whole world is here.

Largely due to its small size and its collective sense of decorum, the BCA is often overlooked in the current debates about immigrants, converts, and the future of Buddhism in the United States. But its members have paid substantial dues in the past, and have justly secured status as the trail-blazers of the American dharma. However the BCA negotiates its current challenges, Jodo Shinshu Buddhists share with a relatively small number of other Japanese and Chinese Americans the unique place of an old-line, middle-class Buddhist ethnic group in the American Buddhist mosaic currently in the making.

CHAPTER SIX

Soka Gakkai and Its Nichiren Humanism

Soka Gakkai International-USA (SGI-USA) is the American branch of a worldwide Nichiren Buddhist movement that has its origins in Japan. For the past half century, its own unique path toward Americanization has been deeply influenced by tensions between a highly traditional Nichiren priesthood and the innovative spirit of the laity. During these decades, priests and laypeople together formed an organization called Nichiren Shoshu of America (NSA). But long-standing conflicts of interest between the two parties erupted in 1991 into a formal schism. Since then, the movement has split into two organizations, the smaller Nichiren Shoshu Temple (NST) led by the priesthood and Soka Gakkai International-USA, a much larger, wholly lay movement. The lay nature of SGI-USA, the energy its members displayed in the wake of the schism, and liberal elements it inherited from its prewar Japanese origins have helped to transform it into one of the most innovative forms of Buddhism on the current American landscape.

There are, however, other variables at work in Soka Gakkai that contribute to its uniqueness. Nichiren Shoshu of America first began to flourish in this country in the 1960s when many Americans embraced Asian religions, but was never as intimately identified with the counterculture as Zen. As SGI-USA, it is primarily a form of convert Buddhism, although there are in it many immigrants, from both Japan and elsewhere in Asia. Japanese immigrants, moreover, played a pivotal role in laying its foundations in this country. But as a result of its successful propagation in American cities, SGI-USA also has a larger proportion of African American and Hispanic American members than other convert Buddhist groups. Many people know that

Tina Turner, the dynamic African American entertainer, is a Buddhist, but most do not understand that she is a Nichiren Buddhist, having embraced the dharma during the heyday of the NSA.

Nichiren is a uniquely Japanese form of Buddhism, named for the thirteenth-century reformer Nichiren, who gave shape to it as a distinct religion. Nichiren's doctrine and practice, however, stand well within the broad Mahayana tradition that is dominant throughout east Asia. Like many other forms of Mahayana Buddhism, it takes its inspiration from the *Lotus Sutra*. Over the centuries, more than thirty Nichiren sects and movements arose in Japan, but Soka Gakkai's most unique characteristics are rooted in mid-twentieth-century Japanese religious history.

SGI-USA currently claims between 100,000 and 300,000 members, the wide margin of error being partially attributable to the home-based nature of the movement. It is a well-organized institution, but many members freely move in and out at the grassroots. Soka Gakkai has little in common with Zen and other traditions embraced by other convert Buddhists, partly due to Nichiren doctrine, which in the past has tended to be strongly sectar-

SGI-USA has a highly articulated institutional structure, but the daily ritual of chanting in a home-based setting forms the foundation for members' dharma practice. These people in a Los Angeles–area home are chanting before an altar that contains a gohonzon, a replica of a mandalalike scroll first inscribed by Nichiren in the thirteenth century.
Soka Gakkai International

ian, and to the style of Nichiren proselytizing, which until recently was highly evangelistic. Attitudes among other convert Buddhists also play a part in this separation. Many of them see Nichiren Buddhists as too devotional in their orientation to practice and too prone to see the dharma as a vehicle for achieving material, as well as spiritual, well-being. They distrust Nichiren's evangelical tendencies and assume its high degree of institutionalization implies authoritarianism. In some respects, however, the gulf that separates Zen and Nichiren Buddhists in this country is based on a mutual lack of understanding and reflects an antagonism between the two groups that has a long history in Japan.

Japanese Historical Background

Many of the underlying forces at work in the Americanization of Nichiren Buddhism today can be traced back to the progressive ideas of Tsunesaburo Makaguchi, the founder of Soka Gakkai. Makaguchi was born in 1871, into a poor family in a small village in northwestern Japan. Little is known about his early life, but by 1893, when he accepted a position as a supervising teacher in a primary school in Sapporo, his lifelong passion for progressive education had already taken shape. Japanese education was at the time highly regimented, having been designed to train loyal citizens to aid in the industrialization and modernization of Japan. But earlier in the century, Japanese intellectuals and educators had exhibited a great deal of interest in progressive and humanistic theories of education imported from the United States, England, and Germany. As a result of his teaching experience, Makaguchi became highly critical of the Japanese educational system and turned for inspiration to these progressive theories.

In 1901, Makaguchi moved to Tokyo where, despite his lack of university training, he hoped to publish in order to gain a scholarly reputation that would enable him to work for education reform. Despite well-received publications on Japanese cultural geography and folk societies, he remained outside the university establishment, working in a variety of editorial positions. In 1913, he returned to education as a primary-school principal in Tokyo. For the next two decades, he was a teacher and administrator in the Tokyo schools, during which time he gathered material for a four-volume collection, *Soka Kyoikugaku Taikei* (*System of Value-Creating Pedagogy*), published in the early 1930s, in which he developed his progressive educational theories.

Makaguchi's theories are one foundation for Soka Gakkai International, and three different secular sources inspired his ideas about *soka* or value creation. One was cultural geography, a scholarly field that had a number of prominent Japanese interpreters around the turn of the century. Makaguchi drew upon their ideas about the reciprocal relation between culture and environment and its influence on the development of the individual. Another was the work of the American pragmatist John Dewey, who was widely hailed in the United States for his ideas about progressive education. The third source of inspiration was modern sociology, particularly the ideas of Lester Ward, from whom Makaguchi derived basic ideas related to values and their creation. Makaguchi envisioned an educational system in which the pursuit of individual happiness, personal gain, and a sense of social responsibility could all work together to foster the development of a harmonious community. The details of his ideas and the soundness of his theories are not important here. Some have dismissed him as a naive idealist, while others have praised him as a visionary.

Nichiren Buddhism became a second foundation for Soka Gakkai International in 1928, when Makaguchi joined Nichiren Shoshu or "The True Sect of Nichiren," apparently sensing a need for a religious dimension to value-creation education. There was little evidence of the impact of religion on his ideas until 1937, when he published a pamphlet entitled "Practical Experimentation in Value-Creation Education Methods Through Science and Supreme Religion." As its title suggests, he began about this time to explicitly link value creation to the Buddhism of Nichiren. The same year also saw the formation of Soka Kyoiku Gakkai (Value-Creation Education Society), the forerunner of today's Soka Gakkai International, with Makaguchi as its first president. Until it was disbanded by the Japanese government in 1943, the Value-Creation Education Society grew increasingly preoccupied with religion. *Kachi Soʐo* (*The Creation of Value*), the group's monthly periodical, published Makaguchi's ideas about value creation alongside testimonials from its members as to how Nichiren religious practices had brought them material and spiritual benefits.

In July 1943, Makaguchi and the entire leadership echelon of the Value-Creation Education Society were imprisoned. The Japanese government accused them of treason for their resistance to wartime efforts to consolidate Nichiren Shoshu with other Nichiren sects and for their militant opposition to State Shintoism. In November 1944, Makaguchi died of malnutrition in prison at the age of 73, having refused throughout his incarceration to recant his dual allegiance to the Value-Creation Education Society and Nichiren Buddhism.

The link between value creation and Nichiren Shoshu was strengthened in the postwar decades by Makaguchi's successor, Josei Toda, a long-time aide and friend who was also incarcerated. In his cell in Sugamo prison, Toda chanted the *daimoku*, a central practice of Nichiren Buddhism, more than two million times, which became the basis for a powerful religious experience that subsequently informed his life's work. After the war, Toda revived the movement under the name Soka Gakkai (Value-Creation Society), dropping the term *kyoiku*, "education," which suggests how he would steer the organization away from secular concerns toward a more profoundly religious emphasis. As Toda worked to revive Soka Gakkai, he also became convinced that the movement had faltered in the prewar years because it lacked doctrinal clarity and discipline, so he began to teach the *Lotus Sutra* and the writings of Nichiren. Toda became the second president of Soka Gakkai in 1951. By his death in 1958, he had transformed it into one of postwar Japan's most vital and vibrant new religious movements, claiming a membership of more than 750,000 families.

Toda's success rested on his skill in implementing *shakubuku*, a form of proselytizing, preaching, and teaching long associated with Nichiren Buddhism, as a way to address the postwar social chaos in Japan, which he likened to the turmoil in Nichiren's day. His religious vision was also informed by Nichiren's idea of *kosen-rufu*, a term that connotes both the conversion of the world to true Buddhism and a utopian vision of world peace and harmony. Toda linked these practices and ideas to value creation in a way that gave meaning both to the personal lives of individuals and to their proselytizing activities. "You carry on shakubuku with conviction," Toda told his followers in 1951. "If you don't do it now, let me tell you, you will never be happy."[1] This kind of exhortation to evangelize in order to achieve personal happiness was central in Soka Gakkai in Japan throughout the 1950s, as it would be later in the United States. "Let me tell you why you must conduct shakubuku," Toda told his followers in Japan.

> This is not to make Soka Gakkai larger but for you to become happier. . . . There are many people in the world who are suffering from poverty and disease. The only way to make them really happy is to shakubuku them. You might say it is sufficient for you to pray at home, but unless you carry out shakubuku you will not receive any divine benefit. A believer who has forgotten shakubuku will receive no such benefit.[2]

Toda's religious convictions played an immense role in shaping the movement, even as he unintentionally laid the groundwork for the later schism. Toda consolidated the institutional relationship between Soka Gakkai and Nichiren Shoshu, which under Makaguchi had proceeded on a more personal level. In 1951, he petitioned to have Soka Gakkai formally incorporated as a religious group. According to its charter, Soka Gakkai and its members became subject to the sacramental authority of the Nichiren priesthood, who were empowered to perform weddings, funerals, coming-of-age rites, and memorial services, and, most important, to issue the *gohonzon*, a religious scroll that is an essential element in Nichiren Shoshu worship. Soka Gakkai also took on the responsibility of registering its members at local Nichiren Shoshu temples and of observing the doctrines as defined by the traditions of the priesthood. Toda also made *tozan*, the pilgrimage to Taisekiji, the head Nichiren Shoshu temple near Mount Fuji, a central element in Soka Gakkai practice.

Toda's linking of Makaguchi's progressive ideals and Nichiren Shoshu institutions created an immensely effective, if inherently unstable, alliance, which resulted in periodic outbreaks of tension between the priesthood and laity. But it was left to Toda's successor as Soka Gakkai president, Daisaku Ikeda, to oversee the tensions result in an outright schism.

Daisaku Ikeda, who is still president of Soka Gakkai International, is considered by many to be among the greatest modern Buddhist leaders, although he has his share of detractors and critics. He converted to Soka Gakkai in his late teens, and for a long time served as the Youth Division Chief. He was prominent in the shakubuku campaigns under Toda, who designated Ikeda as his successor. In 1960, Ikeda became president of Soka Gakkai and, through a succession of terms in office, he has remained the most powerful figure in the lay movement for almost forty years.

During this long tenure, Ikeda has reshaped Soka Gakkai into a more moderate and avowedly humanistic Buddhist movement through a process that seems to have been largely trial and error. From the start, he continued to emphasize the importance of shakubuku, although he gradually modified both the tone and techniques of proselytization. He recast the idea of kosen-rufu to mean the broad dissemination of, rather than the conversion of the world to, Nichiren Buddhism. During this time, Ikeda also transformed Soka Gakkai from a domestic *new religion*, a term generally used to refer to postwar religious movements in Japan, into a worldwide movement with national organizations on every continent.

Ikeda consistently praises Toda as his chief inspiration, but he also returned Soka Gakkai to Makaguchi's emphasis on progressive education. In 1961, he created the Soka Gakkai Culture Bureau, with Economic, Speech, Education, and Art departments that foster value formation. He founded Soka High School in 1968 and Soka University in 1971, both of which are meant to showcase value-creation pedagogy. Ikeda led Soka Gakkai into politics in Japan with the founding in 1964 of Komeito, the "Clean Government Party." Its electoral success led to widespread concerns about the influence of a new religious group on the government and about the violation of the postwar separation of church and state, which in 1970 led Soka Gakkai and the Komeito to legally separate. No comparable effort to directly connect religion and politics has been made in SGI-USA.

Under the leadership of Daisaku Ikeda, Soka Gakkai retained SGI's religious foundations in Nichiren Buddhism while re-emphasizing the humanistic ideas of its first president, Tsunesaburo Makaguchi. The dynamic leadership of Ikeda, shown here at Harvard University, helped to transform what had been a "new religion" in postwar Japan into a worldwide Buddhist movement.
SOKA GAKKAI INTERNATIONAL

Despite his deep commitment to the *Lotus Sutra* and Nichiren's teachings, there is little doubt that Ikeda's brilliance and success helped to precipitate the break between Soka Gakkai and Nichiren Shoshu. Ikeda has long been regarded by his followers as a great *sensei* or teacher. His charisma is such that many have likened him to a new Nichiren, which did not sit well with the Nichiren Shoshu priesthood. On a more fundamental level, however, the rupture occurred because the dynamic growth of Soka Gakkai simply began to outrun the authority, power, and imagination of the Nichiren Shoshu priesthood, particularly once Soka Gakkai began to flourish as an international movement.

Early Developments in the United States

The gradual changes in Soka Gakkai under Ikeda's leadership are reflected in the evolution of the American movement. Shortly after his installation as its third president in 1960, Ikeda made his first trip to the United States, one stop on an initial worldwide mission to set in motion global shakubuku. In a speech he delivered in San Francisco, Ikeda invoked Christopher Columbus and likened his arrival in the New World to the inauguration in the United States of shakubuku. "We have now made the first footprint on this continent as did Christopher Columbus," Ikeda noted. "Yet we face even a greater task than he in driving home the wedge on this tour. Twenty or fifty years from now this day will be marked with great importance."[3]

At about this time, there were in the United States about 300 members of Soka Gakkai, mostly Japanese immigrants, many of them Japanese wives of American servicemen. Stories about the early efforts of these pioneering women have now taken on legendary proportions. But it does seem that much of the diversity now found in the ranks of SGI-USA can be attributed to the audacity of these women, who engaged in shakubuku in a wide range of American neighborhoods.

The first American organization, named Soka Gakkai of America and only later Nichiren Shoshu of America, was founded by Ikeda in 1960. The first English-language meeting was held in 1963, as was the first All-America General Meeting with 1,000 people in attendance. Between 1960 and 1965, tozan or pilgrimage to Taisekiji, the priesthood's temple near Mount Fuji, was made four times by American members. By the middle of the decade, the *World Tribune*, the NSA newspaper, was being published. Throughout this period, NSA operated without a formal leader but grew under the informal direction of Masayasu Sadanaga, a Korean-born immigrant who was raised in Japan but migrated to the United States in 1957. In 1968, Sadanaga was appointed by Ikeda as American General Chapter Chief. Soon afterward, he changed his name to George Williams, apparently at the suggestion of Ikeda, as a way to emphasize the degree to which NSA was committed to Americanization.

As the unrest of the 1960s neared its peak, a growing number of Nichiren Buddhists, both Japanese and non-Japanese, who were committed to shaku-buku and energized by the vision of kosen-rufu, could be found along with Hare Krishnas and other spiritual enthusiasts on America's city streets. NSA's effort to Americanize, however, encouraged a style of proselytizing that was a unique synthesis of shakubuku, American patriotism, and value creation.

The basic form of shakubuku was street solicitation—going out into the streets and inviting people to a Buddhist meeting. This created the opportunity to introduce new people to chanting, which is the basic element of Nichiren practice. In an ensuing discussion, seasoned Nichiren Buddhists would testify to how their practice brought "benefits." These benefits could range from concrete concerns such as financial gain, good health, and good grades to more spiritual matters bearing on insight into the meaning of life. The major thrust of all these testimonials was, however, that Nichiren practice helped people to take charge of their lives and responsibility for their destinies. In Buddhist terms, they enabled practitioners to change poison into medicine, to transform negative elements in life into positive benefits.

Public ceremonies called "culture festivals" were another important part of these early shakubuku campaigns, and gave expression to the more communal element in value creation. They also were strategic devices for Americanization. For a decade and a half, NSA leaders identified Nichiren Buddhism with American values through a series of youth pageants and parades, culminating in highly publicized patriotic celebrations during the American bicentennial.

In 1976, just after NSA's Bicentennial Convention, the organization entered into what was called Phase II. This marked a departure from the highly activist and public phase of the shakubuku campaigns. Street proselytizing was discouraged. The frenetic pace maintained by Soka Gakkai members for a decade slackened. The spirit of the organization began to shift from a collectivism driven by the energy generated by shakubuku, becoming more individualistic and inner directed. Many NSA members turned their attention to the study of the writings of Nichiren and the *Lotus Sutra*, personal growth, and the development of Buddhist families. A number of reasons have been put forward for these changes—a growing fear that NSA was perceived to be a cult; a response to concerns about the number of conversions dropping off; the end of the cultural upheavals of the 1960s. Whatever the case, Phase II was also in keeping with a gradual, broad moderating effect of Ikeda's leadership since 1960.

NSA entered the 1980s claiming a membership of some 500,000, a figure most now concede was inflated. At about this time, NSA also estimated that roughly 25 percent of its members were Asian, 40 percent Caucasian, 19 percent African American, and around five percent Hispanic.[4] In the late 1980s, however, long-standing tensions between the priesthood and the laity reopened, ultimately leading in 1991 to the excommunication of Soka Gakkai from Nichiren Shoshu. At that time, the lay organization adopted its current name, Soka Gakkai International. Those who renounced their ties to Soka Gakkai and allied themselves with the priests took the name Nichiren Shoshu Temple.

Sources of Schism in the Nichiren Practice and Worldview

The alliance between Nichiren Shoshu and Soka Gakkai had been mutually beneficial since its formal establishment under Josei Toda. Soka Gakkai gave to Nichiren Shoshu, a largely moribund sect in postwar Japan, a vital and international new constituency, substantial financial resources, and influence and visibility. Nichiren Shoshu gave SGI legitimacy, cultural authority, and a body of traditional religious texts, doctrines, and rituals that helped it to stand out from the pack of new religious movements that flourished in postwar Japan.

Despite the benefits each gained, there were tensions in the alliance almost from the beginning. But since the early 1990s, relatively minor events in the past have been recast by both parties in often highly dramatic terms. Given the acrimonious charges and countercharges about greedy priests and blaspheming laity, rampant egoism, and scheming power plays, it would seem to outside observers that the final break must have come as something of a relief. The often convoluted and gratuitous nature of these charges, however, should not obscure the fact that at the heart of the conflict was a fundamental dispute about the teaching of Nichiren and that for both parties a great deal was at stake. It is not without reason that the split between the two groups has been likened to the Reformation in sixteenth-century Christian Europe.

The two groups shared and continue to share many essential elements of traditional practice and a religious worldview, much like Protestants and Catholics. But as Soka Gakkai moved with increasing confidence onto the world stage, conflicts of interpretation with the Nichiren Shoshu priesthood inevitably arose over a number of issues discussed below.

Three Great Secret Laws

Nichiren Shoshu Temple and Soka Gakkai International both appeal to what Nichiren called the Three Great Secret Laws of Buddhism, as they are expressed in an age he understood to be *mappo*, marked by the degeneration of the dharma. These three laws are considered by both groups to be the framework of Nichiren's Buddhism. The first law pertains to the gohonzon, a scroll that is considered the chief or supreme object of worship. The second pertains to the *kaidan*, or the high sanctuary of Buddhism, which Nichiren prophesied was to be built in the age of mappo. The third pertains to the daimoku, the true chant or invocation that is the most characteristic practice of Nichiren Buddhism. A consideration of each of these helps to highlight the fundamental conflict between Nichiren Shoshu and Soka Gakkai over the interpretation of basic doctrinal, ritual, and institutional issues.

DAIMOKU   There is little at issue between the two groups pertaining to the daimoku, although NST and SGI have different ways of transliterating it, a point of disagreement that some observers have magnified to an extraordinary degree. In one variant, the invocation or chant consists of the words *Nam-Myoho-Renge-Kyo*, which literally mean "hail to the wonderful dharma *Lotus Sutra*." Congregational chanting of the daimoku, whether in a public temple, at a community center, or before a home altar, is the most basic element in both groups. It is chanted rapidly in unison, sometimes to the accompaniment of drums, creating a dynamic and highly charged atmosphere. In most situations, the daimoku is chanted for fifteen to twenty minutes, after which the chant may change to what is called *gongyo*, the recitation of selected passages from the *Lotus Sutra*. The word *gongyo* means "assiduous practice," and an assiduous practitioner might spend two hours a day chanting, with morning and evening variations in the liturgy.

The daimoku is subject to a variety of interpretations. At its most literal level, it affirms the centrality of the *Lotus Sutra* in the thought of Nichiren. On a more esoteric level, it is thought to be the essence of the dharma, which Nichiren Buddhists often refer to as the "mystic law," as it is manifest in the age of mappo. Nichiren called daimoku the king of all sutras, seeing in it the explanation of the interdependence of all phenomena. Some modern interpreters have likened it to Albert Einstein's formula for relativity, $E = mc^2$. Others see each syllable of the daimoku as revealing rich and diverse depths of religious meaning, one reason why a small variation can become a source of great controversy.

Like the Nembutsu of Jodo Shinshu, the daimoku had a long history of use in Mahayana Buddhism before it gained prominence through its use by a particular sect of Japanese Buddhism. But the daimoku is not chanted out of gratitude and has no relationship to Amida Buddha. Nichiren Buddhists consider it a most effective practice, essential to the attainment of enlightenment.

GOHONZON Very serious matters, however, are at stake in regard to the gohonzon, the subject of Nichiren's second Great Secret Law for the age of mappo. The gohonzon, a term often translated as the true or supreme object of worship, plays a central role in the religious life of the members of both SGI-USA and Nichiren Shoshu Temple. The typical gohonzon in the possession of a lay believer is a small paper scroll that is a consecrated replica of ones originally inscribed by Nichiren. The daimoku is printed on it in Japanese characters, surrounded by the signs of buddhas and bodhisattvas prominent in the *Lotus Sutra*. The gohonzon is enshrined in a home altar and treated with great care. It is thought to embody the dharma and also to embody Nichiren, who, as an incarnation of the eternal Buddha, infused his enlightenment into his original gohonzons. Facing the gohonzon while chanting daimoku, a practice referred to as *shodai*, is considered to be highly efficacious for the realization of one's own true nature and for the attainment of supreme enlightenment.

The gohonzon is also a point of great contention between the priesthood and Soka Gakkai. Under pre-schism arrangements, the high priest at Taisekiji had the ritual authority to consecrate new gohonzons, thereby enabling their mystical dharma nature to come forth. Priests also had the authority to issue gohonzons to all new practitioners through *gojukai* ceremonies conducted at local or regional temples. Nichiren Shoshu doctrine taught, moreover, that the power of all gohonzons flowed from the *dai-gohonzon*, the camphor wood original carved by Nichiren himself, which is housed in the temple at Taisekiji. This meant that not only the authority but also the transformative power and symbolic heart of the religion were in the hands of the priests at Taisekiji. After the schism, the Nichiren priesthood withheld all new gohonzons from members of SGI. It has also vociferously denounced

The Sho-Hondo was built with contributions from the laity to house the dai-gohonzon at
the Nichiren Shoshu temple complex at Taisekiji, on the flanks of Mount Fuji in Japan. In
the wake of the schism, the Nichiren Shosho high priest ordered its demolition, which was
carried out in 1998 amid protests from the international architectural community.
SOKA GAKKAI INTERNATIONAL

gohonzons acquired from other sources as blasphemous counterfeits. These esoteric issues may seem alien, but they are directly comparable to similar controversies about authority and ritual efficacy that deeply preoccupied Protestants and Catholics in Reformation Europe.

KAIDAN Religious conflicts are also raised by doctrines concerning the third of Nichiren's Great Secret Laws, the establishment of the kaidan or highest, most holy sanctuary of Nichiren Buddhism. In its most elementary sense, *kaidan* means "ordination platform," the place where a Buddhist formally takes the precepts. But in Nichiren's thought, the kaidan took on a greater importance because he sought for his movement an authority independent of all other Buddhist religious institutions in Japan. In the course of Nichiren's life, the two other Great Secret Laws—the daimoku and the gohonzon—had been established, but he prophesied the kaidan would be established later, in the age of mappo.

As a result, the kaidan in the Nichiren Shoshu tradition has taken on a mystical, sometimes apocalyptic significance. Its establishment is seen as playing a central role in kosen-rufu, the dissemination of true Buddhism, peace, and harmony throughout the world. The orthodox Nichiren Shoshu interpretation of kaidan identifies it as Taisekiji, the temple founded in the thirteenth century by high priest Nikko Shonin, which has since then housed the dai-gohonzon. Tozan, pilgrimage to Taisekiji to venerate the dai-gohonzon, is seen as an important means of enhancing the efficacy of practice before the household gohonzon.

For Soka Gakkai, the orthodox understanding of kaidan took on a special twist. In 1972, a new, modern sanctuary to house the dai-gohozon, called the Sho-Hondo, constructed largely by the efforts and at the expense of Soka Gakkai, was completed at Taisekiji. Ikeda and others saw it as a sign of a pivotal role to be played by Soka Gakkai in kosen-rufu, one related to its global mission. For Nichiren Shoshu traditionalists, however, this understanding of kaidan was a bald-faced attempt on the part of Ikeda and Soka Gakkai to usurp the traditional and orthodox prerogatives of the Nichiren Shoshu priesthood. After the schism in 1991, SGI loyalists were denied the right to make tozan and were barred from entering Taisekiji. In 1998, the high priest of Nichiren Shoshu expressed his determination to demolish the Sho-Hondo, a noteworthy piece of modern Japanese architecture, in order to erase the memory of Soka Gakkai from Taisekiji. At this writing, demolition is complete, despite an international protest by architects with little invested in the doctrinal conflict between SGI and NST.

Triple Refuge

The potential for doctrinal conflict between the Taisekiji priesthood and Soka Gakkai laity is nowhere more apparent than in the Nichiren Shoshu understanding of triple refuge. In most Buddhist traditions, *triple refuge* refers to the Buddha, the dharma or law, and the sangha or community. Nichiren Shoshu, however, understands the Buddha to be Nichiren himself, whose teachings in the age of mappo supplanted those of Shakyamuni. The dharma or law is thought to rest in *Nam-Myoho-Renge-Kyo*—in the daimoku or chant—but especially in the gohonzon. On both these points, Nichiren Shoshu and Soka Gakkai remain in fundamental agreement.

The Nichiren Shoshu doctrine on the sangha is where the two groups naturally part company. According to Nichiren Shoshu, the sangha is exclusively identified with the priesthood, more particularly with the lineage and person of the high priest at Taisekiji. The integrity of this exclusive lineage is seen as essential to the maintenance of orthodoxy, Nichiren's teachings, the attainment of enlightenment, and the future of kosen-rufu. Despite Ikeda's earlier statements to the contrary, this became an untenable position for Soka Gakkai and its lay members, especially in the United States, as Nichiren Buddhism and value creation came to be increasingly shaped by the ideals of egalitarian democracy.

The schism between Nichiren Shoshu and Soka Gakkai, though involving money, power, and egotism, ultimately rests on fundamental religious issues as they relate to the mission and character of two very different kinds of institutions. To a limited degree, the analogy to the Reformation in Europe is useful. Nichiren Shoshu, like the Roman church, had a centuries-long history during which it came to understand itself as the guardian of orthodoxy. Its doctrines and practices reflected that understanding. To stretch the analogy, all Nichiren Shoshu roads led and lead to Taisekiji. In and of itself, this is no particular problem, as is evidenced by the fact that many individuals, both Japanese and western, remain loyal and fervent practitioners in the Nichiren Shoshu tradition of Taisekiji. But the Nichiren priesthood's lock on doctrine and authority became increasingly problematic as Soka Gakkai developed into a confident and highly dynamic mass movement. Tensions that could be swept aside under Josei Toda, when the organization remained exclusively Japanese, became increasingly unmanageable as Soka Gakkai, under the leadership of Daisaku Ikeda, became a global movement.

Most observers of the schism suggest that the vast majority of American Nichiren Buddhists remained within SGI. Some Nichiren Shoshu Temple members seem to have distanced themselves from the more extreme expressions of emotions that the conflict occasioned, but the pain is such that anti-SGI invective is often found on Nichiren Shoshu websites and in its literature. Rank and file in both camps sometimes seem confused about the issues and dismayed about the break—reminders that many aspects of the controversy make sense in Japan but have little resonance in this country.

It appears that the general response by the Nichiren Shoshu Temple members has been a kind of retrenchment and inward turning. But orthodox Nichiren Shoshu has not lost its religious appeal for some American laity. One stalwart posted an account of a tozan he made in the late 1990s, which conveys the enduring appeal of Taisekiji. Here he describes his first visit to the Sho-Hondo, before it was marked for demolition:

> As the High Priest entered and began to chant Daimoku, the air became filled with electricity once again. I realized at that time that the High Priest is an expert at the practice of Buddhism. We were in awe as the 65 foot high Butsudan doors opened, revealing the golden house of the Dai-Gohonzon. A priest climbed the stairs and reverently flung open the doors, exposing the Supreme Object of The Law.
>
> The daimoku being led by the High Priest felt like a fine-tuned, high performance engine, but it was not raw power, but a gentle yet profound form of energy one could never imagine, and cannot be put into words. The compassion emanating from the Voice of the High Priest was totally unexpected by me as well as most others. It was obvious that the power of the Dai-Gohonzon is absolute. It is we who choose to deviate and cause ourselves needless suffering. That 30 minute span we spent before the Dai-Gohonzon . . . is frozen in time, embedded in my life. . . . I thank the High Priest and the priesthood from the depths of my life for preserving the Dai-Gohonzon, as well as the formalities and doctrines of Nichiren Shoshu Buddhism.[5]

For its part, SGI emerged from the schism energized by freedom from the restraints of the priesthood to face a promising future in the United States. New and old members alike note that the Nichiren Shoshu priesthood never played a particularly important part in their religious lives. Aside from the gojukai ceremony to receive the gohonzon, which was often quite perfunctory, priests had little contact with laypeople. At the peak of its development, Nichiren Shoshu of America had only six regional temples to serve several hundred thousand members spread across the country. Members' homes have always been the movement's central gathering places. Its district organizations have always been organized and run by lay members, who have always occupied every office in SGI-USA, from its headquarters in Santa Monica, California to its many regional and local organizations.

New initiatives inaugurated by Daisaku Ikeda continue to lead SGI-USA in progressive directions. Beginning in the 1990s, he acted as a catalyst for a thorough rethinking of all SGI-USA organizations, urging across-the-board democratization in an effort to dismantle a hierarchical mentality inherited from the earlier era. Sacramental roles are now played by volunteers in nonpaying ministerial offices that are filled on a rotating basis. New initiatives have been put in place to enhance the ethnic and racial diversity of SGI-USA and to give women, who have always played a critical role, a higher profile at the top of the national leadership. Religious dialogue, both interreligious and inter-Buddhist, is now on the SGI agenda, which would not have been the case under the sectarian leadership of the Nichiren Shoshu priesthood. All of these initiatives have contributed to an opening up of Soka Gakkai. A frequent statement in leadership circles is that a new, egalitarian SGI is "a work in progress."

New institutions have also been established that, while infused with the religious spirit of Nichiren Buddhism, are devoted to the kind of progressive and humanistic value creation first outlined by Tsunesaburo Makaguchi. Nonsectarian Soka University of America in southern California was founded by Ikeda in 1987 with a mission to educate an international student body for leadership positions around the Pacific rim. The Boston Research Center for the Twenty-first Century, located in Cambridge, Massachusetts next to Harvard University, is devoted to fostering humanistic values across cultural and religious lines. Since it was founded by Ikeda in 1993, it has sponsored a wide range of conferences, symposia, and research initiatives on such topics as the world's religions and the ethics of ecology, global citizenship and human rights, and development of leadership initiatives among women.

The innovations in SGI since the schism have had different impacts in different countries, but in the United States have helped to transform SGI-USA into a form of lay Buddhism quite in keeping with the tenor and values of a moderate moral and religious current in the American mainstream. Discussion with SGI-USA members reveals that to a striking degree, many American values are also Nichiren Buddhist values. Some members emphasize how Nichiren practice helped them gain control of their lives and brought great material benefits. Others stress increased emotional and physical well-being. But they also repeatedly refer to the importance of Buddhist practice in building character and fostering personal responsibility.

Linda Johnson, a long-time practitioner who is a supervisor in the Criminal Division of the California Attorney General's Office, is among the many SGI members who are articulate about how Nichiren Buddhism has changed their life and given it meaning. Raised a Methodist in the 1950s in an extended family that included Caucasians, Native Americans, and African Americans, Johnson was first drawn to Soka Gakkai in the 1970s, while in law school at the University of Southern California. She was impressed by SGI's ethnic diversity but even more so by the genuine bonds among the people within it. She recalls that the gohonzon and chanting daimoku first struck her as strange, but "I trusted my gut and felt there was something real about these people. They were not faking their happiness. They had something in their life that I knew I wanted and did not have."[6]

One turning point in her practice came during her bar examination several years later, when chanting helped her to focus her mind, control her fears, and tap into her deepest potential, which she refers to as her "Buddha nature." Another, more important turning point came around 1980, when she first met Daisaku Ikeda. As with many others in SGI, his example led her deeper into practice and the study of Nichiren's teachings. "Here was this short Japanese man with a life force that made it seem like he was ten feet tall. He had the most positive energy and was, at the same time, the warmest and most magnanimous human being I had ever experienced. The practice had to be right because of the qualities this man had."

Johnson considers Nichiren Buddhism to be a "difficult practice." She tries to chant daimoku two hours a day, in addition to morning and evening gongyo, saying that it enables her "to meet life head on, moment to moment, to constantly work at overcoming fear, doubt, and negativity, and to plug into the enlightened nature." In her work in the State Attorney General's Office, she often prosecutes death penalty cases before the California Supreme Court. Given the gravity of her work, she finds that chanting helps her maintain clarity of mind and purpose. She understands her role is to enforce the laws of the state of California. But she also knows that the law of cause and effect as taught by the Buddha is also at work in all these cases, unfolding in complex ways among the accused and the victim, families and friends, in ways she is unable to determine. "The mystic law is infinitely more profound than my brain is," Johnson notes, "so I try to suspend my own mental judgment, not figure out how I think the effect should come about, and trust that the higher law will determine the right thing for each person."

During her more than twenty years of practice, Johnson has served in a succession of leadership positions from Junior Hancho (*han* means "group" and *cho*, "leader"), to Hancho and District Leader. She is currently Vice Women's Leader in the L.A. #1 Region and in the Women's Secretariat, where she assists the national head of the women's division. She also heads the Legal Division in the SGI-USA Culture Department, which means that she acts as a kind of spiritual adviser to other lawyers who practice Nichiren Buddhism. Before the schism in 1991, Johnson traveled to Japan at least eight times to meet with other leaders and to see the dai-gohonzon at Taisek-iji, which she considered a powerful experience. "But for me the cause at work in chanting before the dai-gohonzon was pure heart and sincerity of prayer, not the high priest," she recalls. She also thinks that the break, however difficult it may have been for some people, "was a great thing. It enabled us, sometimes forced us, to face issues, to see Nichiren's Buddhism for ourselves. It has enabled the organization to make the equality of all people, our common Buddha nature, more real and concrete."

Ikeda's writings convey the same ardor for character found among members of SGI like Johnson, together with a strong commitment to Nichiren Buddhism. He has written widely and in depth on Mahayana Buddhism, Nichiren, and the *Lotus Sutra*, and has undoubtedly recast many of the doctrines central to the orthodoxy of Nichiren Shoshu. But in his writings and speeches designed for the broader world, Ikeda has called, in very plain language, for nothing less than a new Buddhist humanism that can revolutionize the twenty-first century through the inner transformation of the individual and the reordering of an increasingly interdependent global society. This call is a modern restatement of Nichiren's visions of kosen-rufu, which he first articulated in the thirteenth century. But it also reflects Ikeda's vision of world peace, Josei Toda's commitment to shakubuku, and Tsunesaburo Makaguchi's passion for progressive education.

As the dust settles from the break between NST and SGI-USA, the latter appears to be in a very good position to play an important, ongoing role in the creation of American Buddhism. The Nichiren tradition provides a rich foundation for philosophical reflection and practice. The tenor and tone of the movement are very much in keeping with mainstream American values, while its varied membership gives it a multicultural and multiracial dimension that ought to be an asset in the next century. As a result of adjustments the organization has made since 1991, SGI has a very unambiguous lay orientation, unlike American Zen, for instance, which has lingering unresolved issues related to the monastic character of its practice traditions. At the same time, SGI-USA maintains strong links to its origins in Japan which, as in the case of Zen, can be a source of some tension in the organization. But the connection can also be considered an asset. SGI-USA is in many respects a thoroughly Americanized form of Buddhism, and this could easily lead to a dissipation of its unique energy; the need to be alert to developments in Japan may well serve to maintain the movement as a distinct feature of the American religious landscape.

CHAPTER SEVEN

Zen and Its Flagship Institutions

The Americanization of Zen Buddhism, the most prominent of the Japanese Mahayana traditions in this country, has been fostered by a broad movement to revitalize and modernize Zen institutions and practices that began in nineteenth-century Japan. At that time, Zen monastic institutions came under attack from Shinto nationalists. Income-producing estates that supported Zen monasteries were confiscated and an extensive Zen parish system that served laypeople was dismantled. Zen clergy increasingly abandoned celibacy for marriage and family, with the direct encouragement of the state. Many Zen leaders also were caught up in the rising tide of Japanese nationalism, only to face Japan's defeat in World War II and the challenges of the return to normalcy.

For many Zen clerics, postwar reconstruction meant a return to providing pastoral care to laity, which largely consisted of performing memorial services for the deceased. Most did not pursue meditative practices beyond what was required of them in the course of their ministerial education and training. Others, however, sought to renew the spirit and practice of Zen, often by promoting meditation among Japanese laypeople. Some Zen leaders also began to see the United States as a land of opportunity for Zen, where its ancient genius could be revitalized, unencumbered by its Japanese institutional history.

The work of D. T. Suzuki at the center of the Zen boom in the 1950s was one expression of this interest in America's potential to contribute to the revitalization of Zen. Another was the work a decade later of a number of Japanese teachers, who arrived here steeped in the Zen traditions of Japan but were often critical of its institutions. Once in the United States, they typically encountered Americans seeking authentic spiritual experience but wary of—often in flight from—institutionalized religion. The shared interest of these Japanese teachers and their American students in experiential religion unconstrained by institutions was, in many respects, a perfect marriage. This was particularly the case during the 1960s, when an anti-institutional spirit, epitomized by the counterculture but broadly diffused throughout American society, was in ascendance. This fit between the interests of teachers and students gave American Zen an innovative, sometimes antinomian, spirit that found a home in organizations formed three or more decades ago, often located in rented rooms and meeting halls and then in more substantial settings.

Other factors have contributed to Zen's preeminence and its unique spirit. Zen has the longest American history of any form of convert Buddhism, going back to Shaku Soyen's appearance at the World's Parliament of Religions in 1893. Groups established before World War II laid the groundwork for the Zen boom of the 1950s and positioned Zen to reap many of the benefits of the much broader interest in Buddhism in the 1960s. Zen has also benefited from its substantial literary history in this country. Addresses of Shaku Soyen appeared in print in 1906. D. T. Suzuki and Alan Watts interpreted Zen for a broad American audience at mid-century. Beat poetry, with its marked passion for Zen, is now a part of the American literary canon. *The Three Pillars of Zen: Teaching, Practice and Enlightenment*, published by Philip Kapleau in 1965, and Shunryu Suzuki's *Zen Mind, Beginner's Mind*, published in 1970, are now among America's Buddhist classics. More recently, a publishing boom has given Zen, or at least Zenlike ideas, a high public profile and a great deal of name recognition.

Zen is part of a tradition that was practiced for many centuries within monastic institutions across east Asia. In China it was known as Ch'an, in Korea as Son, and in Vietnam as Thien Buddhism, forms of a shared tradition that are now intermingling with Zen in creative ways in the ferment of American Buddhism. In Japan, Zen was divided into Rinzai, the school that emphasized the use of koans, and Soto, which emphasized sitting meditation. A number of influential Japanese teachers in the 1960s, however, taught both Rinzai and Soto to their American students, which helped to give an eclectic cast to the American practice of Zen, even though the two traditions retain distinct institutions in this country. As a whole, American Zen is primarily a movement of laity who practice monastic disciplines, a trend that has also fostered innovation as practitioners seek to balance rigorous practice with the demands of the workplace and family. The laicization of monastic practice is sometimes hailed as an example of democratization of Buddhism in this country, although it has many Japanese precedents.

Zen is the most popular form of Buddhism among converts who meditate, but their number is very difficult to estimate. Unlike Jodo Shinshu, Zen is not identified with a particular ethnic community, although Zen temples serving Japanese Americans played an important role in its transmission to the United States and remain a part of the American Zen mix. Unlike Soka Gakkai, Zen has no central administration to make estimates of its membership. Many of its most prominent institutions, however, were founded by Japanese teachers and their American students during the 1960s. Collectively, these flagship institutions can be said to represent mainstream American Zen. They help to set the pace for meditation centers across the country and often provide them with teachers. Their leaders are often well-known, well-respected figures in the broader Buddhist community. With few exceptions, the leadership of these institutions passed to a generation of native-born, American teachers in the last decades of the twentieth century, a development hailed by many as the coming of age of American Buddhism. By the turn of the century, these teachers' students had begun to come of age as teachers in their own right, creating a third, in a few cases a fourth, generation of American Zen teachers and leaders.

Mainstream Zen and Its Flagship Institutions

Many of the innovative qualities of American Zen have been attributed to Hakuun Yasutani, who was influential in trans-Pacific Zen circles until his death in 1973. He is seen to have epitomized the modern Japanese Zen reformer—deeply steeped in the traditions of Zen, eclectic in his approach to practicing it, and critical of its institutions. Born in 1885, Yasutani was sent to a Rinzai Zen temple at age five, where he was educated by its abbot. At eleven, he moved to a Soto monastery and became a monk. At sixteen, he moved yet again to study with a well-known Soto leader and commentator on Dogen's masterpiece, the *Shobogenzo*. Throughout his twenties and thirties, Yasutani continued his training with a succession of Buddhist teachers. He also completed his secular education and began a career as an educator. At thirty, he married and began to raise the first of five children.

At the age of forty, Yasutani entered a new phase in his Buddhist vocation. He was soon actively engaged in propagating Soto Zen in Japan, when he met the Zen master Daiun Harada, a teacher of both Soto and Rinzai, and began to practice with him. In 1927, at the age of forty-two, Yasutani attained *kensho*, a breakthrough insight into the nature of Buddha mind. In 1943, he finished koan study with Harada and received dharma transmission, which is essentially a seal of approval given to a student by his or her teacher. Their teacher-student relationship was of sufficient importance that Philip Kapleau, Robert Aitken, and Yasutani's other students are often said to be in the Harada-Yasutani teaching lineage. Yasutani soon turned his attention to training laity, both men and women, an activity that consumed much of his time for the next thirty years. He eventually broke his connections to both Soto and Rinzai Zen institutions and founded his own school, the Sanbo Kyodan, or Three Treasures Association, in 1954, which he viewed as more true to the spirit and form of Dogen's original teaching.

Many of Yasutani's reforms, while controversial in Japan, became taken for granted in a broad swath of the American Zen community. He incorporated both the Soto emphasis on zazen and the Rinzai use of koans into the teachings of the Sanbo Kyodan. He gave lay practitioners the attention and care that had been formerly reserved for monastics and modified the traditional course of training for resident monastics by condensing practice into intensive retreats to fit laypcople's schedules. He particularly emphasized the attainment of kensho as way to start lay practitioners on a path that could be deepened through further sitting and koan study. Yasutani also minimized the ceremonial life of the Japanese temple and adapted what he retained to the practice needs of the laity. For non-Japanese practitioners, both male and female, he greatly eased the linguistic and social barriers that were inherent in traditional, monastery-based training.

Yasutani's impact on American Zen came most directly through two of his American students, Philip Kapleau and Robert Aitken, both of whom played important roles in early, 1960s-era Zen Buddhism. Philip Kapleau was Yasutani's first American student. He had studied with a number of teachers in Japan, but began his formative work with Yasutani in the mid-1950s, practicing in a series of twenty intense, protracted periods of Zen training. After spending eleven years in Japan, Kapleau returned to the United States. In 1965, he published *The Three Pillars of Zen*, a book leagues ahead of Suzuki and Watts in how it addressed the actual practice of Buddhism, which introduced Yasutani and his style to many Americans. In 1966, Kapleau founded the Rochester Zen Center in Rochester, New York, one of American Zen's earliest training institutions. Through his publishing and teaching, he was instrumental in the formation of American Zen. Kapleau made further innovations in the name of Americanization. He encouraged his students to retain American dress, gave them Anglicized dharma names, and used English translations of sutras in the course of training, a particular innovation that drew Yasutani's criticism.

Of Kapleau's students, some went on to form Zen centers in Vermont, Denver, and overseas in Poland. But his best-known student, Toni Packer, eventually broke with Kapleau and the Rochester center, taking with her a number of his students to found Springwater Center, also in central New York. By the 1990s, Packer was among a number of American teachers who had begun to cut Zen loose from its moorings in the doctrine, tradition, and ethos of Japan, seeing them as stifling its capacity to awaken Americans. She established herself as an independent teacher, separate from both the Harada-Yasutani lineage and, more significantly because she represents one trend in the Americanization of Buddhism, the entire concept of lineage. "Truth itself needs no lineage, it is here, without past or future," she told an audience at a Buddhist conference in Boston in 1997. Referring to a koan that emphasized "preserving the house and the gate," that is, the entire tradition of Zen, she said: "That's not what I'm interested in. I wish for Springwater to flourish in its own spontaneous and unpredictable ways, and not become a place for the transmission of traditional teachings."[1] Packer's post-traditional approach is suggested by the general and inclusive name of her organization, the Springwater Center for Meditative Inquiry and Retreats.

Like Kapleau, Robert Aitken had a significant impact on the early stages of American Zen. He first became interested in Buddhism while in an internment camp in Japan during World War II. After the war, he briefly studied with Nyogen Senzaki in Los Angeles and was later introduced to practice in Japanese monasteries. He began serious study and practice with Yasutani in the mid-1950s. In 1974, the year after Yasutani's death, he received dharma transmission from Koun Yamada, Yasutani's successor as head of the Three Treasures Association.

From early on, Aitken and his wife Anne were at the forefront of the Americanization of Zen. They co-founded a Zen sitting group in Hawaii in 1959, later called the Diamond Sangha. They began to lead Zen groups at a time of transition from an earlier, mystical fascination with Buddhism to the more practice-oriented interests that emerged during the 1960s. Aitken recalls that the first retreat he held in Hawaii "saw the tag end of interest in theosophy and general occult things. There were folks who had studied Blavatsky and her successors and who had gone through all kinds of spirit-writing episodes and astrology. The young people didn't start to come until the dope revolution."[2] Since its founding, the Diamond Sangha has grown into a network of affiliated Zen centers in Hawaii, Australia, and California.

Aitken has been described as the dean of American Zen. His translations of sutras and gathas, Buddhist hymns, have been used in many Zen centers in daily services. He has long been an astute observer of grassroots developments in American Zen, and has contributed to its ongoing formation by participating in many conferences and consultations. As a consistent supporter of Native Hawaiian, gay and lesbian, and women's rights issues, he also represents the liberal/left political and social tilt that is conspicuous in many American Zen quarters. With Gary Snyder, one of the most renowned Beat Buddhist poets, and Joanna Macy, a leading American Buddhist teacher and intellectual, Aitken co-founded the Buddhist Peace Fellowship (BPF), a pioneering organization linking American Buddhist practice and social activism. By the 1990s, BPF was emerging as another important American Buddhist organization in its own right.

Due to the early influence of Shaku Soyen, his colleagues, and their students, the Rinzai tradition was most prominent in American Buddhism at the opening of the 1960s. Joshu Sasaki, Eido Tai Shimano, and other Rinzai teachers further contributed to the development of American Rinzai in the following decades. By the late 1990s, Sasaki and Shimano were among the few pioneering teachers from Japan still alive and continuing to teach.

Sasaki arrived in Los Angeles in 1962, and he and his students soon incorporated as the Rinzai Zen Dojo. Over the next two decades, they founded the Cimarron Zen Center in Idyllwild, California, the Mt. Baldy Zen Center in the mountains east of Los Angeles, and the Bodhi Manda Zen Center in Jemez Springs near Santa Fe, New Mexico. His many students subsequently established a network of meditation centers that ranged from Puerto Rico to Vancouver and from Miami, Florida to Princeton, New Jersey.

Shimano began his work in New York City in 1964, where he revitalized the Zen Studies Society, which was originally founded to support the work of D. T. Suzuki. It is now the leading Rinzai Zen institution on the East Coast. He later established International Dai Bosatsu Monastery in the Catskill Mountains on Beecher Lake, a secluded site once the retreat of the Beecher family of Connecticut, which was influential in nineteenth-century Protestant evangelicalism. The monastery serves as a "country zendo" for New Yorkers who sit at its city center in Manhattan; soon after it opened on July 4, 1976, it became one of the important, and certainly one of the most elegant, training institutions in this country.

Both Sasaki and Shimano have been fairly traditional in their approaches to the traditions of Zen. On matters of doctrine and practice, Shimano has been described as a "go slow" Americanizer, and International Dai Bosatsu Monastery appears to be a traditional Zen center transplanted to this country. Japanese visitors, however, readily identify it as American—men and women live and practice together; lay students, who form the bulk of those in training, practice alongside monastics. But a powerful Japanese aura lingers in the design of the monastery, the Buddha images in its meditation rooms, and its landscaping. This mixing of Japanese and American sensibilities remains important in American Zen; its aesthetic appeal can be sensed in Shimano's remarks in 1972, when he consecrated the Beecher Lake property to monastic use in perpetuity.

> I, the Reverend Eido Tai Shimano, the president of The Zen Studies Society, Inc., hereby, with a reverential heart, ask the Deity of Dai Bosatsu Mountain, Lake and Field to hear my declaration.
>
> On behalf of all the Sangha I ask forgiveness for our destruction and pollution of all rocks, trees, grasses, and mosses, and the nature of the Catskill Mountains, particularly by the Beecher Lake.
>
> We ask your permission to establish a Zen monastery on this very site and ask your protection from earth, water, fire, and wind, and any other possible damage.
>
> May this place be peaceful, calm, creative, and harmonious for all the years to come and for all people who may come here, generation after generation.[3]

The Soto lineage moved into prominence in America toward the end of the twentieth century, largely due to the success of Shunryu Suzuki, who founded the San Francisco Zen Center (SFZC), and Hakuyu Taizan Maezumi, who established the Zen Center of Los Angeles (ZCLA). Both teachers were sons of Soto priests. They arrived in this country to serve the Japanese American Zen community, but soon gained a following of other American students. Both made immense contributions to an American tradition of Zen Buddhism. Unlike Yasutani, who had a programmatic approach to the reform of Zen, Suzuki retailored the tradition for America on a trial-and-error basis. Maezumi's approach was from the outset more eclectic, as he had received dharma transmission from Soto and Rinzai teachers as well as from Hakuun Yasutani. Both teachers also established strong teaching lineages. Their students emerged in the 1980s and '90s as among the most prominent native-born teachers of American Zen.

Much of the early history of the San Francisco Zen Center was shaped by the fact that it was at the tumultuous heart of the San Francisco counter-culture of the 1960s. Many countercultural social and political ideals subsequently infused this sangha, giving it a deserved reputation for innovation and creativity. The early death of its founder, Shunryu Suzuki, in 1971 also forced SFZC to confront a range of succession and leadership issues well in advance of most other American Zen communities.

Like many other Zen priests in Japan, Suzuki followed his father into the

Among the most influential Japanese Zen teachers, Shunryu Suzuki taught many American men and women in the San Francisco Bay area during the 1960s, a pivotal era in American Buddhist history. His legacy includes three monastic institutions that now comprise the San Francisco Zen Center, a large network of affiliated practice institutions, and *Zen Mind, Beginner's Mind*, a book of his teachings that is now an American Buddhist classic.
San Francisco Zen Center

clergy, expecting to take over the family temple. After being educated in a Buddhist high school and university, he trained at Eiheji and Sojiji, the two leading Soto training centers in Japan. He later married and began to raise a family. Still in his thirties, Suzuki took a position as head of a network of Soto-affiliated temples.

Suzuki came to the United States in the late 1950s on a three-year, temporary appointment at Sokoji, the Soto Zen temple in San Francisco, where his primary responsibility was to provide pastoral care for the Japanese American community. But from the outset, he also maintained his passion for zazen (sitting meditation), an element of the Soto tradition that held little appeal for most of his parishioners. By the early 1960s, Suzuki was leading between twelve and thirty people, most of them non-Japanese, in zazen each morning. In 1962, this fledgling group of American Buddhists incorporated as the San Francisco Zen Center.

Within a few years, as the Zen boom of the 1950s turned into the Buddhist explosion of the 1960s, the number of people showing up at Sokoji to learn to meditate under Suzuki's leadership dramatically increased. Some rented apartments near the temple, creating the nucleus of a full-blown community. Richard Baker, who later became an influential leader in that community, recalls that prior to this time Suzuki displayed little interest in the rituals and practices found in traditional Zen monasteries. "He thought that real Mahayana practice should be done in the streets and with people in ordinary circumstances." A few years later, however, Suzuki began to require more disciplined monastic-style practice from his students, which he refashioned to suit their unique needs as laypeople, often with families and living in communal settings within the broader Bay area countercultural community. "You have to understand," Baker recalls, about the gradual emergence of a new form of Buddhist institution in San Francisco, "the whole question of residency came up when 'flower power' was in full bloom."

> Everybody was taking acid. Things were a little out of hand. And I felt that we should take more responsibility. The turning point for Suzuki Roshi came when he began to feel that the apartments had become like buildings on the temple grounds; they were part of the temple. At some point his feeling was that Zen Center should accept the responsibility because, in effect, it already had the responsibility. But he always saw common residences as an extension of the temple, not the organization of the community.[4]

In a memoir of these early years, Erik Storlie recounts the circuitous route he followed through the counterculture to Buddhism. Storlie recalls finding himself at Sokoji for the first time in 1964, after an LSD trip on Mount Tamalpais, a favorite haunt of Bay area hippies. He describes the small inner room of the temple, where fifteen men and women sat in a semicircle on folding chairs facing Suzuki, a small man in his late fifties with a shaved head, wearing a simple brown robe and carrying a worn book. Storlie also conveys a sense of the mystique that surrounded both Zen and Suzuki. "He opens the book, and I see that it's filled with rows of oriental characters. The Buddha statue, the flowers, the strange little man, this curious book—I feel transported to some distant time and place, far from the city that begins outside the door on the foggy streets." The inchoate emotions Suzuki evoked in Storlie eventually led him to spend a lifetime as a practicing Buddhist. "Something I can't name is welling up in me. It's the devotion of this small, simple man for an ancient poetry he loves. It is in the images from nature that touch the everyday and the eternal—fish and water, birds and sky—an endless sunlight shedding beauty, sweeping forever through an infinite universe. . . . 'Yes, I'll be here,' I say to myself. 'I'll hear him talk again.' "[5]

At about this time, San Francisco Zen Center also began to take shape as one of America's leading Buddhist institutions. In 1966, the Center acquired Tassajara Hot Springs, an old resort in the coastal mountains several hours south of San Francisco. This was on the eve of the "summer of love," when the counterculture was about to peak and then go into a devastating tailspin. For a time, Tassajara took on the guise of a countercultural institution. Beat poetry readings, Buddhist workshops, and an Avalon Ballroom "Zenefit" featuring the Grateful Dead and Jefferson Airplane were held to pay off a portion of its $300,000 mortgage, although the bulk of the money eventually came from East Coast philanthropists. Tassajara was, however, intended to be a place where Americans could begin to practice Buddhism seriously. Center leaders saw that if Buddhism was to survive the 1960s and the counterculture movement, it would need strong American roots. They envisioned Tassajara as a Zen training institute or monastery.

In 1969, the Center also purchased a building on Page Street in San Francisco, formerly a residential hotel for Jewish women, which enabled the growing community to establish a headquarters independent of Sokoji. Suzuki resigned his post at the temple in order to devote himself full time to his students. Several apartment buildings for Center members were eventually purchased in the neighborhood. During this time, Suzuki began to ordain American students as Zen priests in order to invest them with the kind of status and authority held by Japanese clergy. He also instituted a form of "lay ordination," an innovation meant to address the ambiguous status of most American practitioners, who were neither traditional monastics nor typical laypeople. In 1972, Green Gulch Farm in Marin County, a location within an hour's commute from Page Street, was added to the growing list of properties owned by the Center. For a time, it was a Bay area showcase for Aquarian spiritual sensibilities, in equal parts an experimental farm, a home for Center families, a public lecture hall, and a back-to-the-land retreat.

Shunryu Suzuki died in 1971, but in 1966 he had ordained Richard Baker as both a monk and a priest. Baker was also Suzuki's dharma heir, or spiritual successor, which authorized him to teach. Baker was named the new abbot of SFZC, and he subsequently provided much of the leadership that enabled it to grow into one of America's leading Buddhist institutions. Under his leadership, however, the Center also faced difficulties in making the transition from the Aquarian-age '60s to the Ronald Reagan era. Extraordinary pressures came to bear on Center members as their original idealism was called into question in the 1980s. Resentment about Baker's high-profile leadership and questions about his lifestyle eventually flared into what he later called the "ZCM"—the Zen Center Mess.[6] Amid charges of an abuse of power and sexual misconduct, Baker resigned in 1983, but soon took up the leadership of new Zen communities, first in Santa Fe, New Mexico and then in Crestone, Colorado. Leadership of SFZC shifted to Tenshin Reb Anderson, another dharma heir of Suzuki, who served as its abbot until 1995.

As a result of this traumatic experience, the Center pioneered elective leadership, a cutting-edge development seen as an important turning point in the Americanization of Zen. In the early 1990s, SFZC's Board of Directors adopted a set of "Ethical Principles and Procedures for Grievance and Reconciliation," which reflected the integration of the Buddhist precepts with interpersonal problem-solving and conflict resolution. In the mid-1990s, SFZC undertook an experiment unthinkable in Japan: the establishment of joint leadership of the community by two of Suzuki's students. Zoketsu Norman Fischer was first installed as abbot in 1995, but he was joined a year later by Zenkai Blanche Hartman, who was also named abbot. Hartman was certainly the first Zen abbot to be a mother and grandmother, and she is among a large number of women who have become American Zen leaders and teachers.

At the end of the century, the Page Street Center (now the Beginner's Mind Temple or Hosshin-ji), Tassajara (now the Zen Mind Temple or Zenshin-ji), and Green Gulch Farm (the Green Dragon Temple or Soryu-ji) remained at the institutional core of the San Francisco Zen Center. It also had a large number of affiliates since many of its students had become teachers at centers throughout the United States. In 1998, Center leaders sponsored a high-profile, public-spirited series of lectures and workshops they called "Buddhism at Millennium's Edge," which featured many of the leading Buddhist scholars and practitioners in the convert community—Gary Snyder, Joanna Macy, and Reb Anderson, to name only a few. "As we approach the end of this human millennium, so full of confusion and violence, we're presented with a great challenge: how to repair ourselves and our world," wrote co-abbots Hartman and Fischer. "Buddhism can help. Each of the extraordinary speakers who address us in this series of talks and workshops has created a unique translation of ancient wisdom into contemporary terms. Their insights will inspire us and shine some light on the road ahead."[7]

The Zen Center of Los Angeles (ZCLA) followed a trajectory somewhat similar to that of SFZC in the 1960s and '70s. Its founder, Hakuyu Taizan Maezumi, first served as a priest with the Soto mission at Zenshuji temple in Los Angeles, where he tended to the pastoral needs of Japanese American parishioners even as he began to teach zazen to others. By 1967, ZCLA had moved into a rented house; by 1980, it had grown to 235 members, about 90 of them living in a community-owned complex of houses and apartments that took up an entire square block of west central Los Angeles. In 1976, Maezumi established the Kuroda Institute for the Study of Buddhism and Human Values, a nonprofit educational organization dedicated to promoting Buddhist scholarship. It sponsors conferences and workshops and publishes two series devoted to East Asian Buddhism with the University of Hawaii Press—one scholarly studies, the other translations of classic texts. At about the same time, Maezumi also founded the White Plum Sangha, an association of his students who, by the end of the '70s, had begun to set up Zen centers of their own in various parts of the country. After Maezumi's unexpected death in 1995, the White Plum Sangha was formally incorporated. It now operates as an extended America dharma family that, in the words of its president, Dennis Genpo Merzel, in 1997, works together "with open communication and respect for one another, in fulfilling Maezumi Roshi's dream of establishing the dharma in the United States and world-wide."[8]

ZCLA and its many affiliates represent the kind of diversification that was taking place within American Zen during the 1980s and 1990s. Some of Maezumi's students led monastic-style centers inspired by traditional Zen, while others focused more exclusively on the kind of innovation required to support family practice. Some worked to integrate the dharma and the arts, while others were more directly involved in social action. There are both mountain retreats and inner-city centers affiliated with the White Plum Sangha, and its geographical reach currently extends along the West Coast from Portland to San Diego to Mexico City; east to Salt Lake City, Chicago, and New York; across the Atlantic to Britain, France, and Poland; and across the Pacific to New Zealand.

Like SFZC, the White Plum Sangha includes many women. Among Maezumi's older students, Charlotte Joko Beck, who has taught for many years at the San Diego Zen Center, emerged as an important teacher in the 1980s. Somewhat like Toni Packer, Beck abandoned many of the Japanese elements of Zen, and the spirit of her teaching is conveyed in the titles of her well-received books, *Everyday Zen* and *Nothing Special: Living Zen*, and in the name of her teaching lineage, Ordinary Mind School of Zen. By 1998, the Ordinary Mind School had centers in San Diego, Champaign, Illinois, Oakland, California, and New York City. At about that time, Jan Chozen Bays, who leads a family-oriented practice in Portland but is interested in developing a residential monastic center, began to emerge as a prominent national teacher.

Many centers were also established by men in the White Plum Sangha, two of which represent the complex ways traditionalist and innovative impulses coexist in American Zen today. John Daido Loori moved from Los Angeles to establish Zen Mountain Monastery (ZMM) in the Catskills region of New York State in the early 1980s. Located on 200 acres of fields and forest, ZMM provides Zen training for a lay and monastic community on a year-round basis. Loori, the abbot, has described his approach as "radical conservatism,"[9] by which he means that Buddhism's rich Asian heritage, adapted to the needs of Americans, can serve as the basis for a genuinely alternative form of transformative spirituality.

Loori grounds ZMM programs in what he calls the "Eight Gates of Zen," which include sitting meditation, liturgy, face-to-face learning with the teacher, the study of Buddhism, work practice, the observation of Buddhist precepts, body practice, and the arts. Even though most practitioners at ZMM are laypeople, Loori chose to model his organization on monastic precedents because he and his students wanted the more rigorous monastic lifestyle and practice to set the pace for the entire community. By the 1990s, ZMM had established three distinct tracks for study and practice—secular, for those who sought to cultivate awakened consciousness with no religious overtones; lay Buddhist, for householding practitioners; and rigorously monastic, in the spirit of the Ch'an and Zen traditions of China and Japan.

It had also established a number of Buddhist social programs that ranged from prison mission work to wilderness preservation.

Loori and ZMM have also developed innovative forms of Buddhist educational outreach through Dharma Communications, a not-for-profit corporation dedicated to bringing Buddhism to those without easy access to centers and teachers. Dharma Communications publishes *The Mountain Record*, a quarterly that features articles on Buddhism and art, science, psychology, ecology, and ethics. In 1998, they were about to launch an "Open Monastery," a range of media services including an interactive CD-ROM and online communications, to foster Zen training. ZMM also has a network of affiliated centers called the Mountains and Rivers Order, inspired by Dogen's *Mountains and Rivers Sutra*. It was founded to foster the practice of members in New York City, Albany, New York, Burlington, Vermont, and in three centers in New Zealand.

But Loori keeps this highly articulated organization at the service of the spirit of Zen. "We should really be clear," he noted during his installation as

Hakuyu Taizan Maezumi, shown here with John Daido Loori at Zen Mountain Monastery in Mount Tremper, New York, led the Zen Center of Los Angeles until his death in 1995. Maezumi's students and their own students have formed the White Plum Sangha, a dharma family of Zen teachers who by the 1990s led centers in Mexico, Europe, New Zealand, and across the United States. ZEN MOUNTAIN MONASTERY ARCHIVES

abbot in 1989—in a traditional ceremony during which a new abbot is said to ascend the mountain—"that zazen is not meditation, is not contemplation."

> It's not stilling the mind or focusing the mind, mindfulness or no mind. It has nothing to do with mudras, mantras, mandalas, or koans. Nothing to do with understanding or believing. This zazen I speak of, this sitting Zen, is also walking Zen, working Zen, chanting Zen, laughing Zen, and crying Zen. Zen is a way of using our mind, living our life, and doing it with other people. And yet there's no rule book. This zazen I speak of is the flower opening within the world. So to be in the mountains manifests the freedom that master Dogen is speaking of, the freedom to follow the wind and ride the clouds.[10]

Bernard Tetsugen Glassman, Maezumi's most senior student, has taken the tradition in quite a different direction to become one of American Zen's most well-known innovators. Glassman was an aerospace engineer at McDonnell-Douglas before beginning to study Zen in the 1960s. He moved from Los Angeles to New York in 1979, where he established the Zen Community in New York (ZCNY) in the Greyston mansion in Riverdale, a wealthy section of the Bronx. In 1982, the community opened Greyston Bakery, a gourmet specialties business located in Yonkers, with the goal of securing financial support for the sangha.

By the mid-1980s, however, Glassman decided to pursue a more socially active role in this economically depressed city in Westchester County. ZCNY soon sold its headquarters and purchased an old Catholic convent in Yonkers, which subsequently became the home of the Greyston Mandala, a network of organizations dedicated to developing Zen as a force for social change. Glassman soon expanded the goals of the bakery to include providing employment for the needy, homeless, and unskilled. He and his wife, Sandra Jishu Holmes, then opened the Greyston Family Inn, a homeless housing facility providing shelter, child care, and job training to the Yonkers community. Their vision of the integration of Zen practice with both business and social activism is outlined in Glassman's *Instructions to the Cook: A Zen Master's Lessons in Living a Life That Matters*.

Since then, Glassman has increasingly directed his energy to social transformation as a vehicle for the practice of Zen. He became well known for leading "street retreats" in run-down neighborhoods of New York City, during which participants share the reality of homelessness as a form of

Buddhist meditation. After participating in an Auschwitz retreat sponsored by Nipponzan Myohoji, a Nichiren Buddhist movement best known for its Peace Pagodas and Walks for Peace, Glassman began to lead similar retreats himself, seeing them as a uniquely powerful way to realize the meaning of the Buddha's teaching on death and impermanence. He discusses his vision of social transformation as a way of realization in *Bearing Witness: A Zen Master's Lessons in Making Peace*, published in 1998.

In the same year, Glassman and Holmes left the Greyston Mandala in the hands of senior students and relocated to Santa Fe, New Mexico, where they planned to devote themselves full-time to building a new institution, the Zen Peacemaker Order. In March of that year, Holmes died suddenly in Santa Fe, but Glassman continues to develop the Order and its own unique expression of the American Zen spirit. Its three core tenets are "Not-knowing, thereby giving up fixed ideas about ourselves and the universe; bearing witness to the joy and suffering of the world; and healing ourselves and others." Its members subscribe to four commitments agreed upon by delegates to the Parliament of the World's Religions in Chicago in 1993, the centennial celebration of the original event at which Shaku Soyen and other Asian Buddhists first introduced Buddhism to the United States:

I commit myself to a culture of nonviolence and reverence for life;
I commit myself to a culture of solidarity and a just economic order;
I commit myself to a culture of tolerance and a life based on truthfulness; and
I commit myself to a culture of equal rights and partnership between men and women.[11]

The emphases of Loori and Glassman in their work represent the way Zen is taking on different shapes in this country. Both are men of the same generation, both are students of the same teacher, and both work out of a shared tradition whose leading historical figure is the thirteenth-century Japanese master Dogen. Both have taken it upon themselves to adapt tradition to the needs of Americans. Loori's *Eight Gates of Zen* can be profitably read alongside Glassman's *Bearing Witness*, or the video *Oryoki: Master Dogen's Instructions for a Miraculous Occasion*, produced by Loori's Dharma Communications, can be viewed in light of Glassman's *Instructions to the Cook* to see how Zen is currently following different paths in America, even while maintaining a degree of internal consistency.

American Zen Practice and Worldview

During the last half of the twentieth century, Zen flourished in America and took on institutional forms unlike either Jodo Shinshu or Nichiren Buddhism. But to focus on its leading organizations (and many others could be noted here, from lay-oriented Cambridge Buddhist Association in Massachusetts to the contemplative order at Shasta Abbey in northern California) is not to suggest that Zen in America can be solely identified with its Japanese founders, their students, and their institutions.

First of all, the Asian tradition of which Zen is a part is being reworked in America to a degree that is very difficult to assess as the Ch'an (Chinese), Son (Korean), and Thien (Vietnamese) traditions interact with one another. No discussion of this stream of Asian Buddhism in the United States is complete without attention to teachers such as Hsuan Hua, Seung Sahn, Thich Nhat Hanh, and others, whose contributions are treated in chapters 10 and 12. As important, the literary heritage of American Zen, which has always been closely linked to its spirit, has continued to flourish from Robert Pirsig's *Zen and the Art of Motorcycle Maintenance* in the 1970s to Natalie Goldberg's *Long Quiet Highway: Waking Up in America* in the 1990s. Through essays and poems, Zen and Zenlike ideas have begun to reach into the lives of many Americans who have no commitment to practicing the tradition.

There is in America also a lively phenomenon the Japanese call *bujizen*, a term that in a traditional context refers to self-styled Zen practitioners who disdained the kind of institutional discipline associated with formal traditions and teaching. Seen in a positive light, bujizen is an expression of free-form spirituality and a source of considerable creativity. Much of the artistic expression of Buddhism among the early Beats, as well as the Zen popularized by Alan Watts, might be considered American bujizen. Seen negatively, bujizen is often dismissed as a kind of self-deluded indulgence that mistakes egotism for awakening. However one evaluates self-styled Zen, it suits America's individualist ethos very well and, as evidenced in the explosion of Zen-inspired popular publishing, there is likely to be a great deal more of it in this country.

Committed practitioners, however, continue to hold the traditional disciplines of Zen in high regard, even as they are adapting them to suit the spirit, tenor, and language of American society. The specific forms these disciplines take are often encoded in the practice vocabulary of Zen discussed below, which, while arcane and confusing to the uninitiated, is taken for granted in most monasteries and dharma centers across the country. Some Americans dismiss such vocabulary as an undesirable remnant of Japanese influence, but others see it as an essential part of the tradition to be maintained in the process of cross-cultural translation.

ROSHI In the Japanese tradition, the word *roshi* literally meant "old or venerable master." It has long been a title conferred upon an individual who has realized the dharma, is possessed of honorable character, and has been certified as having passed through years of training under a Zen master. It was assumed a roshi had received *shiho*, or dharma transmission, which is given when a teacher is satisfied that a student has achieved a genuine insight into enlightenment. This is the basis of the "mind-to-mind" transmission of the dharma that is crucial in the formation of Zen lineages. Shiho was also confirmed by a master through *inka*, which means "seal of approval" and connotes a confirmation of enlightenment. In Rinzai circles, inka is associated with the successful completion of koan study.

In some American Zen communities, *roshi* retains this formal meaning, as it does in Zen institutions in Japan. Within communities such as the San Francisco Zen Center and the White Plum Sangha, the founding teachers were called Suzuki Roshi and Maezumi Roshi by their students. The title roshi was subsequently conferred on their students who were recognized as having successfully completed a full course of training. For instance, John Daido Loori is now referred to by his dharma name, as Daido Roshi. Bernard Tetsugen Glassman is referred to as Tetsugen Roshi or, alternatively, as Glassman Roshi. But *roshi* has also passed into more general parlance both in Japan and in the United States. It is often used in a nonspecific way to convey students' respect and admiration for their teachers. As a result, the use of the term varies from community to community.

SENSEI *Sensei* also means "teacher" and is used in different ways in different institutional settings. In the White Plum Sangha, for instance, *sensei* denotes one who has not received inka but has received shiho, or dharma transmission, and thus is called a dharma heir of their teacher. In contrast, a dharma holder has successfully completed part of the course of training with a teacher, but has not received shiho and is thus not yet a full dharma heir. Dharma holder connotes an assistant teacher. Like *roshi*, *sensei* is also used in some settings as a generally honorific term.

The highly formalized monastic practices of Japanese Zen are changing in this country as American practitioners, most of whom are lay-people, begin to reinterpret the forms and language of the tradition to suit a new cultural context. This man and woman at the Hazy Moon Zen Center in Los Angeles are undergoing tokudo, a form of Zen ordination that generally denotes a high degree of commitment to monastic practice. HAZY MOON ZEN CENTER

TOKUDO As in the history of Jodo Shinshu Buddhism, the translation of Japanese terms into English can result in confusion. For instance, the term *tokudo* literally means "attainment of going beyond" and is often translated as "monk's or monastic ordination." It is generally reserved for full-blown Zen monastic practice, a commitment that only a small number of Americans have chosen to make. The terms *monk* and *nun*, however, are used in this country in a variety of ways because, in the absence of institutions with powerful traditions, what it means to make a commitment to Zen is in flux. In any case, the terms *monk*, *nun*, and *monastic* usually do not imply celibacy as they do in the Christian tradition. Nor do they necessarily mean that an individual is expected to reside in a monastic community.

JUKAI A more neutral term that is also translated as "ordination" is *jukai*, which literally means "receiving or granting the precepts." In this country, jukai is a formal rite of passage that marks entrance into the Buddhist community. At that time, a student is given a dharma name, such as Chozen in Jan Chozen Bays. He or she also makes a commitment to the precepts, which are interpreted a bit differently in various communities. The White Plum Sangha follows the Soto tradition, which ordinarily accepts sixteen precepts. These include taking refuge in the Three Jewels; the three pure precepts (to do no evil, to do good, and to do good for others); and the ten grave precepts: 1. Do not kill; 2. Do not steal; 3. Do not engage in sexual misconduct; 4. Do not lie; 5. Do not become intoxicated; 6. Do not speak of others' faults; 7. Do not elevate yourself while demeaning others; 8. Be generous to others; 9. Do not be angry; and 10. Do not slander the Buddha, dharma, or sangha.

ZAZEN In the rich practice vocabulary of Zen, the most important term is *zazen*. The word is derived from *za*, which means "sitting," and *zen*, which means "absorption." In its most classical form, zazen is done seated in the full lotus position on a meditation cushion called a *zafu*, although more relaxed postures and alternative forms of support are commonly used in this country. Zazen is usually done with eyes open, but cast down and lightly focused. In classic Soto centers, it is often done facing a blank wall. Practitioners may follow their breath or work on a koan during zazen. But many do not consider zazen meditation in the general sense of the term because often there is no object on which one meditates. For them, zazen is encountering the mind's incessant activity and, in Dogen's famous expression, learning to "think nonthinking" on a moment-to-moment basis.

KINHIN Kinhin is a form of walking meditation practiced in Zen centers and monasteries between periods of zazen. In the Rinzai tradition, it is done quickly and energetically, sometimes at a jog. In the Soto tradition, it is more often done slowly. In the eclectic style of Zen often found in the United States, it is done both ways. Some teachers use it out of doors with the specific intention of developing attentiveness to nature and the interdependence of all living things in the natural environment.

KOAN Most basically, a koan is a story about or remarks made by earlier roshis, used to instruct Zen students in the dharma. Some practitioners understand koans as paradoxes whose solution requires a cognitive leap that transcends one's normal way of thinking. Others treat them as depictions of situations that must be fully experienced and embraced as having no solution. Systematic koan study is most closely associated with Rinzai Zen, but in the United States koans are used, both formally and informally, in a variety of settings. Here, the term *koan* may also refer to conflicted situations in life that, given proper attention, can aid one on the path of realization. For instance, a lay Zen practitioner might say that his or her attempt to reconcile practice and family is a koan he or she is working on. In this sense, all matters of life and death can be regarded as koans and thus important steps in the process of realization.

DOKUSAN *Dokusan* literally means "going alone to a high place." It refers to a private meeting or interview between teacher and student, the content of which is usually kept secret. Dokusan plays an important role in Zen training. During dokusan, a master will assist a student with problems he or she faces in practice. If the student is working on a koan, it provides an occasion for him or her to display progress in understanding it, which a teacher may confirm or refute. Sometimes an interview is simply an encounter between teacher and student in silence. There are many stories about the enigmatic behavior of teachers in the dokusan room, so the experience can be anxiety-provoking for students. Traditionally, dokusan has been highly ritualized, but in many American Zen centers it has taken on a more informal character.

ORYOKI *Oryoki* literally means "that which contains just enough." The term refers to a set of nested eating bowls that a Zen monk or nun traditionally received at ordination. These bowls, in particular the largest of them, which is called "the Buddha bowl," are considered symbolic of the single one that Shakyamuni allowed his disciples to use in their begging rounds. *Oryoki* also refers to the use of these bowls in meals eaten in silence in Zen monasteries. Eating oryoki-style is a form of Zen practice. Food is first offered to the buddhas and bodhisattvas, and is only then consumed by the community. This kind of practice underscores the conviction that every aspect of life can be the occasion for the realization of enlightenment. Oryoki is a familiar feature in monastically inclined American Zen centers. Some communities eat oryoki-style on a daily basis, others only occasionally. Sometimes oryoki is performed slowly and elegantly and at other times energetically, quickly, even somewhat sloppily.

SAMU *Samu* means "work service" or "work practice." Like oryoki, samu underscores the everyday character of the realization of enlightenment. Most specifically, it refers to the performance of tasks necessary to maintain a Zen center or monastery, which are undertaken in the spirit of service to the community. It is an occasion to perform mundane chores in a meditative state of mind, and it plays an important role in most phases of Zen training. In a more expanded sense, samu is related to right livelihood, one step on Shakyamuni's Eightfold Path. Lay practitioners in this country who need to integrate their work lives with practice often approach their professional activities as a form of samu in a wholly secular setting.

SESSHIN, ANGO *Sesshin* and *ango* are particularly intense and protracted periods of practice. *Sesshin* means "collecting the heart-mind." It is usually a period of three or seven days, held at regular intervals in the calendar of a Zen community, during which students are able to focus on their practice and develop a sustained relationship to their teacher. Sesshins are usually conducted in complete silence. Some take on a ceremonial dimension as well. For instance, a Rohatsu sesshin is held to coincide with the date Shakyamuni is said to have attained enlightenment. In interreligious groups that practice Zen, an Advent sesshin might be held to coincide with the birth of Jesus Christ. *Ango*, which means "dwelling in peace," is a three-month-long period of intensive practice. It is a counterpart to the rainy-season retreats of bhikkhus and bhikkhunis in ancient India.

This kind of vocabulary—and there is a good deal more of it— remains important to American Zen today. It also reflects the complex, ongoing processes at work in the adaptation of Buddhism to this country. As the height of the '60s, very few Americans who were drawn to Buddhism had any knowledge of samu, oryoki, dharma transmission, and the like. From the writings of D. T. Suzuki and Alan Watts, they may have associated Zen with an intuitive approach to the world, as well as paradoxical and enigmatic forms of wisdom. Or their initial exposure to Buddhism may have been the Beat poets, Madame Blavatsky, or Timothy Leary and LSD. At any rate, few grasped what Buddhism in general and Zen in particular entailed as a disciplined way of life and a form of religious commitment.

The Americanization of Zen is often presented as a one-way street, a process of only reshaping a Japanese tradition to suit the tone and tenor of American society. Zen in the United States becomes more informal. It is Anglicized. It is democratized. It is tailored to the middle-class American lifestyle, with its focus on the workplace and nuclear family. As many advocates for Americanization have correctly remarked, Buddhism, and Zen in particular, has throughout its long history displayed a capacity to adapt to a wide range of cultural and national settings. But as a description of the Americanization of Zen, this is curiously incomplete. Many Americans have also been adapting themselves—in fact they have been self-consciously disciplining themselves—to the Japanese traditions of Zen for well over three decades. Zen philosophies, meditation practices, rituals, and vocabularies were taken up by many Americans as they built the flagship organizations of American Zen, a task that required a great deal of labor, money, and commitment and, no doubt, many, many hours of zazen.

There are numerous issues yet to be thrashed out in American Zen. The relationship between American practitioners and the source of their tradition in Japan is much discussed insofar as it bears on practice styles, institutional authority, the legitimacy of the teachings, and a wide range of other questions. It is probably safe to say that there are currently as many positions on how to pursue this relationship—enthusiastic embracing of Japanese models, keeping a respectful distance, maintaining cautious skepticism, and exhibiting outright disdain—as there are Americans seriously engaged in Zen practice.

Some Buddhists are also concerned that Americanization will lead to a decline in the dharma if the aspiration to realize Buddha mind becomes overidentified with psychotherapy, or if practice becomes too accommodating to the economic and emotional needs of the American, middle-class family. Others, however, see precisely those kinds of adjustments as the unique contributions Americans can make to an ancient tradition of philosophy and practice. There are also fascinating questions about how Zen, the leading form of Buddhist meditation in the country, will evolve as it is influenced by the Tibetan and Theravada traditions, which have their own communities of meditating convert Buddhists. It is not possible to forecast these developments, but the fact that they are on the horizon is a reminder that the Americanization of Zen, however much it has progressed in the course of several generations, is far from complete.

CHAPTER EIGHT

The Tibetan Milieu

At least three interrelated forces have been at work in the transmission and adaptation of the Tibetan Buddhist tradition to America over the course of the last several decades. All were set in motion by the Chinese occupation of Tibet in 1950 and by the creation of a Tibetan community in exile in 1959, after the Dalai Lama, Tibet's political and spiritual leader, escaped to India, eventually followed by about a million Tibetans. Given Tibet's unique circumstances, the cross-cultural transmission of its religious traditions has been particularly dramatic, as elements of an entire civilization that was suddenly shattered were selectively transplanted into the vastly different society and culture of the United States.

One of these forces, the campaign for a free Tibet, became a celebrated cause in America's human rights and entertainment communities, a development that brought all things Tibetan to the attention of the American mainstream. What Alan Watts, D. T. Suzuki, and the Beat poets did for Zen in the 1950s, political activists and Hollywood filmmakers and stars did for Tibetan Buddhism in the 1990s. A second, less noticed, but highly significant development was a concerted effort on the part of Asian and western Buddhist scholars and publishers to preserve Tibetan religious texts and disseminate them in the West. This cause was taken up with urgency due to China's determination to eradicate Tibet's religious traditions and institutions. A third force, crosscut by political and preservation concerns, was the establishment of an extensive network of practice centers by lamas and their students, beginning in the 1960s.

Additional factors have helped to create a uniquely Tibetan milieu in this country. Tibetan Buddhism arrived largely untouched by the kind of whole-sale modernization processes that transformed Buddhism in Japan. As a re-sult, its religious worldview remains, for lack of better terms, traditional or pre-modern. Complex mythologies and ritualism are at the center of Ti-betan Buddhism, as is an unapologetic, devotional regard for lamas, many of whom are considered reincarnations of highly realized beings. Another fac-tor is the demographics of Tibetan Buddhism in this country. There are only about ten thousand Tibetan exiles and immigrants in America. As a result, Tibetan Buddhism here is largely a community of discourse that includes lamas living both in this country and in Asia, committed scholars and polit-ical leaders, a small clutch of exiles, and practicing converts, who form the largest part of the community. No figures are available on how many Amer-icans are Buddhists in the Tibetan tradition, but since the 1970s they have been a prominent and very distinctive feature of American Buddhism.

There are differences among Tibetan Buddhism, Tantric Buddhism, and Vajrayana, but the terms are used more or less synonymously in this country. They are part of a broad stream of Buddhism that originated in India but traveled with the Mahayana tradition through China to Japan, taking on a unique form in the Tibetan region of central Asia, where it fused centuries ago with local shamanic traditions. Tibetan Buddhism is structured by a com-plex and sophisticated set of organizations in this country. Its major schools all have budding flagship organizations and are represented by many highly regarded teachers, a few of whom we will come to presently. The trauma re-sulting from the Chinese invasion of Tibet and the resulting emphasis on the preservation of its traditions in exile have given much of the religious activ-ity in the community a conservative slant. At the same time, however, a num-ber of its leaders and teachers, both Asian and American, are regarded as bril-liant innovators.

Politics and Celebrity on the Road to Americanization

Serious interest in the practice of Tibetan Buddhism has been on the rise in the United States since the 1970s, but Tibet momentarily seized the spotlight in America in the 1990s. Much of the fascination with Tibet at that time was infused with romantic idealism, which often obscured the complexity of Ti-betan society and its religious traditions. But through a powerful alliance be-tween Tibet support groups and Hollywood, Americans' awareness of Tibet was greatly heightened, a phenomenon that was also a peculiarly American moment in the history of the cross-cultural translation of the dharma.

At the heart of it all was Tenzin Gyatso, the fourteenth Dalai Lama. His high public profile is based in part on his dedication, charm, and commitment to principles of nonviolence, which have elevated him to Gandhi-like status in the eyes of many Americans. It is also based on the fact that he has been a tireless worker for the Tibetan people since his exile and an assiduous traveler since his first trip to the West in 1973. Both his personal commitment and his work on behalf of his people won him the Nobel Peace Prize in 1989.

The Dalai Lama is seen as a spiritual leader with authority and expertise that appeal to a varied constituency. During a two-week stay in Los Angeles in 1989, for instance, he spoke before a Chinese American audience at Hsi Lai Temple in Hacienda Heights, the largest Buddhist monastic complex in

Tenzin Gyatso, the Fourteenth Dalai Lama, is a Gelugpa monk and the political and spiritual leader of the Tibetan people. His dedication to the cause of Tibet, his religious integrity, and his personal warmth made him among the most popular and charismatic Buddhist leaders in the West in the 1990s. AP PHOTO

the West, where he addressed the assembled as his Chinese brothers and sisters. He spoke to a gathering of American convert and immigrant Buddhists from communities in southern California and gave a public, general-interest lecture to 5,000 in the Shrine Auditorium on the topic of inner peace. In a more practice-oriented vein, he also performed a mass Kalachakra initiation, one of a large number of Tibetan Buddhist empowerment ceremonies, for 3,000 Buddhists and any others who cared to attend. He then addressed medical doctors, scientists, and philosophers, who had requested him to speak on the nature of human consciousness and mind/body relations.

Because the Dalai Lama is also the political leader of his country and an astute statesman, his tours usually balance politics with religion. During a 1997 tour to Washington, D.C., he was particularly concerned with courting the American political establishment, where sympathies for Tibet were warming. He met with President Clinton and Vice President Al Gore at the White House and was hosted by members of Congress, including the chairs of both the House and Senate committees on foreign relations. He was introduced to Secretary of State Madeleine Albright, Speaker Newt Gingrich, Senate Majority Leader Trent Lott, and other congressional leaders. But he also met with American Jewish and Christian leaders, joined an Interfaith Prayer Gathering for Religious Freedom at the Washington National Cathedral, and attended the inaugural Passover ritual held by a movement called Seders for Tibet.

The Dalai Lama's political work in the 1990s received critical support from a wide range of Tibet support groups working both in the upper echelons of American society and at the grassroots. The U.S. Tibet Committee in New York, an independent human rights organization of Tibetan and American volunteers, promoted public awareness of Tibet through lectures, demonstrations, and letter-writing campaigns. The International Campaign for Tibet, located in Washington, D.C., worked primarily with elected officials, but also provided assistance to grassroots groups such as Los Angeles Friends of Tibet (LAFT). LAFT is primarily devoted to public education in Los Angeles, but has been a consultant to the Hollywood studios and coordinated publicity for the Dalai Lama's southern California tours. It is one of many independent, community-based organizations loosely affiliated as Friends of Tibet.

Other support groups used a range of strategies to educate the public about Tibetan issues. Students for a Free Tibet, the leading group on campuses, tapped into the student activism once devoted to the movement to end apartheid in South Africa. It began in 1994 with 45 chapters nationwide, and by 1997 had 350. Students played a key role in helping the London-based Free Tibet Campaign persuade Holiday Inn to pull out of Lhasa, Tibet's capital city. Rangzen, the International Tibet Independence Movement, is headquartered in Indianapolis, Indiana. One of its major activities was to sponsor marches for Tibet's independence. Its 1997 march was a 600-mile, three-month-long trek from Toronto to New York City. In 1998, another went from Portland, Oregon to British Columbia, concluding at the consulate of the People's Republic of China in Vancouver. Both marches were led by Thubten J. Norbu, the elder brother of the Dalai Lama and President of the Tibetan Cultural Center in Bloomington, Indiana.

Other organizations dedicated to Tibet operated across the spectrum of American culture. At the pop end, the Milarepa Fund, founded by Adam Yauch of the rap/hip-hop group Beastie Boys, was best known for its sponsorship of Concerts for a Free Tibet, a series of performances by cutting-edge rock groups designed to introduce Tibetan issues to pop music fans. "For the most part the fans have been really cool and fascinated by the monks, blown away," Yauch noted. "They just emanate so much love and compassion that everyone on the tour and the other bands are drawn to them."[1] A self-identified Buddhist, Yauch was largely responsible for introducing the dharma to a generation more or less untouched by the 1960s-era enthusiasm for Buddhism. At the more establishment end of the spectrum was Tibet House in New York. Founded in 1987 at the request of the Dalai Lama, this cultural center and art gallery educates the public with exhibits, lectures, and workshops about Tibet's living culture and distinctive spirit. Its co-founder and current president is Robert Thurman, the Jey Tsong Khapa Professor of Indo-Tibetan Buddhist Studies at Columbia University, a former Tibetan monk, author, and outspoken American Buddhist leader.

Hollywood added both the luster of celebrity and a powerful dose of publicity to the campaign for Tibet, which reached a critical mass in 1997, the annus mirabilis for Tibetan issues. Between October and December of that year, Hollywood propelled Tibet into the public eye with the release of *Red Corner*, a movie trashing the Chinese justice system, starring Richard Gere, one of America's long-time, high-profile Buddhists; *Seven Years in Tibet*, starring box-office idol Brad Pitt; and *Kundun*, a story about the childhood of the Dalai Lama directed by the eminent filmmaker Martin Scorsese. Each premiere served as the occasion for interviews, protests, nationwide campaigns, and Tibet-related appearances by celebrities.

The release of *Seven Years in Tibet* also prompted *Time* magazine to run a cover story, "America's Fascination with Buddhism," that despite its glibness ("All over the country, pop goes the dharma") and star-struck tone ("Bodhisattva Brad?") signaled a resurgent Buddhist vogue reminiscent of the '50s Zen boom. In the same year, moreover, Penor Rinpoche, head of the Nyingma school, announced that he had recognized Steven Seagal, the action-adventure film hero, to be a tulku, the reincarnation of a seventeenth-century monk and lama whose teachings had been destroyed by the Chinese. This elicited so much cynical commentary about celebrity Buddhists in general and Seagal in particular (one journalist dubbed him "the homicidal tulku"[2]) that Penor Rinpoche soon issued a press release to clarify issues. "Some people think that because Steven Seagal is always acting in violent movies, how can he be a true Buddhist," he wrote from Namdroling Monastery in India.

> Such movies are for temporary entertainment and do not relate to what is real and important. It is the view of the Great Vehicle of Buddhism that compassionate beings take rebirth in all walks of life to help others. Any life condition can be used to serve beings and thus, from this point of view, it is possible to be both a popular movie star and a tulku. There is no inherent contradiction in this possibility.[3]

All the publicity evoked cautious responses from much of the convert Buddhist establishment, where many people who had been practicing the dharma for thirty years seemed put off by all the attention. *Tricycle*, a respected Buddhist review, asked in a cover story: "Hollywood: Can It Save Tibet?" In a piece on the image of Tibet in films from Frank Capra's 1937 classic *Lost Horizon* to the present, one author concluded Hollywood was "relevant—maybe even critical" to the outcome of Tibet's political struggle.[4] Similarly cautious applause came from Stephen Batchelor, an influential British Buddhist who was in New York for a forum with Philip Glass, the avant-garde composer and long-time Buddhist who wrote the score for *Kundun*. "Perhaps it doesn't matter how Buddhism—the dharma—filters into the culture," Batchelor told the *New York Times*. "What matters is whether people take it up and change their lives."[5]

Tibet support groups made use of all the coverage but considered it both temporary and superficial, and they anticipated that corporate America, with eyes to China's vast markets, would soon put a lid on the media's pro-Tibet sympathies. But as Larry Gerstein, co-founder of Rangzen with Thubten J. Norbu, noted in the midst of it all, the media attention had some positive effects: "We'll have to see whether all this publicity translates into broad-based, public support. But at least people now know why we are marching. A few years ago a lot of folks asked, 'What's Ty-bet?' "[6]

Preservation and Dissemination of Texts

A second, very different avenue for the transmission of Tibetan Buddhism to the United States has been the effort of many people to preserve Tibetan religious texts and disseminate them in this country. When refugees fled Tibet for India, they left behind great works of art, ritual paraphernalia, and a vast number of Mahayana and Vajrayana texts, all of great importance to the study and practice of Buddhism, and a great many unknown in the West. Over the next twenty years, an estimated 6,000 monasteries, plus temples and other landmarks, were demolished. Art was destroyed and monastic libraries were burned. Monks and nuns were tortured and imprisoned, and hundreds of thousands of Tibetans were killed in the course of a campaign aimed at the extinction of a civilization. China's policies gave the work of preservation and transmission of the Tibetan tradition a particular urgency. If Tibet were destroyed, its traditions would live on only in religious texts and in a generation, perhaps two, of exiled Tibetans.

The arduous task of collecting, preserving, translating, and disseminating Tibetan texts was first taken up in this country in the 1960s by lamas in exile and their students. More than teachers from other traditions, these lamas encouraged their students to take advanced degrees in Buddhist Studies and to seek jobs in the academy. Among the most influential of these students-turned-academicians is Jeffrey Hopkins, whose writing, research, and teaching in the Buddhist Studies program he founded at the University of Virginia have been critical in advancing the study of Tibetan Buddhism in this country. The rise of Tibetan studies helped to change the evaluation of Tibetan Buddhism in the West, where it had been dismissed by many scholars as a corrupt form of the dharma. In the 1970s, a range of Buddhist presses became selectively engaged in the distribution end of the preservation and translation work. Whereas in 1960, only a few older translations of classic texts such as *The Tibetan Book of the Dead* were readily available in American bookstores, by the mid-'90s a wide range of philosophical and liturgical texts were on the open market, many of which had been considered secret teachings for centuries.

A number of publishing concerns, all with strong links to the American Vajrayana practice communities, played a central role in this activity. Wisdom Publications is a nonprofit organization associated with the Foundation for the Preservation of the Mahayana Tradition (FPMT), an international network of practice centers founded in the 1970s by Lamas Thubten Yeshe and Thubten Zopa Rinpoche. Wisdom is dedicated to the publishing of the work of the FPMT founders as well as translations of sutras, tantras, other Tibetan texts, and a range of general Buddhist literature.

The premiere English-language publisher of scholarly and trade books about Tibet and Tibetan Buddhism is Snow Lion Publications, located in Ithaca, New York. Formed in 1980, Snow Lion is closely associated with the Gelugpa tradition and its spiritual leader, the Dalai Lama, whose North American monastic headquarters, Namgyal Monastery, is also located in Ithaca. Since 1984, Snow Lion has published fourteen books by or about the Dalai Lama. But its extensive Tibetan material also includes translations of philosophical, ritual, and devotional texts, and books devoted to Tibetan history, art, and culture. Snow Lion has been instrumental in distributing the work of a pioneering generation of scholars of Tibetan Buddhism, but it maintains a popular profile as well by distributing Vajrayana-related audio-visual material, T-shirts, posters, and ritual and decorative paraphernalia.

Shambhala Publications is the foremost general-interest publisher in the American Buddhist community. Founded in 1969, it has been a part of the Buddhist phenomenon among the baby-boom generation almost from the start and, together with *Tricycle: The Buddhist Review*, it is a significant public voice of the convert community. Among its most successful titles are *The Tassajara Bread Book*, now a Zen standard from the counterculture era, and Fritjof Capra's *Tao of Physics*, a pioneering popular book about the interface between science and Asian religion. Shambhala is also well known as the publisher of the works of Chogyam Trungpa Rinpoche, a teacher who played a key role in the Tibetan part of the convert community throughout the 1970s and into the '80s. Its first publication was Trungpa's *Meditation in Action*, released while he was still in England. In 1973, it published his *Cutting Through Spiritual Materialism*, a path-breaking book at the time and now an American Buddhist classic. Shambhala continues to maintain a full line of Trungpa's work in print, but it also has a history of publishing a broad range of Asian and western spiritual texts in a variety of paperback and pocket-sized editions. Since 1974, its distribution agreement with Random House has enabled it to make an unusually significant contribution to the introduction of Buddhism into mainstream America.

In contrast, Dharma Publishing, founded by Lama Tarthang Tulku in Berkeley, California in 1971, is run by the lama's nonsalaried, long-time stu-

Chogyam Trungpa, whose book *Cutting Through Spiritual Materialism* is an American Buddhist classic, was one of the most innovative of the many Tibetan lamas to come to the United States during the Buddhist boom of the 1960s. He is shown here teaching at Naropa Institute in Boulder, Colorado, one of the institutions that are part of his legacy in this country. SHAMBALA SUN

dents and takes a quasi-monastic approach to texts. Dharma Publishing has many projects, but one ongoing effort has been the creation and distribution of a limited edition, 128-volume collection of the *Kangyur* and *Tengyur*, the canonical scripture of Tibetan Buddhism. Each atlas-sized volume weighs ten pounds, is hand bound, and is printed on acid-free paper to ensure its survival for centuries. Each contains about 400 gilded pages of photocopied block print texts, a Tibetan sacred painting called a *thangka*, line drawings of a founder of one of the Tibetan schools or lineages, historical maps, and an image of one of Tibet's many buddhas, all selected to honor the wisdom contained within the text and to delight readers. This attention to detail reflects the devotional regard in which the *Kangyur* and *Tengyur* are held by

Tibetans, who display the volumes above the central altars in shrine rooms and prostrate themselves before them as a devotional exercise. Dharma Publishing is now located at Odiyan, an extraordinary monastic complex in northern California designed by Tarthang Tulku, which serves as a study and retreat center for his practice community.

A monastic spirit also infuses the Asian Classics Input Project (ACIP) directed by Geshe Michael Roach, a Gelugpa monk and the first American to receive the geshe degree, the Tibetan equivalent of a doctorate in philosophy. But ACIP is working to produce a scholarly edition of the *Kangyur* and *Tengyur*, together with philosophical commentaries and dictionaries related to them, in a searchable format on CD-ROMs, which are made available at a nominal cost to scholars, research institutions, and practice communities. For more than twenty years, Roach studied with Geshe Lobsang Tharchin, the abbot of Sera Mey monastery, once located in Lhasa but rebuilt in south India after the Chinese occupation of Tibet. Young monks in exile now perform data entry for ACIP at Sera Mey, a task that helps to support the impoverished monastic community. The marriage of ancient wisdom and high technology epitomized in the work of ACIP is captured in the poem "In Praise of the ACIP CD-ROM: Woodblock to Laser," by Gelek Rinpoche, another tulku who is a highly regarded teacher and the founder of Jewel Heart, a network of Buddhist centers in half a dozen cities here and abroad.

> *A hundred thousand*
> *Mirrors of the disk*
> *Hold the great classics*
> *Of authors*
> *Beyond counting.*
> *No longer*
> *Do we need*
> *To wander aimlessly*
> *In the pages of catalogs*
> *Beyond counting.*
> . . . .
> *With a single push*
> *Of our finger*
> *On a button*
> *We pull up shining gems*
> *Of citations,*
> *Of text and commentary,*

Whatever we seek;
This is something
Fantastic,
Beyond dreams.[7]

The Vajrayana Practice Network

The campaign to free Tibet and the preservation and dissemination of texts have been central to the transmission of Tibetan Buddhism to America, but the living heart of the process is found in a practice network built by lamas and their American students. By and large, Tibetan centers in this country are not highly politicized, although the issues surrounding Tibet in exile necessarily pervade the community. But the unique circumstances created by the need to preserve Tibet's religious life have given a traditional cast to much of their activity. Prayers flags, prayer wheels, thangkas, butter lamps, and the cultivation of Vajrayana meditative practices in gemlike shrine rooms help to re-create a uniquely Tibetan ethos in the West that is devotional, highly festive, and contemplative.

The first lamas in exile began to arrive in America in the late 1950s, but Tibetan Buddhism became popular only in the late '60s and '70s. At that time, pioneering teachers such as Kalu Rinpoche, Dilgo Khyentse Rinpoche, and Chogyam Trungpa Rinpoche began to draw large numbers of students both in America and in Europe. For many westerners, the discovery of these lamas was a transforming experience, much like that of Americans who first encountered Japanese Zen teachers. For many in an older generation of American practitioners, these lamas retain a legendary aura and status, as is suggested in this poem by a student of Kalu Rinpoche written in 1997:

Kalu in '72
sat still,
spoke Tibetan quietly,
and I of course didn't
understand a word.
exotic melodious sounds
filled my body.
translation wove itself in
voices and color . . .
dark red robes, small thin body,

occasional slight smile on the calm
weathered face.
the unforgettable face . . .
I didn't know then how many times
Kalu would appear in dreams of
golds and deep reds,
that decades later in another city
I would echo the ancient bodhisattva vows,
Kalu again before the room,
even more gaunt now,
old thin yogi wrapped in folds of red.[8]

Throughout the 1970s, the foundations of the Vajrayana practice network were laid as students gathered around teachers, rented temporary
dharma halls, and began to purchase property, a process much like that in
American Zen, only a few years later. Like American Zen, Tibetan Buddhism in this country has no central administration. Its practice centers are
organized as schools and along the spiritual lines of specific teaching and
practice lineages. There are four main schools in Tibetan Buddhism, the
Gelugpa, Kagyu, Nyingma, and Sakya, but within these are many different
lamas who run centers more or less in accord with the traditions of their
teacher and his or her lineage. While one can speak of an American Vajrayana community as a whole, it is really more a patchwork of small sub-
communities often quite separate from each other, but all maintaining living
links through their teachers to the broader Tibetan community in exile.

A brief look at the Kagyu, a school with well-developed American institutions, suggests the organization of this network in all its fascinating complexity. The Kagyu school is a cluster of teaching and practice lineages associated with the tenth-century Indian king Tilopa, the Tibetan master
Marpa, and his great student, the ascetic Milarepa. Kalu Rinpoche was
among the earliest and most important Kagyu lamas to teach in America,
during a number of tours he made between 1971 and his death in 1989. He
first gathered students around him for teachings on a temporary basis in a
number of American cities.

Shortly after, resident lamas arrived to lead these ad hoc groups and to
continue teaching. In San Francisco, for example, Lodru Rinpoche, a lama
who had studied under Kalu and a number of other Kagyu teachers, was
appointed by the head of the school to develop a group that now goes by
the name of Kagyu Droden Kunchab (KDK). It occupies an apartment

building in San Francisco where local members practice daily, but Lama Lodru also maintains satellite centers in Marin Country, Arcata, Sacramento, and Palo Alto, in part by means of teleconferencing. These five groups constitute the KDK teaching and practice community, a small portion of the Kagyu network, which itself is but one component of the larger American Vajrayana community.

Other Kagyu communities have a more complex structure, such as Karma Triyana Dharmachakra (KTD) in Woodstock, New York. It was founded in 1979 by the sixteenth Gyalwa Karmapa, traditional head of the Karma Kagyus, a prominent lineage within the Kagyu school. At the highest level of organization, KTD is the North American seat of the Gyalwa Karmapa, an office occupied by a succession of reincarnated lamas. It is therefore closely affiliated with Rumtek monastery in Sikkim, the home of the Gyalwa Karmapa in exile, and with Tsurphu monastery in Tibet, the ancient monastic center of the Kagyus. At the same time, however, KTD operates as an American monastery, and its grounds include solitary retreat cabins, staff quarters in a rambling wood-frame farmhouse, and a monastery building constructed in the 1980s, which contains a residence for the Gyalwa Karmapa and two community shrine rooms. Under the direction of its *khenpo* or abbot, Karthar Rinpoche, and Bardor Tulku Rinpoche, KTD maintains a daily practice schedule for staff and guests and regularly offers both introductory and advanced classes.

But the lamas of KTD also lead more than two dozen meditation centers in about nineteen different states (as well as a number overseas), where small groups of American students practice Kagyu teachings, sometimes with a resident Tibetan instructor but more often independently. For them, KTD is a kind of continuing-education home base, which they may visit from time to time to take instruction during a weekend or week-long retreat. KTD also maintains a rural center for the three-year, three-month-long instructional and practice retreat that is a fundamental rite of passage for the advanced student. Its network also includes a stupa, a Buddhist reliquary mound and pilgrimage site, at Karma Thegsum Tashi Gomang in Crestone, Colorado, where the community plans to build an institute for the study and practice of traditional Tibetan medicine and monastic retreat facilities.

Shambhala International, another institution primarily associated with the Kagyu school, is organized similarly to KTD, but has a more complicated relationship to the Tibetan lineages. The headquarters of its far-flung network of North American and European practice centers is in Halifax, Nova Scotia. Its major retreat facility is at Rocky Mountain Shambhala Cen-

The Great Stupa of Dharmakaya at Rocky Mountain Shambhala Center represents both the high regard for tradition and the willingness to innovate found in much of Tibetan Buddhism in America. Its design is in accord with Tibetan precedents and its construction was marked by elaborate rituals, but the Americans who have dedicated years to building it have also adapted selected elements, such as cutting-edge concrete technology and a ground-floor public space, for contemporary uses.
GREAT STUPA OF DHARMAKAYA

ter in Colorado, where the community is creating one of the wonders of the
American Buddhist world, the Great Stupa of Dharmakaya. Thanks to its
founder, Chogyam Trungpa Rinpoche, Shambhala is a unique blend of Vajrayana traditionalism and American innovation. Trungpa was a tulku of the
Trungpa lineage of teachers within the Kagyu school, but he was also trained
in the Nyingma tradition and was an adherent of the *rimed* (pronounced
re-*may*) movement, a modern ecumenical or nonsectarian form of Tibetan
Buddhism. As a result, Shambhala is considered to be in both the Kagyu and
Nyingma lineages and draws upon a wide range of Tibetan traditions.

Shambhala's uniqueness also owes much to Trungpa's brilliance as an in-
novator and interpreter of Tibetan Buddhism. Trungpa arrived in America
in 1970 after studying at Oxford in England, where he relinquished his monastic vows and married. Throughout the '70s, he was deeply involved with
the countercultural movement, first in Vermont and then in Colorado, and
his capacity to combine the cultivation of enlightenment with the outra-
geousness favored in that decade became legendary. During this period of
intense activity, Trungpa laid the foundation for a range of educational, arts,
and practice institutions that would eventually evolve into Shambhala International. In the 1980s, however, he shifted his base of operations to Halifax,
Nova Scotia, and many of his students followed him there. His death in Halifax in 1987 led to a period of strife and confusion for his students. But the
many developments in Trungpa's community during these decades—the
founding of the Jack Kerouac Chair of Disembodied Poetics in 1974;
Trungpa's cremation at Karme Choling, the Vermont center where he started his movement, in 1987; and the death of his regent Osel Tendzin (a convert named Thomas Rich) from AIDS in 1990—were among the most dramatic moments in the cross-cultural transmission of the Tibetan dharma to
the United States.

In 1995, Shambhala came under the leadership of Trungpa's eldest son,
who was enthroned as the movement's leader and is now generally referred
to as the *Sakyong*, or earth protector. Shambhala has since then clarified its
institutional structure and mission by developing three distinct gates or
paths to practice, which reflect different aspects of Trungpa's lifelong passion for the cultivation of awakened living. *Nalanda* is a path for the cultivation of wisdom through the integration of art and culture, which can be
pursued through a range of disciplines from photography and dance to
archery, poetry, and the medical arts. Nalanda is most closely associated with
Shambhala's educational activities, such as its Sea School and elementary
schools in Nova Scotia and Naropa Institute, a fully accredited liberal arts

college in Boulder, Colorado. A second path, *Vajradhatu*, is the most traditionally Tibetan, but it also reflects Trungpa's interests in Zen and Theravada Buddhism and his concern with adapting Vajrayana to the needs of western students. This path is cultivated in a network of local practice centers
called Shambhala Meditation Centers. A third, more thoroughly innovative
path is Shambhala Training, which will be discussed below.

Shambhala International is among America's most complex and innovative Buddhist institutions, but it remains intimately linked to the broader Tibetan ethos and community. The Sakyong is referred to as Mipham Rinpoche because he was recognized by Penor Rinpoche, head of the Nyingma
school, to be an incarnation of Mipham Jamyang Namgyal, a revered meditation master and scholar. Thrangu Rinpoche, the abbot of Shambhala's
Gampo Abbey in Nova Scotia since 1986, is a highly trained Kagyu tulku
and teacher who also heads a convent in Nepal as well as Buddhist study centers in Benares, India, and at Rumtek monastery in Sikkim. He is currently
rebuilding the monastery of the Thrangu lineage in Tibet and leads a network of his own centers in America, Asia, and Europe. At the same time,
however, Pema Chodron, an American student of Trungpa, a mother and
grandmother, and director and resident teacher at Gampo Abbey, is both a
fully ordained Kagyu nun and a highly respected and popular teacher in the
broader American convert community.

These three institutions give only a small picture of the larger Kagyu
network in this country, one that is more or less replicated among the Nyingma, Gelugpa, and Sakya schools. All together they form the institutional
foundations for American Tibetan Buddhism and the means by which teachings and practices are being transplanted to this country, by Tibetan lamas in
exile, American students, and a rising generation of American-born lamas.

Tibetan Buddhist Practice and Worldview

On a popular level, Americans are engaged with the religious traditions of
Tibet in a wide variety of ways. Some are casual visitors to culture and practice centers, where they partake of the spiritual aura of Tibetan Buddhism.
Others take refuge and identify themselves with the community, but limit
their activities to basic meditative practices. Many hold Tibetan lamas in the
highest regard and find being in their presence both inspiring and edifying,
a lay devotional attitude with a long history in Tibet. The disciplined core
of the community in this country, however, is made up of those students and

teachers who make a serious and sustained commitment to meditation, which requires a great deal of diligence, energy, and years of practice. The variety and complexity of these practices are such that it is best to say too little about them rather than too much. But the basic practice vocabulary, understood by all the members of the community, gives a sense of the unique quality of American Vajrayana.

Shamatha and Tonglen Meditation

Shamatha, or *shamatha-vipashyana*, meditation is a basic element in Tibetan practice. It resembles zazen in form, with similar postures and attention to the breath, but its specific goal is the cultivation of tranquility of mind. Shamatha meditation is usually set within a ritual framework that opens with taking refuge and reciting the bodhisattva vow and concludes with a dedication of the merit accrued from the practice to all sentient beings. The cultivation of openness, healthy-mindedness, and calm make shamatha an essential introduction to higher practices, whether visualizations or higher kinds of meditation such as Dzogchen and Mahamudra, which are often compared to Zen. However, shamatha meditation can also be the central, lifelong practice of Americans who consider themselves Buddhists in the Tibetan tradition.

Tonglen, or sending and receiving practice, is a particular method of meditation in which the altruism intrinsic to shamatha is made more explicit. In tonglen, the practitioner takes in the confusion, paranoia, and suffering of the world with each inhalation and neutralizes them in mind and spirit. With each exhalation, he or she concentrates on sending goodness, health, wholesomeness, and sanity into the world. Tonglen meditation is taught by many Tibetan lamas, but it has also been made familiar to Americans by Pema Chodron in her book *Start Where You Are: A Guide to Compassionate Living* and other writings.

Empowerments

Abhisheka is a Sanskrit term translated as "initiation" or, more frequently, "empowerment." It refers to a ritual process in which a lama introduces students to a particular teaching and empowers them to practice it. In traditional Tibet, such empowerments were essential to studying or practicing secret tantric teachings and they remain so in serious practice circles today.

The secrecy and strict procedures that once surrounded empowerments were relaxed in the nineteenth century, when lamas began to encourage laity

to cultivate selected monastic practices. The current boom in publishing esoteric Tibetan texts has further contributed to this openness, which seems to
trouble some lamas a great deal but others not at all. As a result of these
changed circumstances, however, the importance placed on empowerments
seems to be in flux. The Asian Classics Input Project has agreed to release
some texts on computer disk only to those who have been appropriately empowered to study them. But the Kalachakra empowerment, which was formerly meant for experienced practitioners and in Tibet was held only infre-
quently, has become a large-scale, public event promoted by the Dalai Lama
as a meritorious experience for everyone in attendance. Some Americans receive a number of empowerments from lamas but have little expectation of
diligently practicing the teaching. This collection of empowerments often
draws criticism from serious students, but others consider it a form of meritorious activity, one particularly well suited to the religious needs of the laity.

Ngondro

Ngondro (pronounced nundro) means "something that precedes" and refers
to practices used to clear away negativity and accumulate merit in preparation for higher Vajrayana practices, and to cultivate right view. Ngondros
vary from lineage to lineage, but usually consist of a series of four practices
that include rituals, prayers, and physical and mental methods of purifying
body, speech, and mind. The first ngondro is taking refuge in the form of
full-body prostrations before an image, altar, or painting to discipline the
body and heart. The second is the visualization of Vajrasattva, a buddha associated with purification of thoughts and actions, and the recitation of his
hundred-syllable mantra. The third is a mandala offering, a sequence of ritualized offerings of saffron rice ornamented with coins, jewels, and semi-
precious stones arranged on a round plate. These are visualized by the practitioner as containing the universe and all its most desirable things, which are
offered to the buddhas and bodhisattvas. The fourth ngondro is called guru
yoga. In this practice, a student visualizes their teacher as an embodiment of
the Buddha and the wisdom of all the teachers in a practice lineage, a process
that involves the memorization and recitation of lengthy litanies.

Ngondros are considered only preliminary, but even so, they are not for
the faint of heart. Depending on the lineage, the first three are performed
100,000, 108,000, or 111,000 times, and guru yoga is done in 1,000,000,
1,080,000, or 1,110,000 repetitions. Needless to say, not all Americans in the
Tibetan Buddhist community take up ngondro practices, or may do so only

sporadically. Ngondros are, however, fundamental for students who want to advance to the primary forms of Vajrayana practice. Over the course of several years, students will routinely "work on their ngondro." Those Americans who become lamas repeat ngondros periodically in the course of their lifetime practice.

Sadhana

Sadhana, or "means of accomplishing," is a form of Vajrayana meditative practice based on visualizations. It is a ritual procedure during which a practitioner visualizes one or another fully realized buddha or bodhisattva, the choice depending on his or her teacher and lineage. All sadhanas serve as tools to accomplish the same end—the cultivation of total liberation or fully enlightened consciousness by identifying body, speech, and mind with the attributes of a fully realized being.

The procedures in performing a sadhana can be summarized in three basic steps. The first is the taking of refuge and the dedication of merit resulting from the performance of the sadhana to the enlightenment of all beings. The second step, which is the core of the practice, is the visualization of a buddha or bodhisattva in detail —the palace or mandala in which they reside; their apparel and ornaments; and their posture and characteristic gestures, which are called mudras. Throughout a visualization, a practitioner also chants mantras identified with the buddha or bodhisattva in question.

One can get a sense of the visualization process in the following excerpts taken from a Medicine Buddha sadhana offered at an empowerment by Geshe Khenrab Gajam at Osel Shen Phen Ling, a Gelugpa center in Missoula, Montana, in 1990.

> In the space in front of you is the divine
> form of Guru Medicine Buddha. He is seated
> on a lotus and moon cushion. His body is
> in the nature of deep blue light, the color of lapis lazuli.
> He is very serene and adorned with silk robes and magnificent
> jewel ornaments.
>
> Guru Medicine Buddha's right hand rests on his right knee,
> palm outward in the gesture of giving realizations. His left
> hand rests in his lap, holding a nectar bowl of medicine that
> cures all ills, hindrances and obstacles.

Later in the sadhana, the visualization process continues, but with an emphasis on the purification of all obstacles on the path to enlightenment and a vision of the clarity of fully awakened consciousness.

> *From the heart and holy body of the*
> *King of Medicine, infinite rays of light pour down completely*
> *filling your body from head to toe. They purify all your*
> *diseases and afflictions due to spirits and their causes, all*
> *your negative karma and mental obscurations. In the nature of*
> *light, your body becomes clean and clear as crystal.*
> . . . .
> *At the heart of Medicine Buddha appears a lotus and moon*
> *disc. Standing at the center of the moon disc, is the blue*
> *seed-syllable OM surrounded by the syllables of the mantra.*
> *As you recite the mantra, visualize rays of light radiating*
> *out in all directions from the syllables at his heart. The*
> *light rays pervade the sentient beings of the six realms.*
> *Through your great love wishing them to have happiness, and*
> *through your great compassion wishing them to be free from*
> *all sufferings, they are purified of all diseases,*
> *afflictions due to spirits and their causes, all their*
> *negative karma and mental obscurations.*[9]

The third and concluding step is sometimes referred to as the "carryover practices." In this step, the practitioner dissolves the visualization completely, rests in the awakened state evoked in the course of practice, and prepares to carry the insight into everyday life. To conclude the sadhana, he or she dedicates the merit accrued from performing it to all living beings.

There are a relatively small number of Americans, several thousand perhaps but certainly not more than ten thousand, who routinely perform this kind of sadhana expertly. The ngondros and the three-year, three-month retreat are daunting disciplines that tend to select out all but the most committed. Those Americans who have become accomplished at performing them, however, hold the distinction of being among the first generation of native-born teachers of Tibetan Buddhism in this country.

The process of establishing Tibetan Buddhism in America has been undertaken by numerous teachers, both Tibetan and American. Most are religious teachers at work within particular communities, in dharma centers or monasteries, or in more public educational facilities like Naropa Institute. A number of them are also academics, some of whom work as scholars and professors in research universities. Given the circumstances that surround Tibet, much of their work is traditional in character, if not conservative, devoted to the collection, preservation, and interpretation of texts and to perpetuating the teachings. Some have taken up work that is more directly political. A number of teachers, however, have made a conscious attempt to cast Tibetan Buddhism in western terms and are among the communities' most prominent innovators.

For instance, Tarthang Tulku was among the first of the pioneering generation of lamas to recast elements of the Tibetan tradition, including its visualization techniques, into essentially secular terms. His Time, Space, Knowledge Association, which was founded in the 1970s, has its own body of texts and a small but dedicated following.

Chogyam Trungpa's Shambhala Training is a more well-known secular path for the cultivation of contemplative living. The inspiration for Shambhala Training came to Trungpa in a series of dreams and visions in the early 1980s. As a result, they are considered *terma*, a form of teachings thought to be hidden centuries ago by the great sage Padmasambhava, only to be revealed at a later date that was determined by karma. Thus Trungpa is considered to be a *terton* or treasure-finder, who discovers and reveals hidden teachings. The details of Shambhala Training are closely held by the practice community, but its basic elements are outlined in Trungpa's book, *Shambhala: The Sacred Path of the Warrior*, published in the 1980s. Shambhala Training is currently cultivated in classes offered by Shambhala teachers in various locations across the country. It is considered a path in its own right, but many Shambalians go on to study Vajradhatu, the more traditional form of practice offered in Shambhala International.

Two Americans, Lama Surya Das and Robert Thurman, have also emerged as innovative voices in the Tibet community. Surya Das (Jeffrey Miller) is a religious teacher primarily associated with the Nyingma tradition, but, like Chogyam Trungpa, he was also ordained in the nonsectarian rimed movement. He first encountered Tibetan Buddhism when traveling in India in the 1960s and '70s. He studied with lamas there for a number of years. Then in 1980 he traveled to France, where he completed two three-year, three-month retreats under the guidance of Dudjom Rinpoche and Dilgo Khyentse Rinpoche, renowned lamas of the Nyingma lineage.

Over the course of the 1990s, Surya Das joined other leading native-born teachers from a range of traditions at the forefront of a movement to consciously forge American forms of the dharma. He was instrumental in organizing the Western Buddhist Teachers Network, a loose affiliation of Vajrayana, Zen, and Theravada teachers from America and Europe who are wrestling with the challenges of adapting Buddhism to the West. In 1991, he established the Dzogchen Foundation in Cambridge, Massachusetts to serve as his home base. *Dzogchen*, which means "natural innate perfection," is a Zen-like form of meditation considered the highest form of practice in the Nyingma tradition. In the late '90s, he published *Awakening the Buddha Within: Tibetan Wisdom for the Western World*, which is among the most accessible in a new generation of books designed to introduce Buddhism to Americans.

Robert Thurman, co-founder of Tibet House and professor of Indo-Tibetan Buddhist Studies at Columbia University, probably has the highest public profile of any American Buddhist, other than celebrities such as Richard Gere. In 1997, *Time* magazine named him one of the twenty-five most influential Americans. Like Surya Das, Thurman traveled to Asia in the early '60s, when he was ordained a Buddhist monk by the Dalai Lama. After four years of practice and a return to the United States, he relinquished his vows and entered the academic field of Buddhist Studies. Like others in his generation whose personal commitment to monasticism waned, he married and began to raise a family, seeing lay life as a way to follow the bodhisattva path. "I didn't make that much progress as a monk," he told the *Utne Reader* in 1997. "I learned a lot more after coming back and having to deal with the nitty-gritty. It's comparatively easy to be a monk in a quiet monastery, but the bodhisattva tries to engage with all the noise of the world."[10]

In most respects, Thurman is in a class of his own—a well-respected scholar, confidante of the Dalai Lama, and provocative public Buddhist intellectual. Despite his own decision to leave the Gelugpa order, he is an outspoken defender of monasticism who sees the establishment of the monastic traditions of Asia in the West as a prerequisite for the successful transmission of the dharma. He is also a well-known advocate for what he calls "the politics of enlightenment," which he outlined in his 1998 book, *Inner Revolution: Life, Liberty, and the Pursuit of Real Happiness*.

As its title suggests, *Inner Revolution* is a manifesto for an exuberantly American Buddhism. Much of its power comes from Thurman's ability to tap into an idealistic strand in American culture that can be traced back to the revolutionary period and to link it to '60s-era politics, giving them both a distinctly Mahayana Buddhist twist. Much of the book's appeal for American readers is its activist, democratic, social agenda and its affirmation of the importance of the individual. "History's enlightenment movements tell us we can transform ourselves and our world," Thurman writes.

We can start by allowing that it might be possible to make an enlightened society, one individual at a time, starting with the obvious: ourselves. If, once we enter into the process of enlightening ourselves, we find it possible to help other people move in the same direction, so much the better. . . . If we don't see the whole move into a buddhaverse manifestation in our lifetimes, at least we will have been part of the potential solution rather than of the problem.[11]

But in his sweeping interpretation of global history, Thurman also envisions the twenty-first century as a time when the "outer modernity" of the West can be transformed by the "inner modernity" of Buddhist Asia. Ultimately, he suggests nothing less than that a path of enlightenment first discovered by America's founding fathers in their revolt against the British can be fulfilled by the dharma, which was brought to its highest development in Tibet as a science of spirit and a model for enlightened society. Presenting the idea that the American revolution invested kingly power in the individual, Thurman concludes that:

We must reaffirm the democratic mission to restore a piece of the jewel crown of the natural royalty of every individual to every person on this planet, letting the authoritarian personalities of dictators and dictated melt in the glow of the human beauty and creativity released by freedom.[12]

The idealism expressed by Thurman and others played an important role in raising the public profile of Tibet in America in the 1990s. But the future of Tibetan Buddhism in this country depends on its lamas in exile and its American teachers, the dedication of their students, and, in large part, the future of Tibet. Some lamas express the conviction that the invasion by China was determined by karma to disseminate the dharma worldwide. By the 1990s many had lived and taught in the West for most of their lives. However, a new generation of Tibetan teachers were moving into prominence, who did not share with their elders the experience of living in old Tibet and were more in tune with the West. If Tibet becomes free once again, many lamas and other Tibetans in exile will no doubt be drawn home to build a new society. But even if that occurs, Tibetan Buddhism will remain a permanent part of the American Buddhist landscape, with its uniquely rich and highly distinctive forms of philosophy and practice.

CHAPTER NINE

The Theravada Spectrum

Theravada Buddhists in this country can trace their origins to the World's Parliament of Religions of 1893, when Anagarika Dharmapala presented a stirring vision of the Buddha as a religious reformer whose teachings could heal the modern schism between science and religion. But America's first Theravada temple, the Buddhist Vihara Society in Washington, was established only in 1966, and it functioned primarily as a center for diplomats and foreign visitors to the capital city. Since then, the tradition has assumed a very prominent role in American Buddhism and, due to its size and complexity, it is likely to have an immense impact over the long term. There are, however, at least three distinct tiers to American Theravada Buddhism, so it is less a single community than a spectrum of positions along which different kinds of Buddhists practice the dharma under institutional and cultural conditions that vary considerably.

South and southeast Asian Theravada immigrant communities are at the traditional end of the spectrum, where the dharma is being Americanized by perennial forces in immigration history such as Anglicization and generational change. Asian Theravada is conservative in many respects, but has undergone significant alterations in the modern period. One trend has been the growth of institutions of higher education for bhikkhus, which has led some monks to adopt roles as progressive social and political leaders. Another is the emergence of the retreat center, where monastics and laity set aside their traditional social and religious roles and devote themselves to meditation. A forest ascetic movement has also been important in the past century and a half, introducing rigorous forms of Buddhist practice into the south and southeast Asian hinterlands; some immigrant and native-born American Theravadans follow this practice in the United States. New religious roles have also begun to emerge among Theravada women. There are numerous female renunciates in south and southeast Asia even though the bhikkhuni lineage died out in the tenth century. Questions about whether to reestablish this lineage are a source of lively contemporary debate among Buddhist women both in Asia and in the United States.

Convert Buddhists in the Insight or vipassana meditation movement are at the other end of the spectrum. Many of these Buddhists studied in retreat centers in Burma and other countries in southeast Asia in and around the 1960s, then returned to the United States to become teachers. In most important ways, these Buddhists identify themselves with Zen practitioners and other European American converts who engage in sitting meditation. They share a strong interest in adapting the dharma to the needs of western laity. Ritualism and the traditional ceremonial cycle of Buddhist holidays tend to be kept to a minimum, and there is little interest in or sympathy for the concept of merit-making. As with other forms of American Buddhism emerging among converts, this kind of Theravada Buddhism is often highly influenced by western secular humanism and psychotherapy; the movement as a whole is both applauded and criticized for its many innovations.

Theravada immigrants and converts live in very different social and cultural worlds and have different religious priorities, which militates against the creation of a unified American Theravada community. However, a number of significant developments led by monastics tend to blur the boundaries between these two large camps. Some university-educated Asian monks have taken up work in this country that bridges the two communities. Other connections are being made by westerners who, having undergone lengthy monastic training in south or southeast Asia, are able to move between the two worlds as teachers and leaders. Relative to the immigrants and converts, they do not comprise a particularly large group but represent a creative synthesis between the two, and one model for the integration of tradition and innovation.

Additional variables give a great deal of texture and variation to Theravada Buddhism in this country. The first is country of origin. Among immigrants are Sri Lankans, Thais, Cambodians, and other national groups whose communities in this country are often distinct, although their Buddhist traditions share a strong family resemblance. Another variable is mode of entry. Most Theravada Buddhists are immigrants, but others are refugees, which often has a significant influence on the shape and mood of a particular community.

A third, more complex variable is related to the distinction between monastics and laity. In traditional communities, Theravada bhikkhus follow the vinaya, the regulations that order life and practice in the monastic sangha, and they usually retain the high status accorded them in Asia. There are lay-based immigrant groups in this country, but most Asian American laity continue to practice their religion through rituals and devotional expressions that are understood to be occasions for merit-making. In convert communities where the majority of Buddhists are laypeople who meditate, the monastic model has been by and large abandoned, although monks sometimes play prominent roles as exemplars and teachers.

Theravada in the Immigrant Community

Immigrant Theravada monastics and laity have been working for about thirty years to build a network of Buddhist institutions that is now among the most extensive in the country. Paul Numrich, one of the few scholars to direct sustained attention to recent immigrant Buddhism, estimates that there were between a half and three quarters of a million Theravada immigrants at the time of the 1990 census. In 1996, he confirmed the existence of about 150 organizations functioning as Theravada temples, called *wats* (Thai) or *viharas* (Sri Lankan), in more than thirty states, but mostly in California, Texas, New York, and Illinois, which have absorbed the bulk of the Asian immigrants. Many of these have been formally recognized by one or another Asian Theravada sect as consecrated temples. Others are monastic residences that also serve as communal religious facilities. Many more informal temples probably exist in apartments and houses in immigrant and refugee communities.

Upon arriving in the United States, Theravada immigrants were first preoccupied with social adjustment, economic survival, and the emotionally complex processes involved in Americanization. Religious life in the temple was often rudimentary. Many viharas and wats were first formed as Buddhist societies by laity, often from different ethnic and national traditions, who then worked with religious authorities in Asia to arrange for monks to immigrate. Much of their energy was channeled into attempting to reconstitute the religious life of their homelands. In the early years, tensions often arose around ethnic and sectarian issues. Different parts of the community reacted in different ways to legal, social, and religious questions raised in the course of adapting their traditions to a radically new setting. Some tensions became long-standing as differences emerged among ethnic and national groups and as monks and laypeople disputed who should hold authority in religious communities. Questions also emerged about the degree to which temples were to be strictly religious or to serve a range of social, cultural, and religious functions. All these conflicts tended to foster the differentiation of Theravada religious life, as new temples were formed to meet the needs and aspirations of particular constituencies.

By the mid-1980s, many communities had passed into another phase, in which the most pressing concerns were related to second-generation issues. As children and grandchildren became thoroughly Anglicized and Americanized, the process of translating Theravada traditions into American forms began in earnest, with the establishment of after-school programs, Buddhist summer camps, and Sunday dharma schools. At about that time, many Theravada communities also entered into a "brick and mortar" stage of Americanization. With financial resources more readily available, new temples could be purchased or built, often in suburban locations, to more satisfactorily meet the needs and aesthetic tastes of their congregations. Other communities, however, did not have this luxury. Roughly 40 percent of Theravada Buddhists arrived in the United States as refugees, including hundreds of thousands of Laotians and Cambodians fleeing war and revolution in southeast Asia. They encountered many emotional obstacles on the road to Americanization, and have tended to remain clustered in low-rent, inner-city neighborhoods in cities like Chicago and Long Beach, California.

During this entire period, Americanization had a unique impact on immigrant bhikkhus struggling to live in accord with vinaya regulations regarding dress, food, and money. "Los Angeles certainly wasn't made for Theravada village monks," notes Walpola Piyananda, abbot at a vihara in southern California. "When I first arrived, food was quite a problem. Of course I had no money and no notion of cooking for myself." The challenges monks faced on a personal level also had repercussions for the entire community. Sri Lankan immigrants in Los Angeles, he recalls, "expected me to be an ideal, perfect village monk. They didn't want to see a monk wearing shoes, socks, or sweaters. They couldn't bear to see a monk even shaking hands with women. This was difficult, as in dealing with Americans, if I refused to shake hands, people took offense." He further reflected on the difficulties presented by the urban environment. "I constantly faced the challenge of meeting the social customs of the U.S. head on, dealing with things

While many Theravada temples are located in houses, old school buildings, or storefronts, Wat Thai in Los Angeles is one of many new temples constructed across the country since the 1980s. Here the community is celebrating Vesak, the Buddha's birthday, one of the most important holidays in the Buddhist calendar. DON FARBER

that did not seem to coincide with the letter of the Vinaya. . . . I needed to drive, as Los Angeles is virtually uninhabitable if you can't get around, and certainly it makes a monk useless if he cannot reach his community."[1]

Even weather reshaped the life of the monastic community. In 1990, Robert W. Fodde, the American security officer at a wat near St. Louis, wrote to the head of the Mahanikayas, a Thai monastic order in this country, pleading for an alternative to monastic dress. While cotton robes were suited to south Asia, he argued that their continued use during midwestern winters put monks at serious risk. "It is easy to picture a car-load of monks being driven to a meeting during the cold winter months, having their car break down and freezing to death before help could arrive. Easy to see the possibility of a furnace breaking down, and monks hospitalized with hypothermia," he wrote. "It is clear that a modified uniform is not a luxury, but a necessity."[2] Fodde suggested that the monks abandon their monastic robes and adopt the kind of uniform worn by Christian clergy, an idea Mahanikaya leaders rejected. But the order soon permitted adjustments in dress, and bhikkhus now wear thermal underwear beneath their robes, knit caps, heavy sweaters, and socks with their sandals in winter, usually dyed the traditional ochre of the Theravada sangha.

Some of the stark challenges that often faced refugees are recounted in *Blue Collar and Buddha*, a documentary about Laotians in the mid-1970s arriving in Rockford, Illinois, a rust belt city with high unemployment. The film focuses on the anger and resentment directed at Laotians by vocal groups in Rockford, who viewed them as competitors both for welfare and for low-paying jobs in a troubled economy. Others frankly expressed their hatred for people they associated with the defeat of the United States in southeast Asia. The film's second focus is on the religious life in the temple, a small wood-frame farmhouse set amid cornfields at the edge of the city, which became the target of bombings and shootings in the 1980s. With its fenced-in compound, some locals viewed the temple as a symbol of the Laotians' unwillingness to assimilate. Others feared that nefarious activities went on there, mistaking the temple, with its monks in robes and sandals, for an Asian kung-fu training center.

For the Laotians, however, the temple provided social and religious continuity. The film's narrator, a Laotian artist who worked as an upholsterer for Goodwill Industries, describes how a festival drawing several hundred people to the temple expressed a variety of religious meanings. "The New Year's festival is important for people of my country," he notes, as men, women, and children are shown offering trays of rice, fruit, and vegetables, as well as toilet paper and Twinkies, to monks ranging in age from the late teens to the fifties. Some offerings had personal intentions. "They celebrate by bringing food to the monks and money for the temple. . . . People don't have money. People don't have jobs. But they want to give food and money because it brings them merit. This will help them to be reborn in a better state." Others had a more communal emphasis: "Or they may give this merit to people who have died," he continues.

> If their parents have died this merit can help them wherever they have been reborn. When monks eat the food, people feel that the spirit of the dead mother or father enjoys that food too. They give food to make these spirits happy. After the monks and spirits have eaten, everyone else eats that food too.[3]

Temples are often points at which the traditional Theravada worldview and American culture intersect, as at Wat Promkunaram near Phoenix, where in 1991 a tragedy disrupted the community's quiet march toward Americanization. The wat was founded as a home temple by Thais, Laotians, and Cambodians in 1983. In 1985, the prospering community purchased five acres of land to build a new, $300,000 suburban wat with an office, a monastic residence, and a large shrine room. The new temple opened in May 1989 and shortly thereafter hosted the thirteenth annual conference of the Council of Thai Bhikkhus, one of a number of Theravada monastic organizations in this country. In 1991, nine people lived in the wat—six monks, one novice, one nun, and a young man described as "a temple boy to chant and recite Buddha's teaching and sit in meditation in the morning and evening."[4] But in August of that year, two Thai women arrived at the wat to cook meals for the residents, a form of meritorious religious activity, and found all nine murdered in the shrine room.

The tragedy built bridges between Wat Promkunaram and the broader community, even as it underscored the differences between them. Temple leaders educated reporters as they answered questions about theft as a motive for the killings: monks do not wear jewelry; they are not even allowed to touch money; the Buddha image in the shrine room was not solid gold, but gilded concrete. The Thai ambassador met with the governor of Arizona and the local investigative team. Monks and relatives flew in from Asia and children returned home to help parents cope with the tragedy.

But at the same time, the Theravada community was confronted with alien American mores. The shrine room was cordoned off for a week as a crime scene. The nine bodies were taken to the morgue for autopsies, and it cost the community $30,000 to secure their release. When they were returned to the temple from the funeral parlor, their faces were heavily made up. "In my village when a monk died we put poison herbs in the body's mouth," said one woman, a waitress at a Thai restaurant, "and the spirit returned and told the monk who killed him. Here they won't let us touch the bodies."[5] Some recalled omens foreshadowing the crime and others had dreams that offered clues to its solution. One man attempted to contact the deceased monks in meditation. Two highly Americanized young men related to the victims made plans to go to Thailand for ordination in order to dedicate the merit to their deceased relatives.

Few immigrant communities experienced such devastating developments, but most faced probing questions raised by local zoning boards, which often served as immigrants' first encounters with American bureaucracy. Can a monk's home in a residential neighborhood be considered a public temple? Is it an appropriate place for communal religious festivals? Who is to be held responsible for parking problems and traffic congestion? Are gilded spires on wats and viharas in keeping with community aesthetic standards? Is sutra chanting through the night a public nuisance or an exercise of the constitutionally guaranteed freedom of religion? These were the fundamental issues of the Americanization process for many Theravada immigrants during the 1980s and '90s, as they built a network of temples in a range of national traditions, all with common elements of ritual and religious etiquette. A grasp of some of these elements is essential to understanding the distinct form of Buddhism found within the Theravada immigrant community.

Theravada Practice and Worldview

Prostrations

Making prostrations is a basic ritual of respect in Theravada temples. Before entering a shrine room, both laity and monks remove their sandals or shoes. Upon entering, they make a prostration before the Buddha image, kneeling with palms together at the level of the chest or head, then bowing forward to the floor three times. Laypeople also make ceremonial prostrations before monks, because they are thought to embody the triratna or Triple Gem. In the course of teachings and rituals, monks normally teach from a raised platform, while laity sit lower, on the shrine room floor, as a sign of respect.

Chanting

Chanting is central to the religious life of the temple. Virtually every rite begins with three chants: the first is the *Namo Tassa*, which means "homage to the blessed one"; the second is the *Tisarana* or the Three Refuges. The third, the panca sila, is the recitation of the five precepts. These provide an introductory framework for a range of additional rituals performed on specific occasions. Most of the chanting is done by the monks in Pali, but some responsive chanting between monks and laity is done in the vernacular—Thai, Sinhalese, another southeast Asian language, or, increasingly, English. Monks conduct morning and evening sessions of chanting in Pali, which may or may not be attended by laypeople. Laity may also conduct their own chanting sessions, sometimes in English. These sessions often include a period of meditation, perhaps twenty minutes to a half hour long, often the only occasion laity meditate.

Buddha Puja

Buddha puja, which is roughly translated as "Buddha homage," is an integral part of the religious life of the Theravada temple. Like prostrations, it is done more as a sign of respect and veneration than worship as understood in Christianity. Buddha puja can be done as an individual act: a devotee will place a small gift of water, incense, or flowers on the altar before the Buddha image. In the context of a collective ritual meal, small portions of each dish are arranged on a tray and passed among the congregation so that each can touch it. The tray is then placed on the altar as a collective offering.

Other forms of puja common in south and southeast Asia are found in American Theravada communities. *Deva puja* (roughly, "god homage") is a form of veneration given to a wide range of animistic deities. Although not entirely orthodox, these rituals and deities were long ago incorporated into popular Theravada practice. There is some indication that the veneration of these deities, who are intimately associated with particular Asian locales and regions, will not be successfully transplanted to the United States. *Bodhi puja*, another popular practice with a long history that dates back to ancient India, is the ritual veneration of bodhi trees, in honor of the pipal tree under which the Buddha gained enlightenment.

Sanghika Dana

Sanghika dana (or *sangha dana*) means "offering or gift to the sangha." Laity who prepare and serve meals to monks are performing one form of sanghika dana, as are those who donate goods deemed requisite for monastic practice by the vinaya. The most basic gifts are robes, begging bowls, belts, razors, and a few other items, but they may include money, groceries, toothpaste, and other necessities. Sanghika dana is a central element in Kathin, one of the major festivals shared by all Theravada national traditions. During Kathin, laypeople replenish the stores of the monastic community by making gifts, especially gifts of robes, in the first months after the rains retreat, a time when monks traditionally gather in a communal setting. But sanghika dana is also done on an individual basis when a lay donor seeks counsel from a monk, commemorates the death of a loved one, or comes to have his or her fortune told or palm read. In response to lay gift-giving, monks perform rituals of blessing such as chanting Pali texts or, in the Thai tradition, whisking water over a donor's head.

Lay Vows and Ordination

On some occasions, special vows are taken by laypeople, both men and women. They take eight precepts (the panca sila plus no eating after midday, no worldly amusements, and no luxurious sleeping arrangements, which includes maintaining celibacy) and spend from a day to a week living a contemplative life in the temple. In some Theravada traditions, young men have the opportunity to be temporarily ordained into the sangha as bhikkhus for varying lengths of time. During this period, they are instructed in the dharma and monastic principles and practices to prepare them for their adult lay lives. A higher ordination is also sometimes taken by adults, who are then considered a part of the monastic sangha for a period of time varying from a few days to several years.

Some temples are experimenting with "lay ordination" for American converts who join the temple. This functions as a rite of passage into the serious practice of Buddhism, but does not require maintaining celibacy or adhering to other monastic regulations found in the vinaya. Few Americans have taken full monastic ordination. Among those who have, there is a tendency for many to later relinquish their vows or to move to Asia, where there are fewer distractions from the pursuit of a monastic vocation. A new generation of Americans who became interested in Buddhism in the 1990s, both women and men, appeared to have fewer qualms about taking full ordination; if this trend continues, it may significantly influence the development of Theravada in this country.

Vesak

Vesak or Visakha is a spring celebration that commemorates Buddha's birth, enlightenment, death, and passing into nirvana. It is the most important Buddhist holiday in Asia, although its observance varies according to national tradition. In this country, it has become the occasion for a common celebration that unites different Buddhist traditions and schools. It is also the traditional festival most frequently attended by non-Asian Buddhists. At Dharma Vijaya Buddhist Vihara in Los Angeles, for example, Vesak extends over a weekend and draws hundreds of people. The temple and its compound are first thoroughly cleaned and then festooned with lights and streamers, and a Buddha image is installed on the porch of the temple. A pavilion is also constructed where monks will sit and engage in hours of chanting. The opening hours of Vesak are devoted to more or less secular activities, such as performances by the children of the dharma school, award presentations, and orations. The religious core of the festival consists of an all-night program that includes chanting, Buddha puja, ordinations, and a range of other rituals, all of which come to an end the following morning with a communal meal served to the monks by hundreds of laypeople.

Vipassana Meditation

Vipassana is translated as "insight" and denotes the highest form of Buddhist meditation in the Theravada tradition. There are, however, a variety of ways vipassana techniques are taught in different traditions and groups. In some Theravada traditions, primarily the Burmese and Sri Lankan, vipassana is used to promote moment-to-moment awareness of the fleeting phenomena in the mind and body. In others, primarily the Thai forest tradition, vipassana is not seen as a distinct technique but as a quality of awareness that comes from developing insight into the laws of karma while cultivating mental tranquility. Traditionally, vipassana meditation was the province of monastics, but lay meditation movements have become increasingly important in modern Theravada countries in south and southeast Asia.

The Vipassana or Insight Meditation Movement

The vipassana or Insight Meditation movement among convert Buddhists stands at the opposite end of the spectrum from immigrant Theravada Buddhism. It originated in lay-oriented meditation retreat centers in south and southeast Asia and is among the most powerful and popular forms of convert Buddhism in the United States. The dynamics of immigration, distinctions between monks and laity, and ritualism have played only a small part in the creation of the American movement. The most prominent teachers are lay Americans who traveled to Asia in the 1960s, where they trained with a variety of Theravada teachers, some of them monks and others laypeople. These Americans later returned home and began to teach one or another form of vipassana meditation, more or less divorcing it from traditional monastic and lay elements in the religious life of Theravada immigrant communities. These teachers also developed an eclectic style in their efforts to indigenize the dharma, freely drawing upon other schools of Buddhism, other religions, and humanistic psychotherapy to create readily accessible forms of Buddhist practice.

Ruth Denison is among the American pioneers of this movement. She and her husband first became interested in Asian religions in the 1950s. They traveled to Asia in 1960, spending time in Zen monasteries before studying Theravada forms of meditation at a center in Burma. After returning to America, Denison frequented the Zen Center of Los Angeles but continued to return to Burma for training, at a time when Theravada meditation traditions were virtually unknown in this country. Denison began teaching in 1973 and soon gained a reputation for her energetic approach to practice and her use of music, movement, and rhythm, emphases she attributes both to her background in humanistic psychology and to Theravada meditation techniques that focus on sensory awareness. This approach to meditation, she told *Insight*, a movement journal, means

> Never a dull moment,—and a demand for total participation from the students and the teacher. This in turn cultivates a wonderful spirit of genuine communion. Most of all, I encourage people to go into their difficulties and to cope with the change that's taking place even as they are paying attention to it. Our life is nothing but change and it is to this change that I bow deeply. I bow to this change, I bow deeply to life itself.[6]

In 1977, Denison bought a desert property near Joshua Tree, California, which eventually grew into Dhamma Dena, an important movement retreat center since the early '80s.

The year 1975 was an important turning point in the movement: Sharon Salzberg, Jack Kornfield, Joseph Goldstein, and others, all having trained with Theravada teachers in Asia, founded the Insight Meditation Society (IMS) in Barre, Massachusetts. Salzberg first went to India at age 18, and eventually studied Buddhism with teachers from India, Nepal, Bhutan, Tibet, and Burma. Kornfield became interested in Asian religions during his undergraduate years at Dartmouth College. After graduating in 1967, he joined the Peace Corps and worked in Thailand, where he met the first of a number of meditation teachers. Several years after returning to the United States in 1972, he began teaching and eventually took a Ph.D. in clinical psychology. Goldstein also became interested in Buddhism as a Peace Corps worker in Thailand and in 1967 took up vipassana meditation, subsequently studying under a number of Asian teachers. He began to teach in 1974, the year before IMS was founded. For over a decade, IMS was the flagship of the movement; then, in 1988, Kornfield helped to found a West Coast counter-

The founding of the Insight Meditation Society in 1975 was an important event in the development of Theravada-based lay practice in this country. Here IMS founders Jack Kornfield, Sharon Salzberg, and Joseph Goldstein are shown teaching together in the Barre, Massachusetts center in 1977. INSIGHT MEDITATION SOCIETY

part at Spirit Rock in Marin County, California, which has since become an integral part of the San Francisco Buddhist community.

Unique characteristics of the Insight Meditation movement have helped it grow into one of the most popular forms of American Buddhism. Like Zen, it is a movement of laity engaged in the meditative practices traditionally associated with monasticism. But in contrast, it is less associated with the vocabulary, history, and literature of one particular Asian tradition, a factor that has helped it to assimilate quickly to the style and ethos of the American mainstream. At the same time, many of the books written by its teachers, which are readily available on audio cassettes, have an appealing devotional and inspirational tone reminiscent of the heartfelt piety found in comparable popular movements in Judaism and Christianity. But as a whole, Insight Meditation is not presented as a religion but as an awareness technique fostering awakening and psychological healing through the use of practices taught by the Buddha.

As in the case of Zen, the tenor of the movement has changed over the course of the past three decades. In the 1970s, leaders focused on insight or vipassana meditation, which in Theravada is considered the culmination, not the beginning, of training. It is used to realize the Buddha's teaching on the insubstantiality of the self, the impermanence of the universe, and the universality of suffering.

In the 1980s, Insight Meditation began to emphasize *metta* or lovingkindness meditation, the starting point for practice in traditional Theravada training. This shift is reflected in books such as Salzberg's *Lovingkindness: The Revolutionary Art of Happiness* and *A Heart as Wide as the World*, and in Kornfield's *A Path With Heart: A Guide Through the Perils and Promises of Spiritual Life*. Some teachers also began to absorb Mahayana ideas about the bodhisattva's compassion in a way that underscored the movement's basic orientation to western humanism and American idealism. "We now begin by awakening the heart of compassion and inspiring a courage to live truth as a deep motivation for practice," Kornfield wrote. "This heart-centered motivation draws together lovingkindness, healing, courage, and clarity in an interdependent way. It brings alive the Buddha's compassion from the very first step."[7] This blending of West and East, humanism and Buddhism, is also prominent in the teaching of Sylvia Boorstein, a well-known figure long associated with IMS and Spirit Rock. Her books, such as *It's Easier Than You Think* and *Don't Just Do Something, Sit There*, are among the movement's most widely known introductory classics.

Over the course of the 1990s, some leaders of the movement, especially Jack Kornfield, advocated the idea that a distinct style of Buddhist practice was already emerging out of the often tumultuous experience of the 1960s. "I do not want to be too idealistic. There are many problems that Buddhist communities must face—unhealthy structures, unwise practices, misguided use of power, and so forth. Still, something new is happening on this continent," he wrote in 1998.

> Buddhism is being deeply affected by the spirit of democracy, by feminization, by shared practice, and by the integration of lay life. A North American vehicle is being created. Already this vehicle draws on the best of the roots, the trunks, the branches, the leaves, the blossoms, and the fruit—all the parts of Buddhism—and it is beginning to draw them together in a wise and supportive whole.[8]

IMS and Spirit Rock are teaching, retreat, and training centers that have produced a second generation of instructors now at work in a wide range of independent centers. There are no estimates of the number of people who participate in the movement, but Theravada-based meditation centers doubled in number between 1987 and 1997, from 72 to more than 150.[9] A few are affiliated with immigrant temples and others with Asian lay teachers working in this country, but the mainstream of the movement is articulated by the teachers of IMS and Spirit Rock, their students who have become teachers, and other lay Americans who have trained in south and southeast Asia. Overall, Insight Meditation maintains a low institutional profile. Many of its centers are "living room sanghas" with fewer than twenty-five members. Spirit Rock has developed a Kalyana Mitta (Spiritual Friends) Network of small dharma support groups that sustain contact among practitioners in informal and intimate settings. The most important institutional form in the movement is the retreat, whether held for one day, a weekend, or three months. Retreats are usually held in silence and involve sitting and walking meditation, periods of work practice, and a sermonlike dharma talk by the retreat leader. The Cambridge Insight Meditation Center has developed a unique form called the "sandwich retreat," which consists of five weekday nights of practice "sandwiched" between two weekend-long intensive sessions.

Inherent in American Buddhist movements like Insight Meditation and Zen is a creative tension that gives them much of their appeal and dynamism. On one hand, the primary inspiration for their practice is Buddhist monasticism, an intrinsically elite undertaking due to the rigorous, lifelong demands of monastic discipline. On the other hand, laity must necessarily accommodate their commitment to practicing the dharma to the demands of householding. This combination of monastic practice and lay lifestyle is not a strictly western or American phenomenon, but it strongly influences the way converts are shaping distinctly American forms of Buddhism. An important question, however, is whether lay-based practitioners can seriously pursue the extraordinary goal of enlightenment, which throughout most of Asian history was done by monks and nuns living in celibate monastic communities. For some American Buddhists, this is no real problem. Adjustments in the dharma made to accommodate lay practitioners are seen as setting American Buddhism on an egalitarian foundation. For others, however, such a leveling of practice poses a threat, however unintended, to the integrity of the original teachings of the Buddha.

Joseph Goldstein addressed some of these questions as they arose among Insight Meditation teachers in the early 1990s, at a time when mid-course corrections were being made in the movement. Unlike many, he considered this a serious issue facing lay American Buddhists. "As householders we're busy and we have a lot of responsibilities, and the work of dharma takes time. The view that it [householding] is as perfect a vehicle as monasticism doesn't accord with what the Buddha taught. He was very clear in the original teachings that the household life is 'full of dust.' " Goldstein questioned whether Americans were maintaining the excellence of the Buddha's teachings. "I wonder whether we, as a generation of practitioners, are practicing in a way that will produce the kind of real masters that have been produced in Asia. I don't quite see that happening." In a specifically Buddhist context, he was raising an issue that American Protestants have long called *declension*, the gradual loosening of doctrine and practice over successive generations. "I wonder how much connection there will be to an authentic lineage of awakening in another twenty years. The amount of time that people spend training to be a teacher is getting less and less," Goldstein observed.

> In Asia, people will often practice for as many as ten or twenty years before teaching. Most of us who came from practice in Asia to the West started teaching much sooner than that, but it was still after a substantial period of training. There are people teaching now who have practiced for only a few years.[10]

The Monastic-Led Middle Range

One end of the Theravada spectrum is grounded in the traditionalism of the immigrant community; the other is the more innovative movement among converts associated with IMS and Spirit Rock. But there is also a range of people and places that blur the lines between these two communities and may in the long run provide creative examples for the development of a full-bodied and fully American Theravada Buddhism. Some of these are what Paul Numrich called "parallel congregations,"[11] small groups of American converts who study and practice Buddhism with monks at immigrant temples, while remaining largely aloof from the cultural life of the immigrant community. Other examples are found among some leaders in the Insight Meditation movement, who are continually reexamining the relationship between traditional monastic practice and the spiritual needs and desires of the American lay community. But the most concrete expressions of this middle range are found where a number of Asian and European American monks are working from monastic foundations but extending themselves beyond the boundaries of ethnic communities.

A number of Asian-born, university-educated bhikkhus are important teachers and leaders in the broad reaches of the American Buddhist community. One of these is Henepola Gunaratana, a Sri Lankan monk who leads the Bhavana Society, a practice center located in the Shenandoah Valley of West Virginia, based on Theravada monasticism but incorporating American adaptations. Born in Sri Lanka in 1927, Gunaratana was ordained at the age of twelve, trained as a novice for eight years, and then took full ordination as a bhikkhu. After completing his education, he left Sri Lanka to work as a missionary in India and then as an educator in Malaysia. He first came to the United States in 1968 to serve at the Buddhist Vihara Society in Washington. Once there, he earned an M.A. and Ph.D. in philosophy at American University, where he served as Buddhist chaplain, and taught courses on Buddhism at Georgetown, the University of Maryland, and elsewhere. In 1980, he was appointed the president of the Buddhist Vihara Society. In 1982, he founded the Bhavana Society, for which he served as president. During the 1990s, he was a prominent figure in the Insight Meditation movement overseas.

The Bhavana Society is a residential retreat center for both laypeople and monastics, where Gunaratana leads a small core group of Asian, American, and European monks and nuns. Visitors on retreat can undertake intensive meditation, study the Buddha's teachings as applied to daily life, or engage in the kind of meritorious work traditionally associated with laity. Vinaya regulations are central to practice, but are modified when necessary. Monks and nuns drive cars and shop when no one else is available to do it and work side by side, which, by southeast Asian standards, is considered innovative. Gunaratana favors reestablishing the bhikkhuni lineage and granting full ordination for women, but thinks that this practice will first take root in the United States and only then gain wide acceptance in south and southeast Asia.

Gunaratana sees the United States as providing an opportunity for making adjustments in practice because Buddhism is still so new here, but he is by no means an avid Americanizer. Unlike some in American Theravada circles, he does not support monks and nuns abandoning their robes as a means of adapting the vinaya to this country. He sees monastic dress as protecting monks from worldliness and reminding them of their religious duties. He is also critical of how some Americans attempt to cultivate serious practice while ignoring the Buddha's teachings about craving and the passions by continuing to engage in casual sexual activity. "Every rule prescribed by the Buddha is for our own benefit. Every precept we observe is in order to cleanse the mind. Without mental purification, we can never gain concentration, insight, wisdom, and will never be able to remove psychic ir-

Havanapola Ratanasara, a Sri Lankan American monk, is a Theravada leader who works among the various Buddhist communities in the United States. He is shown here with Karuna Dharma, said to be the first American woman to receive full bhikkhuni ordination, during an ecumenical ordination ceremony at the International Buddhist Meditation Center in Los Angeles. DON FARBER

ritants." He also considers highly problematic the way America and its free-wheeling, materialistic lifestyles are transforming values overseas. "America is still like a teenager, a juvenile, just trying to grow, and that spiritually immature state has been taken as a standard for the whole world to follow. I don't think that is a healthy way of thinking."[12]

Havanpola Ratanasara is also a university-educated bhikkhu working in the broader American Buddhist community. A Sri Lankan monk who resides in Los Angeles, he is largely associated with a series of local, regional, and national institutions that have pioneered Theravada educational and ecumenical initiatives in this country. Ratanasara entered the monastic order in Sri Lanka at the age of eleven. Much later he received a B.A. degree in Pali

and Buddhist philosophy at the University of Ceylon, then attended Columbia University and the University of London, where he earned a Ph.D.
in education. After teaching education and Buddhist Studies in Sri Lanka, he
was appointed delegate to the twelfth General Assembly of the United Nations in 1957, the first Buddhist monk to hold such a position. Ratanasara
emigrated to the United States in 1980, and he was among the founders of
Dharma Vijaya Buddhist Vihara, one of the earliest Theravada temples in
Los Angeles.

Ratanasara's many different administrative hats give an indication of his
work both within and among American Buddhist communities. He helped to
found the Interreligious Council of Southern California, a path-breaking
ecumenical organization, and served as its vice president. He has been president of the Buddhist Sangha Council of Southern California, an organization founded in 1980 in an effort to mediate disputes between monks and
laity in a local temple. Since that time, the Sangha Council has sponsored
inter-Buddhist celebrations of Vesak and participated in a wide range of interreligious initiatives in southern California. Ratanasara later played a key
role in the formation of the American Buddhist Congress (ABC), an organization devoted to many of the same goals as the Sangha Council, but on a
national scale.

Ratanasara is also the president of the College of Buddhist Studies in
Los Angeles, which was founded by the Sangha Council in 1983. The College provides opportunities to study Buddhism from a nonsectarian point of
view and at a depth that cannot be provided by individual temples. Its cur-
riculum is designed to promote understanding among different schools and
traditions that find themselves in close proximity in this country, many for
the first time in Buddhist history. As part of an overall effort to Americanize
the dharma, Ratanasara is working to steer Buddhism in progressive directions, but from a position grounded in traditional monasticism. Together
with other monks in Los Angeles, he has been reviving full ordination for
women. Only fully ordained nuns can ordain other women, so the reestab-
lishment of a Theravada lineage requires cooperation with those Mahayana
Buddhist traditions whose women's lineages have not become extinct. To
this end, Ratanasara played a prominent role in initiating ecumenical ordination ceremonies in this country involving monks and nuns from a wide
range of national traditions.

Ajahn Amaro and Thanissaro Bhikkhu are two European American
monks who represent a tradition of forest ascetics that has been a powerful
religious reform movement in southeast Asia. Both are fully ordained and

observe the regulations of the Theravada monastic vinaya, although they have different institutional affiliations and attempt to adapt traditional practices to the American Buddhist community in somewhat different ways. Both began to develop significant public profiles in the broader convert Buddhist community in the 1990s. Amaro was among the few Theravada monastics to teach regularly on the Insight Meditation circuit, an effort motivated in part by his interest in exposing Americans to the monastic lifestyle. Thanissaro taught at the Barre Center for Buddhist Studies, associated with IMS, and became well known as the author of a number of scholarly books, including *The Mind Like Fire Unbound* and *The Buddhist Monastic Code*, and as the translator of meditation guides written by Asian teachers in the forest tradition.

Ajahn Amaro was instrumental in creating a forest monastery in northern California, which is the center of a largely lay, convert Buddhist community based in the San Francisco area. Born in England in 1956, he traveled to Thailand after graduating from the University of London and began to study and practice at Wat Pah Nanachat, a forest monastery established for western students by Ajahn Chah, a monk in the Mahanikaya order and a teacher in the forest lineage. Amaro was ordained in 1979 and later returned to England, where he became associated with Chithurst and Amravati monasteries, two forest tradition centers. During the early 1990s, he began to make teaching trips to northern California, where he developed a circle of friends and students interested in building a community around the monastic practices of the forest tradition.

At about this time, Hsuan Hua, a Chinese Mahayana teacher and founder of the California City of Ten Thousand Buddhas (see chapter 10), donated 120 acres of undeveloped land in Mendocino County to Amravati Monastery for use as a forest retreat, with the aim of fostering ties between the Mahayana and Theravada monastic communities. In turn, Amravati assigned stewardship of the land to the Sanghapala Foundation, a California lay organization, with a mission to develop it into a forest retreat center eventually named Abhayagiri Buddhist Monastery. In the mid- to late '90s, Abhayagiri became the center of a Buddhist community in a lineage that ran from Ajahn Chah through Chithurst and Amravati in England to northern California. Amaro was named its abbot, an office he has shared since 1997 with Ajahn Pasanno, a Canadian with a long record as a teacher and leader in the movement. For a number of years, Abhayagiri has run annual, long-term winter retreats for monastics that, in keeping with tradition, have been supported by the efforts of American laity.

Thanissaro Bhikkhu went to Thailand in the early 1970s after graduating from Oberlin College. He began to practice meditation with Ajaan Fuang Jotiko, a teacher in one of a number of Thai forest lineages; took monastic ordination in 1976; then continued to study and practice in Thailand after his teacher's death in 1986. In 1991, he relocated in California, where he helped to establish Metta Forest Monastery (Wat Mettavanaram or more simply Wat Metta) in the mountains north of San Diego, where he is known as Ajaan Geoff. Under the spiritual direction of a senior Thai monk in the Dhammayut order, Thanissaro has served as the abbot of Wat Metta since 1993. Unlike Abhayagiri, Wat Metta is a part of the larger Thai Buddhist institutional network in this country.

In some respects, Wat Metta functions like other American Buddhist retreat centers by offering short-term, residential practice sessions on major holiday weekends and short- and long-term retreats on an individual basis. But Thanissaro has emphasized forming a stable monastic community, so Wat Metta also serves as a devotional and practice center for Thai and Laotian Americans living in the surrounding area and for convert Buddhists, many of whom are affiliated with regional meditation groups such as the John Wayne Dhamma Center and the San Diego vipassana community. In keeping with the orthodox tenor of the forest tradition, Ajaan Geoff and the other monks live strictly in accord with the vinaya. As a consequence, Wat Metta is run by the principles of a gift economy. Laity contribute what they can to its maintenance, while monks give freely of their teachings. Ajaan Geoff regards this as an important alternative to the retreat model, which is often based on the payment of fees. "There is no way that the dharma can survive as a living principle unless it can be offered and received as a gift," he wrote in *Tricycle*. A gift economy creates an "atmosphere where mutual compassion and concern are the medium of exchange, and purity of heart the bottom line."[13]

Thanissaro made a conscious decision not to join the circuit of teachers in the Insight Meditation movement. This was due partly to his commitment to a monastic way of life at Wat Metta, and to his own conviction that Theravada practice requires a sustained rigor not readily available in the retreat center mode. Moreover, he sees the critical importance of establishing a wilderness tradition in the United States. "Buddhism has always straddled the line between civilization and the wilderness," he wrote in 1998. "The Buddha himself was raised as a prince, but was born in the forest, gained Awakening in the forest, and passed away in the forest."

Over the centuries, many courageous men and women have rediscov-
ered the dharma by going to the forest. The dharma has survived not
simply by adapting to a host culture but also by standing apart from it—
and the wilderness has been a place to stand apart. It teaches many of the
personal qualities—heedfulness, ingenuity, resilience, and harm-
lessness—that are needed for finding the dharma in the heart and mind.[14]

Given its wide range of expressions, the Theravada tradition is in an excellent position to make long-term contributions to the formation of American Buddhism. Its unique strength rests in the many different avenues
through which it is approaching Americanization—the extensive network of
immigrant temples, the strong practice movement associated with IMS and
Spirit Rock, and the monastic-led institutions in between. All these approaches, however, do not amount to a concerted effort; a wide range of
questions face people in the different strata of the community.

Monastic-led communities and groups must address issues such as the nature of the monks' role in American society, to what degree the vinaya should
be altered to suit the American context, and the desirability of forging ecumenical ties with other forms of Buddhism. Lay immigrants must continue to
wrestle with the myriad complexities of communicating their tradition to
their children and grandchildren. It is doubtful that Asian Americans or European Americans will soon choose to seek full ordination in significant
enough numbers to create a native-born monastic sangha. Therefore, Asian
monks are certain to remain prominent for a number of generations, providing living links to tradition and slowing any tendencies toward wholesale
Americanization.

Lay leaders of the Insight Meditation movement will have to continue to
weigh questions about how to make Buddhism accessible to a middle-class
constituency while maintaining the depth of their teaching. They also need
to develop sufficiently strong institutions and a lineage-like mechanism between teachers and students to attract and sustain another generation, comprised of either their own children or a new wave of American seekers.

CHAPTER TEN

Other Pacific Rim Migrations

Immigration and the complex social forces associated with it gave rise to the Japanese Jodo Shinshu community, which through the trials and errors of successive generations has struck a balance between being ethnic Buddhist and mainstream American. Immigrants formed the original Nichiren groups in this country, and they still contribute to the rich multiculturalism of Nichiren Shoshu Temple and SGI-USA. Tibetan lamas, whether as alien residents, exiles, or new citizens, are essential to the practice of Tibetan Buddhism and Vajrayana in the United States. And despite the impact of literature in generating interest in Zen in this country, Japanese immigrants were the first practice-oriented teachers. The importance of immigration to Theravada Buddhism in this country cannot be overstated.

Migration has also been the driving force behind the formation of Korean, Vietnamese, and Chinese American communities, which are contributing a variety of elements to the American Buddhist mix. Koreans and Vietnamese have been in the United States in large numbers only since the 1970s. Chinese Buddhists have been part of the religious life of this country since the mid-1800s, although they did not form large, enduring religious institutions until more recently. Korean, Vietnamese, and Chinese Buddhism are all in the Mahayana tradition and thus have much in common, but each draws inspiration from its own regional traditions and folkways.

Historians have yet to focus sustained attention on the religious lives of these groups, so it is difficult to do more than sketch some of the ways they are adapting Buddhism to American society. Buddhism plays an integral role in the formation of personal and social identity. It provides many immigrants and their children with emotional stability and a sense of continuity. As a result, religion in these communities is intimately linked to broader patterns of social and cultural adaptation, generational change, and Anglicization. However, some religious leaders within each of these traditions have reached beyond their respective ethnic groups to make vital connections with American Buddhist converts and contributions to the general development of Buddhism in American society.

Chinese Diaspora Communities

Buddhism has been practiced by Chinese in America since the middle of the nineteenth century, when immigrants from the mainland first arrived in California, or Gold Mountain as it was called in China, drawn by the Gold Rush of 1848. The first social organizations formed by the Chinese were based on kinship and linguistic groups and mutual aid societies. In the absence of regularized diplomatic ties between the United States and China's Manchu government, these voluntary associations, later consolidated into merchant organizations called the Six (or Seven) Companies, became influential, particularly when anti-Chinese violence flared up on the West Coast in the post–Civil War decades.

For much of Chinese American history, these merchant groups were the primary sponsors of the community's religious life. The first Buddhist temple in San Francisco was founded by the Sze Yap Company in 1853. A rival company founded the second a year later. Each temple was housed on the top floor of the company's headquarters, a pattern that can still be observed in older Chinatown temples today. By 1875, there were eight temples in San Francisco. By one generous estimate, there were more than four hundred Chinese temples, often small shacks or home temples, at the end of the nineteenth century across the western states, only a few of which still exist today. The religion practiced in these temples was a complex mixture of Confucian ancestor veneration, popular Taoism, and Pure Land Buddhism that typified Chinese popular religion. Devotion to Amitabha, Kuan Yin, and other bodhisattvas was introduced to this country by Chinese Buddhist pioneers.

Most Chinese Buddhism in this country today is of more recent origin. Chinese immigration was drastically curtailed in the late nineteenth century, and as a result, estimates of the population in the twentieth century have run as low as 150,000 in 1950. But changes in immigration law in the 1950s and '60s encouraged a dramatic increase. By the mid-1990s, there were well over three

quarters of a million ethnic Chinese immigrants in this country, from mainland China, Taiwan, Hong Kong, and other centers in the Chinese diaspora
around the Asian Pacific Rim. Many arrived as Christians, and some no doubt
are nonreligious. But many are Buddhist, and there is no question that they are
adding considerably to the complex cultural profile of Buddhism in America.

Some scholars estimate that by the 1990s there were more than 150 Chinese Buddhist organizations in this country, some very small, others extensive. In contrast to the sectarian model prevalent in Japan, most share the
tendency of Chinese Buddhism toward doctrinal and ritual eclecticism. A
form of practice in most groups is *nien-fo*, devotional recitation of the
names and attributes of the buddhas and bodhisattvas, especially that of
Amitabha, who in Japan is known as Amida. In many of these organizations,
the taking of bodhisattva vows and the cultivation of compassion are of central importance, and this encourages altruistic social action that can include
charity and disaster relief work, maintaining a vegetarian diet, and practicing the ritual release of captive animals. Most groups also practice sutra
study and chanting. Few give exclusive emphasis to the kind of sitting meditation associated with Zen.

Aside from these general characteristics, it is clear from the available
data that Chinese American Buddhism is also highly diverse. Most organizations serve ethnic Chinese exclusively, but a few have a significant number of other members and participants. Some are monastic in orientation,
while others, to give free rein to the religious aspirations of laity, have
no monastic sangha at all. A considerable variety is found within Chinese
American Buddhism today, with varying elements drawn from the national
traditions of Burma, Vietnam, and Tibet. There are also important class
variables at work. Some temples serve working-class Chinese living in
urban Chinatowns, while others address the needs of doctors, engineers,
entrepreneurs, computer programmers, and other professionals who are
more likely to live in suburban communities. A number of Chinese temples
and associations are directed by nuns, whose constituencies are largely composed of laywomen. Brief sketches of a few organizations can only suggest
the richness and complexity of the forms of Chinese Buddhism currently
thriving in this country.

Eastern States Buddhist Temple of America

Located in the heart of New York's Chinatown, Eastern States temple was
founded by James Ying (My Ying Hsin-jiu) and his wife Jin Yu-tang. In 1963,

it became the first New York Chinese American organization with a monk in attendance, and it subsequently played an important role in bringing to this country many of the Chinese monks currently presiding over temples in New York City. The temple is also familiar to many tourists because its street-level shrine room, bookstore, and museum are a frequent stop on the city's guided bus tours. Other areas of the temple remain closed to visitors. In 1971, Eastern States opened Temple Mahayana as a retreat in the Catskill Mountains north of the city. Several monks live in residence at the Temple and laypeople use it as a retreat facility. On special festival days, buses shuttle hundreds of pilgrims to Temple Mahayana from New York City.

Cheng Chio Buddhist Temple

This temple in the Pure Land tradition was founded in 1976 by Fa Hsing, a Buddhist nun from mainland China who had been forcibly laicized by the communist government in 1956 and put to work in a factory. She eventually emigrated to Hong Kong, where she remained for seventeen years before moving to Canada. At the invitation of the Eastern States Buddhist Temple, she came to New York City in 1973. Despite the objections of some area monks, she soon established her own temple in a rented apartment, which she later moved after raising funds to purchase a three-story building. By the early 1990s, Cheng Chio temple had more than a hundred members, including five resident nuns. About 80 percent of the members are women. Each Sunday they gather to chant, then share a vegetarian lunch. Once a month they celebrate a liturgy for Bhaisajyaguru, the Medicine Buddha. The temple also conducts ancestral rites, weddings, and funerals.

Buddhist Association of Wisdom and Compassion

This lay association in Akron, Ohio was founded in the late 1980s by Ted He Tang, a medical doctor born in Taiwan who has lived in the United States for many years. The group has about fifty members in the Akron area, with branches in Detroit, Columbus, and Cleveland, and between 400 and 500 participating members nationwide. It has no ties to a monastic sangha and no formal temple organization. Members consider these to be distortions of the original teaching of the Buddha, which they understand to be the cultivation of wisdom and compassion and social service. Meetings are held either in private homes or in rented spaces. Members engage primarily in the Pure Land practice of chanting the names of Amitabha. Their social service consists of making donations of money and goods and providing health care for area poor and needy. They also chant sutras for the ill and deceased in members' families, which in case of serious illness is done on a twenty-four-hour basis.

Tzu Chi Foundation

The Buddhist Compassion Relief or Tzu Chi Foundation was founded in Taiwan in 1966 by Master Cheng Yen, her followers, and five disciples. They began their charitable work with daily donations from members and the proceeds from the sale of baby shoes sewed by the disciples. Like many other charities, Tzu Chi channels religious sentiments into philanthropic work, the spirit of which is captured in its slogan, "To relieve with compassion, to give with joy." Since its founding, the movement has attracted more than 4 million members located in Chinese diaspora communities worldwide. There are about 16,000 members in the United States, affiliated with chapters located in 11 states. The Tzu Chi Foundation has done extensive disaster relief work around the world. In this country, it runs an academy, a publishing concern, and a free clinic in Alhambra, California. It also actively promotes bone marrow transplants and recruits donors for patients in need. Since 1993, it has maintained the Taiwan Marrow Donor Registry, which is now the third largest registry in the world and the largest in Asia. In Canada, Tzu Chi joined forces with the Vancouver Hospital and Health Sciences Centre in developing a clinical facility devoted to research and public education in alternative and complementary medical care.

Most Chinese Buddhist organizations operate within the boundaries of their ethnic groups, but a number are also active in the broader Buddhist community. Most convert practitioners seem not to be aware of the many contributions these groups are making to the creation of American forms of the dharma. The work of some of them is carried on at the leadership level of different ethnic and national immigrant Buddhist communities. But they all, in one way or another, have been building bridges between American Buddhists and Buddhist communities overseas.

Ch'an Meditation Center

The Ch'an Meditation Center is part of a network of organizations founded by Sheng-yen, a Ch'an master who is currently the abbot of Nung Ch'an Monastery and the founder of the Chung-Hwa Institute of Buddhist Studies and the International Foundation of Dharma Drum Mountain, all in Taiwan. It operates both as a small monastery where fully ordained monks and nuns live in accord with the vinaya and as a public study and practice center. Its constituency consists largely of Chinese Americans, but includes other ethnic groups as well, among these many European Americans who attend classes and lectures on Buddhist scriptures and philosophy and engage in chanting, liturgy, and sitting meditation.

Sheng-yen was born in rural mainland China in 1931 and became a monk at the age of thirteen. In 1949, he fled the mainland for Taiwan, where he continued to practice and study. He eventually earned a Ph.D. in Buddhist literature from a Japanese university and received dharma transmission in the 1970s. He started the Ch'an Meditation Center in 1976 as a meditation group at the Temple of Great Enlightenment in the Bronx, where the Buddhist Association of the United States (see below) has its headquarters. Within two years, the group established its own center, which is now located in Elmhurst, New York. Sheng-yen frequently travels between Taiwan and the United States, but also has students in the United Kingdom. He is highly regarded in international Ch'an/Zen circles and is the author of a number of books and a translator of sutras. His stature is such that he was invited to engage in a public dialogue with the Dalai Lama in New York during the latter's spring 1998 American tour.

Fo Kuang Buddhism

Fo Kuang Buddhism is perhaps the largest Chinese Buddhist movement in this country. It was founded in 1967 by Master Hsing Yun, a prominent figure in the ongoing revival of Buddhism in Taiwan. Born in Chiangsu province on the mainland in 1926, Hsing Yun became a monk at the age of twelve and was fully ordained in 1941. Seven years later, he followed the Nationalist government to Taiwan. There he witnessed the emergence of a booming economy and experienced firsthand the kind of social transformation that accompanies rapid economic progress. This prompted him to redefine elements of the Chinese tradition to address the needs of daily life in an increasingly consumer-driven, urban, and industrial society. Hsing Yun's philosophy has been described as "humanistic Buddhism," in which the Pure Land tradition has been recast as an optimistic vision for the betterment of human society. The tenor of these ideals is expressed in the name by which the movement is known in this country, the International Buddhist Progress Society.

The international headquarters of the society is at Fo Kuang Shan ("Buddha's Light Mountain"), a monastery in Taiwan, where the movement also has sixteen other affiliated temples. Temples or associations are also found in South Africa, France, Germany, Canada, and in Asian countries around the Pacific Rim. Buddha's Light International Association, the lay wing of Fo Kuang Buddhism, was inaugurated in 1991 and reports one million members, mostly ethnic Chinese, in fifty-one countries.

Hsi Lai, or "Coming to the West," temple is an extensive monastic compound in the Los Angeles metropolitan area that serves as the American headquarters for Fo Kuang Buddhism and its affiliates in San Francisco, San Diego, Dallas, Houston, Austin, Las Vegas, Kansas City, and New York. In addition to religious programs and retreats, these centers offer classes in Chinese language and literature, martial arts, painting, and singing. Most members are ethnic Chinese, but Caucasians, African Americans, and others are encouraged to participate and become members. Some have taken lay precepts. Hsi Lai temple also plays a role in American Buddhist ecumenism by frequently helping to organize events such as the 1997 Buddhism Across Cultures conference, co-sponsored by the Buddhist Sangha Council of Southern California and the American Buddhist Congress.

In late 1996, Hsi Lai became embroiled in scandal after hosting an event that set off a controversy about fund-raising by the Democratic National Committee. Many Asian Americans saw in the press reactions—which included sly, winking references to Charlie Chan and hand-wringing about Asian money on the Potomac—a renewal of the "yellow peril" rhetoric of the last century. Others expressed bewilderment about the confusing ways Americans juggle courtesy, good will, political support, and money. The *Los Angeles Times* quoted one Hsi Lai temple nun who dismissed the affair as "a storm in a teacup," but Hsing Yun himself took a darker view. "How could something that is a good thing turn into something that is a bad thing?" he asked. "The more we Asians try to participate, the more we get criticized. . . . We asked ourselves, 'What is our mistake?' " he told one reporter. "The only mistake I can think of is that we were Asian."[1] The cast of characters involved in the controversy, their varied motives, and the details of the Senate investigations are not of the essence here. But for Fo Kuang Buddhists, the funding controversy was a powerful, if painful, wake-up call to how race, religion, money, and power can be a volatile mix in the American political mainstream.

Dharma Realm Buddhist Association (DRBA)

The Dharma Realm Buddhist Association is the Chinese Buddhist group most intimately connected to the broader convert Buddhist community. It was founded by Master Hsuan Hua, who was born in Manchuria and taught in Hong Kong before coming to the United States. He arrived here in 1962 at the invitation of several of his Chinese disciples living in San Francisco. Like Shunryu Suzuki and Taizan Maezumi, he soon began to reach beyond his immediate circle to teach European American students interested in Buddhism in the late 1960s. But from the outset, Hsuan Hua emphasized the importance of the monastic precepts as the foundation for spiritual life, which appealed to many students who were disaffected with the excesses of the counterculture. In 1968, five of his American disciples, three men and two women, received full ordination at Haihui monastery in Taiwan, forming the core of what would later become DRBA. Over the next two decades, full ordinations were held in this country at DRBA centers, first at Gold Mountain Dhyana Monastery in San Francisco and later at its new headquarters at the Sagely City of Ten Thousand Buddhas in northern California.

Hsuan Hua, who died in 1995, charged DRBA with a fourfold mission. A first priority was to build a properly instituted monastic sangha of fully ordained, precept-holding monks and nuns. A second was to develop a body of able translators to make the entire Buddhist canon available in English and other western languages. Hsuan Hua was also an educational reformer. His vision of fusing traditional Buddhist values with innovative education has inspired the DRBA to build schools and produce educators to serve both Buddhists and the broader American community. Hsuan Hua also placed a strong emphasis on interfaith dialogue, a goal that DRBA now pursues with people of other religious faiths and with critical thinkers in the natural sciences.

Throughout his long teaching career, Hsuan Hua drew disciples from both West and East. Students from a wide range of cultural and religious backgrounds now live and work together in DRBA's institutions, which include ten monasteries in the United States and Canada, an elementary and secondary school, Dharma Realm Buddhist University, and the Institute for World Religions in Berkeley, California. At the City of Ten Thousand Buddhas, there are about 350 full-time residents, including 150 precept-holding monks and nuns, families, and live-in students from America, Europe, and the Asian Pacific Rim. This environment fosters face-to-face relations and creative exchanges between Asians and westerners, monastics and laypeople. Dharma Realm Buddhist Association holds a unique place in American Buddhism and in the vibrant, polyglot Buddhist community of the San Francisco Bay area.

Under the leadership of C. T. Shen, the Buddhist Association of the United States has developed an extensive complex for practice and scholarship at Chuang Yen monastery north of New York City. The Great Buddha Hall, pictured above, was formally dedicated in the spring of 1997 by the Dalai Lama in the course of a three-day-long ceremony.
BUDDHIST ASSOCIATION OF THE UNITED STATES

Buddhist Association of the United States (BAUS)

BAUS is the largest Chinese Buddhist organization in metropolitan New York, founded in 1964. Its approximately 700 members tend to be well-educated, Mandarin-speaking Chinese, most of them first-generation immigrants from Taiwan. The headquarters of BAUS is at the Temple of Enlightenment in the Bronx, but the organization also maintains Chuang Yen monastery in rural Kent, New York, about an hour north of the city. Construction of the 225-acre monastery began in 1981. It now includes residences for monastics and lay guests, dining facilities, an extensive library of Buddhist texts, and practice halls situated around Seven Jewels Lake, a small body of water in which stands a 12-foot-high statue of Kuan Yin. The centerpiece of Chuang Yen is the Hall of Ten Thousand Buddhas Encircling Buddha Vairochana, which has a seating capacity of 2,000 and a 37-foot statue of a seated Buddha, the largest in the western hemisphere. It was formally dedicated by the Dalai Lama in three days of ceremonies in May 1997, after which His Holiness conducted several days of teachings for the Buddhist community.

Chia Theng Shen is the major force behind BAUS. Born in Chekiang, China in 1913, Shen spent many years in manufacturing and international trade in Asia. He moved with his family to the United States in 1951 and started a shipping business. In 1972, he became the chairman and CEO of American Steamship Company until his retirement in 1980. Since arriving in this country, the Shens have been important philanthropists in the Buddhist community, donating land in the Bronx and Kent to BAUS and acreage in Woodstock, New York to Karma Triyana Dharmachakra, the monastery that is the North American seat of the Gyalwa Karmapa. C. T. Shen also donated the land for the Buddhist Text Translation Society in San Francisco, whose work is carried on by the monastic community of the DRBA.

Shen is also a scholar, public lecturer, and authority on the *Diamond Sutra*, an important text in east Asian Buddhism known for its penetrating analysis of nondualism, impermanence, and emptiness. His understanding of Buddhism's contribution to America is suggested in the address "Mayflower," which he gave on a number of occasions to commemorate the bicentennial in 1976. In the speech, he likens the *Mayflower* crossing, a charter event in American history, to a verse from the *Diamond Sutra*, which he considers the charter of the American Buddhist community.

All the world's phenomena and ideas
Are unreal, like a dream,
Like magic, and like a reflected image.
All the world's phenomena and ideas
Are impermanent, like a water bubble,
Like dew and lightning.
Thus should one observe and understand
All the world's phenomena and ideas.

For Shen, the power of the *Diamond Sutra* as what he called "our Mayflower" is in the wisdom it teaches about realizing a luminous and compassionate state of mind unlimited by the dualistic thinking that gives rise to confusion, hatred, and strife. "This service will soon be over. It is impermanent. Tomorrow your recollection of this occasion will be nothing more than a dream. It is unreal," he told a New Hampshire audience.

But I hope my message has boarded you onto your own Mayflower.
Please carry this message to your family, friends, and the whole nation.
Let us sincerely hope that in the tricentennial year, your children and

your children's children will meet here again in a society where lovingkindness, compassion, joy, and equanimity prevail.[2]

A Korean Buddhist Minority

Korean Buddhism is entering this country in two distinct but familiar ways.
The first is through the establishment of traditional temples in Korean immigrant communities in major cities—New York, Chicago, Atlanta, and,
most prominently, Los Angeles, where there is an extensive Koreatown in
the center of the city. The second is through Korean immigrants, who have
been teaching for over three decades in the convert community.

Most Korean immigrants have arrived in this country as Christians. Of the
approximately 150,000 Koreans in the Los Angeles area in 1988, only an estimated 10 to 15 percent identified themselves as Buddhist. At this time, there
were about 15 Korean Buddhist temples in southern California, but an estimated 400 Christian churches serving the immigrant community. In the late
'80s, the abbot of the Kwan Um Sa temple in Los Angeles estimated that there
were 67 Korean Buddhist temples nationwide with an active membership of
25,000. Most of these temples conducted services in Korean and were devoted
to addressing the needs of first-generation Korean immigrants.

Korean temples began to appear in major American cities as immigration
from Korea rapidly increased in the early 1970s. The first temple, Dahl Ma Sa,
was established in Los Angeles in 1973. Most temple practice centers around
pophoe, a Sunday service that consists of scripture reading, ceremonies,
chanting, and a sermon. Services are not considered obligatory, so attendance, which tends to run from fifty to one hundred people each Sunday, reflects only a small portion, perhaps as little as a fifth, of a temple's formal
membership. Greater numbers regularly attend special festivals such as the
Buddha's birthday. In contrast to Christian church services, Korean congregational worship is quite informal, with people entering and leaving throughout. Most temples focus on devotional rather than meditative practices because the latter do not appeal to their lay constituency. Some offer members
a range of social services such as marriage and youth counseling, hospital vis-
itations, and assistance with negotiating government bureaucracies.

The future of these Korean temples depends a great deal on how they
negotiate many problems typical of immigrant religious communities. As of
1990, Korean temples lacked an effective administrative structure in this
country. Most were loosely affiliated with the Chogye order, the major mo-

nastic organization in Korea. Others were Won Buddhist temples, part of a sectarian movement that began in the first part of this century. Many temple leaders lacked English language skills, which put them at a particular disadvantage in dealing with second-generation issues. Clergy often faced financial difficulties. Lacking the kind of institutional support found in Korea, many needed to work outside the temple, a practice that was often viewed with suspicion by many laypeople. Once in this country, many monks chose to leave the clerical profession to pursue other vocations, a phenomenon that is fairly common in American immigration history.

As is the case with other groups, the links between immigrants in this country and the homeland play a powerful role in shaping the life of the community. The large Korean immigrant community in southern California has experienced a number of peaks and valleys as it has attempted to balance strong attachments to Korea with pursuit of the American dream. Hopes of quick success vanished for many in the mid-1980s with a severe downturn in the Los Angeles real estate market, which effectively trapped many Koreans in this country. At the same time, South Korea rose as an economic tiger, which became for Korean Americans a source of both pride and envy. In the early 1990s, the Northridge earthquake and then the Los Angeles riots, in which Koreatown was severely damaged by arson and looting, left many in the community reeling, questioning the wisdom of ever having left Korea. But by the late '90s, the tide turned once again as the Korean economy, along with those of the other southeast Asian tigers, went into a tailspin. Katherine Kim, a Korean American journalist, reflects on what she calls the emotional roller-coaster ride experienced by Korean Americans during the 1997 currency crisis. "Sadness rolls in with the loss of pride. It affects ethnic Koreans—whether in America or in Korea—for it is happening to our country, 'woori nada.' "[3]

A number of Korean immigrant teachers have also made an impact in the broader American Buddhist community. Kyungbo Sunim (*sunim* is Korean for "monk") is often cited as the first Korean teacher in this country. He visited Columbia University in 1964 and stayed in America for six years, moving from one city to another and lecturing on Korean Buddhism in temporary temples located in rented houses. Upon his return to Korea, one of his disciples, Kosung Sunim, came to America and founded Korean-style meditation centers along the East Coast. Kusan Sunim, an influential Korean Buddhist leader, made his first trip to the United States to inaugurate the Sambo Sa temple in Carmel, California in 1972, a visit that served as the occasion for him to cultivate an American following. Students he gathered on that trip returned with him to Korea to form the core of what later became the International Zen Center at Songgwang Sa temple, an organization that subsequently trained a number of western students, among them Stephen and Martine Batchelor, two Buddhist leaders who primarily work in the United Kingdom but are influential in America.

Two teachers, Samu Sunim and Seung Sahn Sunim, achieved particular prominence in this country in the 1980s and '90s. Both teach the dharma in the Korean Son Buddhist tradition, a stream of practice related to Ch'an and Zen but often noted as having an earthiness, informality, and humor characteristic of the Korean national tradition. While the teachings and organizations of Samu and Seung Sahn are in some ways quite distinct from those of classical Zen, they and their students are generally seen as a part of the broader Zen movement in this country.

Samu Sunim emigrated to Montreal, Canada in the late 1960s. In 1972, he relocated to Toronto, where he "lived in a basement apartment on Markham Street. It was dark, damp, and cool, but the place was as quiet and as secluded as a mountain cave." He lived there for seven years, spending much of his time alone, engaged in meditation. During an illness, he was "discovered" by older immigrant women, most of whom had migrated to Canada from the Korean countryside. They cared for him, while he began to hold service for them on Sundays. "Occasionally, I took them to visit other temples in Toronto in order to help them understand the different aspects of world Buddhism," he recalls. "Buddhism is an endless journey. Buddhists are pilgrims on this endless journey toward the liberation of all. The journey is endless because sentient beings are innumerable." At some point, however, "it dawned on me that I was on a pilgrimage to the contemporary Buddhist movement in North America."

Samu Sunim then began in earnest to visit many Buddhist centers while traveling throughout Canada and the United States.

> I had a special feeling for every Buddhist place I visited and each Buddhist I met. Their struggle and difficulties in establishing new temples and spreading dharma in the foreign land naturally evoked a great respect and deep appreciation in me. I felt grateful and indebted to them for their dharma work. In those days, I had no particular ambition. I thought I would be living in the basement permanently. Looking back, I feel I was like a humble servant who knelt before a Buddhist monument in the making and enjoyed himself with meditation and prayer.[4]

Shortly thereafter, he moved from the basement and, together with other Buddhists, purchased a "flophouse" in Toronto, which they converted into a teaching center.

In subsequent years, additional centers were established in Ann Arbor, Michigan, Chicago, and Mexico City, linked together in a modest-sized but vibrant organization called the Zen Lotus Society, today the Buddhist Society for Compassionate Wisdom. Samu Sunim's interests prompted him to host the Conference on World Buddhism in North America at his temple in Ann Arbor in 1987, at which many prominent leaders, both converts and immigrants, gathered to discuss the challenges they faced in propagating the dharma in the West. He also served on the International Advisory Board for the Council for a Parliament of the World's Religions held in Chicago in 1993.

Seung Sahn Sunim was born in North Korea in 1927, of parents who were Protestant Christians. During World War II, he was in the underground working for Korean independence from Japan. After the war, he became interested in Buddhism when a friend of his, a monk in a small mountain temple, gave him a copy of the *Diamond Sutra*. In 1948, he was ordained as a monk and practiced on his own until meeting Ko Bong, a master in the Korean tradition who became his teacher and later gave him dharma transmission. When Seung Sahn came to the United States in 1972, he began to teach in an apartment in the inner city of Providence, Rhode Island, slowly developing a dynamic style by combining sitting meditation, koans, dharma talks, chanting, and prostrations. His fledgling organization soon drew the attention of students at Brown University. In the course of a few years it grew rapidly, and by the early 1980s he was said to be training as many as 1,000 students both in the United States and overseas.

In 1983, Seung Sahn founded the Kwan Um School of Zen. As of 1998, it claimed more than sixty practice centers worldwide, most of them in the United States and Europe, loosely overseen from its headquarters in Cumberland, Rhode Island. As of that date, Seung Sahn had given dharma transmission to seven students, who are now Zen masters in the Kwan Um school. He has also authorized about fifteen senior students, who in the movement are called Ji Do Poep Sa Nims or Guides to the Way, to teach. Among Seung Sahn's best known works are *Ten Gates*, which treats the ten koans most frequently used in teaching in the Kwan Um school; *Dropping Ashes on the Buddha: The Teaching of Zen Master Seung Sahn*, which contains material related to his biography; and *The Compass of Zen*, an engaging presentation of the Buddhist tradition from the perspective of Zen.

Seung Sahn's charismatic teaching style has great appeal for many Americans. He has called his enigmatic method of teaching "Don't Know Zen," which evokes the example of Bodhidharma, the first Chinese patriarch in the Ch'an tradition of China. In one ancient tale, Emperor Wu of Liang, who was affronted by Bodhidharma's apparent impudence, angrily demanded to know who he was. Interpreters of Ch'an have long taken Bodhidharma's reply, "Don't Know," to be a reference to the Buddha mind that exists prior to all thinking and is luminous in its emptiness. Seung Sahn has also encouraged experimentation in Americanizing Buddhism, a liberty that many of his students value highly and find to be a source of genuine creativity. "Many people have fixed ideas about what is American," he noted in an address at the second annual congress of the Kwan Um school in 1984, "but in fact there are countless ideas."

> Some of these ideas lead to difficulty, and some may help people. If we cling to one idea of what is American, we become narrow minded and the world of opposites will appear. . . . The true American idea is

Seung Sahn, pictured here with students from his Kwan Um School based in Rhode Island, is among several influential Korean Buddhist teachers who have been at work in the convert community since the early 1970s. A distinct tradition in the Ch'an school of Buddhism, Korean Buddhism as taught by Seung Sahn is considered part of the multifaceted Zen tradition flourishing in the United States. KWAN UM SCHOOL OF ZEN

no idea. The true American situation is no situation. The true American condition is no condition. . . . The direction and meaning of our school is to let go of your opinion, your condition, your situation. Practice together, become harmonious with each other, and find our true human nature."[5]

By the late 1980s, Seung Sahn had begun to turn over much of the teaching in the Kwan Um school in this country to his students as a way to foster Americanization. "Before, everybody was my student," he noted in 1989, "but now the Ji Do Poep Sa Nims have their own students. Now the Ji Do Poep Sa Nims will decide the Kwan Um School of Zen's direction; they understand American mind better than me. I taught only Korean style Buddhism; now the Ji Do Poep Sa Nims are teaching American style Buddhism."[6]

Vietnamese Exile Communities

In the years after the defeat of the United States in Vietnam and the fall of Saigon in 1975, well over a half million Vietnamese arrived in America. Most came as part of an "acute" rather than "anticipatory" refugee movement, meaning that their flight was unplanned and chaotic, a response to the rapid collapse of American military power in southeast Asia. A few were airlifted by helicopter from the roof of the besieged American embassy in Saigon. The vast majority, however, began long, often tortuous journeys to this country through squalid refugee camps in southeast Asia and by sea as boat people in overcrowded floating death traps.

Andrew Lam, a Vietnamese American author and journalist who arrived in this country as a young boy, recalls the sense of tragedy and loss that for decades pervaded Vietnamese exile communities. "The saddest date in the Vietnamese exile calendar was, of course, April 30, 1975, known as 'Ngay mat nuoc'—the day of national loss."[7] The Vietnamese exile narrative "tells of families torn apart; fathers lost in communist gulags, children drowned at sea, sons executed by Viet Cong in front of distraught fathers, wives and daughters raped by Thai pirates on crowded boats, sons and daughters abandoning senile mothers and now wracked by sadness and guilt." In Vietnamese coffee shops in San Francisco and other exile communities in this country, "songs with titles like 'Mother Vietnam, We Are Still Here,' and 'Those Golden Days in Vietnam' still echo nostalgically on the speakers."

Despite the trauma of defeat and the refugee experience, the Vietnamese have been successful at negotiating the obstacles on their path to Americanization. A new era in the Vietnamese community began in 1995 when President Clinton normalized relations between the United States and Vietnam. At about the same time, a second generation began to come of age for whom Vietnam represented less a tragic element in the past and more a future opportunity. The 1990s saw the emergence of a new phenomenon Lam calls "a reverse exodus." "The gap between father and son, between generations, grows wider," Lam writes. "Ironically, while my father's generation find it harder to return home, we children have returned many times, searching for ways to help and influence the future of our homeland." Despite continued political and religious repression in the homeland, "Vietnam and America, the two divergent ideas, are converging. I see an old legacy ending and the hyphen of my identity stretching like a bridge across the deep blue sea."

The new era in the Vietnamese American community is also reflected in the maturation of Vietnamese religious institutions, some Roman Catholic, most Buddhist. As in Theravada ethnic communities, many Vietnamese temples were first established in suburban homes or small storefronts and mini-malls across the country. More recently, grand new edifices that reflect the social and economic confidence of the community have been erected in many places, from Minneapolis to Oklahoma City. By one count, there are now more than 150 Vietnamese Buddhist temples in this country.

Most Vietnamese settled in California, where they have become an integral part of a new Pacific Rim ethnic, racial, and religious mosaic in the making. Many are located in northern California and have found the computer industry of Silicon Valley, which many Vietnamese refer to as "the Valley of Golden Flowers," to be an excellent vehicle for upward mobility.

Thanh Cat temple, located close to Stanford University and affluent Palo Alto, and in the midst of the freeways of Silicon Valley, epitomizes in its history the saga of this country's Vietnamese. Thich Giac Minh, abbot of the temple, arrived in the United States just after the war ended. Working as a licensed acupuncturist, he donated his earnings, as did others in his community, to aid refugees. Construction of Thanh Cat temple was repeatedly deferred so that surplus funds could be used to sponsor boat people to come to this country. After a few years, however, the situation had stabilized and construction could

Chua Vietnam, which occupies an apartment building in central Los Angeles, was founded in the wake of the fall of Saigon as a refugee center. It is the oldest of the Vietnamese Buddhist temples in California, but many more are now found to the north in the San Francisco Bay area and to the south in Orange County, as well as elsewhere around the country. Don Farber

begin. Thanh Cat was completed in 1983, and is now one of a number of temples in the area offering a range of religious services—Sunday gatherings, daily chanting sessions, meditation, and ceremonies to commemorate ancestors. But Mrs. Luong Nguyen, who with her husband is a long-time lay supporter of the monks and nuns of Thanh Cat, also notes that "The temple is more than a place of worship. . . . We come here to feel anchored. We share news about our lives and we support each other . . . and if possible, we get our children married."[8] Thanh Cat also serves as the headquarters and training center for monks and nuns affiliated with the Vietnamese Buddhists of America, an organization of about one hundred ethnic temples scattered across the country.

In nearby San Jose, Chua (Temple) Duc Vien is among a number of temples in this country run by Vietnamese nuns. Dam Luu, its head, operated a home for war orphans in Vietnam before the fall of Saigon. After the communist takeover, she eventually escaped on a small boat with 200 other people, making a grueling six-day trip, with no food or water, to Malaysia. By 1980, Dam had found her way to San Jose, where she rented a small house to serve as a temple. Over the course of the next decade, she accumulated $400,000, earned from recycling newspapers, cans, bottles, and cardboard and from donations made by laity, which she used to make a down payment on a new temple. In the early 1990s, Chua Duc Vien, a million-dollar, 9,000-square-foot temple, opened with nine resident nuns who live in a very modest wood-frame house next door.

One of the most vibrant Vietnamese communities in this country is in Orange Country, California, about twenty miles south of Los Angeles. As recently as 1975, this area of Westminster and Garden Grove was little more than a cluster of aging mobile home parks and auto repair shops set in the midst of strawberry fields. But in the past two decades it has been transformed by the Vietnamese, many of whom arrived in this country through a refugee center at Camp Pendleton, about thirty miles to the southeast. The area of settlement "literally exploded," Westminster Mayor Chuck Smith told an *Asian Week* reporter in 1996. "The development there was just unbelievable. It's been very positive for the city."[9]

In the early 1990s, local entrepreneurs began to develop this thriving business district into Little Saigon, which they envision both as a national showcase for Vietnamese culture and as a tourist attraction to draw crowds that visit nearby Disneyland and Knott's Berry Farm. "The Asian Garden Mall is a mall like no other," the reporter observed. "On a concrete pedestal near the entrance of the two-story building, a statue of a Happy Buddha extends its arms in warm welcome. Behind it are stone statues of the gods of Longevity, Prosperity, and Fortune. . . . Saigon, once known as the Paris of the Orient, is, in a sense, thriving here in Westminster." Tony Lam, a member of the Westminster City Council and a Little Saigon pioneer, is quoted as saying, "Old Saigon is no more, the Communists have seen to that. . . . We wanted to create something here in America to remind us who we are."[10] Little Saigon's many restaurants and shopping arcades, its Confucian-culture court and Buddhist-themed mall architecture, reflect a newfound public optimism and confidence among the largest concentration of Vietnamese Americans in this country.

Moreover, tucked within the sprawl of the surrounding communities are at least fourteen temples that reflect stages of development in Vietnamese American Buddhist history. Chua (Temple) Truc Lam Yen Tu, reportedly the oldest temple in the area, is housed in a small, neat brick cottage whose attached garage has been renovated to serve as an intimate shrine room. Chua Hue Quang and its monastic community are housed in a cluster of wood-frame cottages that once sheltered migrant workers. The temple complex contains Little Saigon's oldest and largest bodhi tree, at the foot of which devotees place incense, fruit, water, and other offerings. By 1997, however, fund-raising efforts for a new temple, including a gala concert featuring Vietnamese pop stars at the Anaheim Coliseum, were underway.

Chua Lien Hoa began as a home temple. After protracted litigation over local zoning ordinances, Dao Van Bach, the monk who heads the temple, converted the original ranch house into a monastic residence. He constructed a new shrine room in a small backyard that also serves as a social space for afternoon tea and a garden for contemplation. During the installation of a fifteen-foot statue of Kuan Yin, a female bodhisattva of compassion, Bach compared her to the Statue of Liberty. "Both are international symbols of love, peace, and democracy," he noted. "It is this unity of thought that establishes the unbreakable tie between America and her Vietnamese inhabitants."[11] Less than a half mile across town, Chua Vietnam and Chua Duoc Su, the latter run by Vietnamese nuns, are multimillion-dollar edifices completed in the mid-1990s. They serve Orange County Buddhists both as vital religious centers and as testimonies to the accomplishments of the entire community.

The civic boosterism that is a part of the Vietnamese coming-of-age in America can, however, disguise persistent tensions within the community. Emotions still run very high about a wide range of homeland issues. Political, religious, and economic relations between Vietnamese Americans and

Vietnam are likely to remain complex, sometimes volatile, for years to come, like the continuing passionate concerns of Cuban exiles in Miami about issues in the Caribbean. On the domestic scene, many elderly Vietnamese suffer deeply from the emotional scars of their exile, never having adjusted to the freeways and suburban sprawl of California.

It also remains to be seen how Vietnamese Buddhism will fare among the younger generation for whom the American way of life is second nature. Reports of temple life are often studies in contrast. The *Los Angeles Times* reported on a 1991 ceremony for members of Vietnamese families held at Chua Vietnam. While eight monks in saffron and yellow robes prayed, young people milled about eating box lunches and listening to soft rock music. Many elders are concerned about how America's free-wheeling, consumer-driven lifestyle is eroding the deference and respect Vietnamese children have traditionally held for their elders. Ton-That Niem, a Cerritos, California psychiatrist, notes, "The older generation is trying their best to keep traditional values going. . . . There's always a kind of conflict. We try our best and be flexible. I believe with love we can do it."[12]

Nam Nguyen, editor-in-chief of *Viet Magazine*, a San Jose-based bilingual publication often called the Vietnamese *Newsweek*, expressed concerns about both the erosion of traditional values and the loss of ethnic identity. "The way I see it, we've passed the survival phase and we're now a thriving overseas community entering our entrepreneurial age," Nguyen told Andrew Lam of *Jinn*, the online magazine of the Pacific News Service. "What I worry about is the second-generation Vietnamese Americans who are both smarter and more privileged than their parents but may not be driven in the same way. I wonder whether they will simply meld into American life or retain their ethnicity. . . . We need artists, writers, social scientists to balance out our preoccupation with the high tech field. Maybe the new generation will fulfill this need."[13]

Over the course of several decades, a number of Vietnamese Buddhist leaders have reached beyond their ethnic group to make a significant impact on the broader American Buddhist community. Among the earliest was Thich Thien-An, a monk in the Vietnamese tradition who also received training in the Rinzai tradition of Japan. He arrived in southern California in 1966 as an exchange professor at the University of California at Los Angeles. His students there encouraged him to teach Buddhist meditation, which led him to found the International Buddhist Meditation Center (IBMC) in Los Angeles in 1971. After the fall of Saigon, when Vietnamese began to enter the United States in large numbers, IBMC devoted much of its energy to refugee issues. As a result of his twofold interests, Thich Thien-An was instrumental early on in building bridges between the American convert and Vietnamese Buddhist communities. He died in 1980, but his progressive legacy continues in the meditation center he founded, now under the direction of Karuna Dharma, said to be the first American woman to be fully ordained as a bhikkhuni. IBMC remains at the center of the complex, multiethnic, multinational Buddhist world unfolding in Los Angeles today.

Thich Nhat Hanh, another Vietnamese monk, has a stature in the American Buddhist community comparable only to that of the Dalai Lama. A progressive poet, spiritual teacher, and political leader, he is among the few figures to have wide recognition in both the convert and the immigrant Buddhist communities. He has had tremendous influence in this country first as an advocate for peace in Vietnam and later as a central figure in the emergence of Buddhist social activism, which will be dealt with in chapter 12.

Despite Nhat Hanh's importance in this country, he is more the patriot in exile familiar from the anticolonial struggles of European history than an Americanizing Buddhist leader. Born in central Vietnam in 1926, he entered a Zen monastery in Hue at the age of seventeen, where he studied Zen and Pure Land Buddhism. He was fully ordained in 1949 and shortly thereafter began to take up a range of progressive causes in the monastic community in Saigon, formulating ideas that would later emerge as socially engaged Buddhism. In 1961, he made his first trip to the United States, during which he studied religion at Princeton and lectured on contemporary Buddhism at Columbia. He returned to Vietnam in 1964, shortly after the fall of Ngo Dinh Diem's regime, and became deeply involved with the Unified Buddhist Church of Vietnam, a religious organization attempting to find peaceful solutions to the struggle between north and south. In 1965, he founded the Tiep Hien Order, the Order of Interbeing, an organization embracing laity, monks, and nuns that in subsequent years grew into an international movement.

In 1966, in an effort to encourage a peaceful resolution to the war, Thich Nhat Hanh began a nineteen-nation tour during which he met with numerous political and religious leaders. This tour prompted him to write *Vietnam: Lotus in a Sea of Fire*, a book that was significant in shaping the American public's increasingly critical view of the war. Warned not to return to Vietnam due to the danger of assassination, Nhat Hanh went into permanent exile in France. In 1969, he formed the Vietnamese Buddhist Peace Delegation, a group that worked behind the scenes during the Paris Peace Talks, while also working and teaching at the Sorbonne.

After the fall of Saigon, Thich Nhat Hanh rededicated his monastic vocation to Vietnamese refugee work, the plight of political prisoners, and rebuilding relations between Vietnam and the West. In 1982, he established
Plum Village, an international residential community dedicated to spiritual
and social transformation, located on eighty acres of land in the Bordeaux
region. Since that time, his influence in the United States has grown steadi-
ly. In the early 1980s, a number of western Buddhists began to be ordained
in the Order of Interbeing. In 1983, the Community of Mindful Living, a
Berkeley, California-based nonprofit organization, was formed to support
the practice of mindfulness by conducting retreats, developing programs,
and encouraging the establishment of residential retreat centers. There are
now more than two hundred Communities of Mindful Living worldwide,
the majority in the United States. Thich Nhat Hanh also pioneered mindfulness retreats as a way to address suffering caused by war, especially
among Vietnam-era veterans still wrestling with the legacy of the conflict in
southeast Asia.

Over the past three decades, Nhat Hanh has published sixty books that
range from scholarship to poetry. These include *The Miracle of Mindfulness*,
a wartime book he wrote for his students in Vietnam, and *Being Peace*, which
introduced the principles of socially engaged Buddhism to western peace activists. More recently he published *Living Buddha, Living Christ*, a reflection
on the ways of holiness and compassion as expressed in the two great contemplative religious traditions. The Mahayana principles informing Thich
Nhat Hanh's work are the interrelatedness of all living things and the non-
judgmental expression of universal compassion. One of his frequently cited
poems, "Please Call Me By My True Names," expresses these ideals powerfully and succinctly. It reads in part:

> *I am a member of the politburo, with*
> *plenty of power in my hands,*
> *I am the man who has to pay his*
> *'debt of blood' to my people,*
> *dying slowly in a forced labor camp.*
>
> *My joy is like spring, so warm it makes*
> *flowers bloom in all walks of life.*
> *My pain is like a river of tears, so full it*
> *fills up the four oceans.*

Please call me by my true names,
so I can hear all my cries and my laughs
at once,
so I can see that my joy and pain are one.

Please call me by my true names,
so I can wake up,
and so the door of my heart can be left open,
the door of compassion.[14]

It is easy to say that the influx of Chinese, Koreans, and Vietnamese Buddhists into the United States over the past thirty years, whether as immigrants, refugees, or exiles, is contributing a great deal to American Buddhism. But, as is the case with Theravada immigrants, it is far more difficult to determine precisely what, in the long term, these contributions will turn out to be. The religious life of immigrant communities typically stabilizes in the third generation, after a pioneering generation has laid down traditional institutions, a second generation has rejected them, and a third begins to look back appreciatively to the accomplishments of their grandparents. By the end of the 1990s, it was clear that whatever Buddhism in this country is to become in the twenty-first century will be significantly shaped by the contributions of multicultural sanghas from China, Taiwan, Vietnam, and Korea.

Part Three

SELECTED ISSUES

CHAPTER ELEVEN

Gender Equity

Between 1960 and the turn of the century, immigrants and converts wrestled with questions from how to incorporate temples in accord with American law to the economics of sustaining dharma centers and the education and training of subsequent generations. But the most extensive public discussion about how to adapt the dharma to America and its ideals took place among converts, who saw the emergence of the first generation of native-born teachers in the 1980s as signaling the coming of age of their community. An examination of three issues—concerns about gender equity, the means of orienting Buddhism to social issues, and religious dialogue between Buddhists and non-Buddhists—gives a sense of some of the forces at work in the creation of New World Buddhism in the last decades of the twentieth century.

A drive for gender equity among Buddhists over the course of the 1980s and '90s reflected the egalitarian idealism associated with the 1960s as it continued to play out within the convert community. Women have played significant and diverse roles in the transmission of Buddhism to the United States from the start. One of the earliest, Helena Blavatsky, put her own idiosyncratic stamp on the dharma before transforming it into a popular and important alternative religious movement. Others played supporting roles, such as Mrs. Alexander Russell, an American housewife who hosted Shaku Soyen on one of his American tours. Ruth Fuller, a central figure in the Sokei-an circle in New York in the 1930s, was among the first Americans to travel to Japan and practice in Zen monasteries. A few decades later, women like Ruth Denison and Jiyu Kennett, founder of California's Shasta Abbey, studied in Asia and were authorized to teach well before Buddhism turned into anything resembling an American mass movement. But between the '60s and the '90s, American women became a major force as practitioners and as teachers, intellectuals, and leaders in ways quite different from women in Asia. Virtually all commentators within the Buddhist community now note that one hallmark of American Buddhism is the way in which the dharma is being transformed in terms of gender equity.

Concern about equity became particularly acute in the wake of a series of scandals, beginning around 1980, that rocked those convert communities most closely associated with the counterculture. The nature and extent of those scandals remains in question. Some people maintain that sexual improprieties, the excessive consumption of alcohol and drugs, and abuse of power were widespread, while others see these episodes as isolated incidents. A few events, however, are universally recognized as amounting to gross negligence. For instance, a bisexual American teacher in a Tibetan Buddhist community engaged in unprotected sex for three years, while knowingly infected with the virus that causes AIDS.

These scandals had a number of important consequences for the development of convert Buddhism. To some extent, they were leadership crises that occurred as the free-wheeling, no-holds-barred spirit of the 1960s and '70s ran aground on the conservative mood of the Reagan years. Some commentators within the community saw them as a healthy dose of cold water for Americans whose pursuit of transcendence through psychedelics, sex, and meditation had obscured more fundamental concerns like mental health and a sense of responsibility. The scandals helped bring to an end the countercultural era in American Buddhist history and the ill-conceived attempt, inherited in part from the Beats, to wed the dharma to experiential excess.

As important, these events dashed overly romantic assumptions about Asian religions held by a generation of western students. Many began to criticize what Kathy Butler, a long-time practitioner at the San Francisco Zen Center, called "an unhealthy marriage of Asian hierarchy and American license that distorts the student-teacher relation."[1] They saw how dharma centers had often operated like dysfunctional families, with power and control issues swept under the rug in the name of collective spiritual discipline, a situation Butler called "a lineage of denial." "When our teacher kept us waiting, failed to meditate, or was extravagant with money, we ignored it or explained it away as a teaching," she wrote in 1990, comparing this behavior to what alcoholism counselors call enabling.

A cadre of well-organized subordinates picked up the pieces behind him, just as a wife of an alcoholic might cover her husband's bounced check or bail him out of jail. . . . It insulated our teacher from the consequences of his actions and deprived him of the chance to learn from his mistakes. The process damaged us as well: We habitually denied what was in front of our faces, felt powerless and lost touch with our inner experience.[2]

The ensuing controversies had important institutional consequences. The San Francisco Zen Center established democratic mechanisms for leadership and guidelines for teacher/student relations, and other organizations soon followed suit. Disaffected journalists from a variety of traditions founded independent outlets for the expression of their opinions, most significantly *Tricycle: The Buddhist Review*. In its premiere issue in 1991, a lead article cut to the chase on a central issue—authority and exploitation—by featuring a conversation among Robert Aitken; David Steindl-Rast, a Catholic monk; and Diane Shainberg, a psychotherapist who used Buddhist teaching in her practice. The three discussed "the tension inherent between egalitarian imperatives and the authority required in order to pass on spiritual teaching."[3] Their conversation focused on how many students brought to practice hopes for a mystical transformation, the ease with which these hopes could be exploited, and the need for centers to operate like healthy families. In the often emotion-charged atmosphere of the practice center, Aitken noted the need "to establish a ground of trust in the milieu between teachers and students. . . . Good teachers have, by and large, recognized that the sangha is a family and that the teacher has an archetypal place in that family as father or mother, and that sexual betrayal, seduction of a student by a teacher, is incest."[4]

The scandals and controversies also hastened the Americanization of Buddhism, even as they raised questions about what Americanization was to mean. The pain many felt in the wake of events made clear that meditation might not address intimate issues such as childhood wounding, guilt, and low self-esteem, a realization that encouraged some to increasingly identify the dharma with psychotherapy. Some began to call into question the goal of Buddhist practice. To achieve total liberation? To become self-realized? Healthy-minded? Or simply stress-free? As a result, the emphasis in much of convert Buddhism shifted from a 1960s-era preoccupation with transcendence to the safer ground of ethics. "Enlightenment—oddly enough—has become all but a dirty word among American Zennists," wrote Helen Tworkov, editor of *Tricycle*, in 1994.

The quest for enlightenment has been derided of late as the romantic and mythic aspiration of antiquated patriarchal monasticism,
while ethics has become the rallying vision of householder Zen. To
pursue the unknowable state of enlightenment is now often regarded as an obstacle to practice that emphasizes "everyday Zen," a state
of mindful attention in the midst of ordinary life.[5]

More to the point here, the scandals served as a wake-up call for women
by setting their quests for transcendence through meditation in a gender-po-
litical setting. Throughout the 1970s, women had been active in the community as leaders, teachers, and students. But they now had a context in which
to make sense of negative experiences. Affairs with teachers, whether devastating or merely problematic, could be examined in terms of the power implicit in teacher-student, male-female, and often Asian-European American
relationships. The discomfort they experienced in some practice centers,
where the atmosphere was militant if not militaristic, could be understood as
coming from male-centered practice regimes created by teachers trained in
hierarchical monastic traditions who had little or no experience teaching
women. Many women also saw clearly the secondary roles they often played
in running dharma centers and the deference expected of them by male
teachers as evidence of a more or less consistent secondary status.

The liberation ethos inherited from the '60s, the reaction to the scandals,
and the power of feminism in the broader culture coalesced in the 1980s to
place gender equity at the top of the agenda in the convert community. This
development was most conspicuous in Zen centers and in the Insight Meditation movement, where overt Americanizing tendencies had been strongest
from the outset. But the ideal of gender equity infused most of the convert
community over the course of the 1980s and 1990s, a good deal later than in
the more progressive quarters of American Judaism and Christianity.

Soon Buddhist gender commentary, written with an eye to the emotional and spiritual needs of Americans, emerged as practitioners experienced in
dealing with issues of sexuality and women's spirituality turned their critical
attention to Buddhism. One ground-breaking study was *Turning the Wheel:
American Women Creating the New Buddhism*, published by Sandy Boucher in
1988. Boucher, a long-time feminist activist, lesbian, and author familiar
with many forms of women's spirituality, was introduced to Buddhist practice in 1980 by Ruth Denison at Dhamma Dena. In *Turning the Wheel*, she
looked at ways in which women, both heterosexual and lesbian, were practicing Buddhism in a wide variety of traditions and communities, helping to

uncover the diversity of women's involvement with American forms of the dharma. She also began to catalogue the kind of issues that became important to women in the wake of the scandals—the problems they encountered with male teachers; the distinct modes and styles of practice and teaching they pursued; and the unique character of women-led practice centers.

Turning the Wheel helped to set in motion a broad and highly varied exploration of women's unique contributions to American Buddhism, in books from Lenore Friedman's *Meetings With Remarkable Women: Buddhist Teachers in America* to Karma Lekshe Tsomo's *Buddhism Through American Women's Eyes* and Marianne Dresser's *Buddhist Women on the Edge: Contemporary Perspectives from the Western Frontier*. In 1997, Boucher published *Opening the Lotus: A Women's Guide to Buddhism*, in which she gave voice to a form of liberal, feminist Buddhism practiced by many Americans, both men and women, in the '90s, and provided a resource guide for women's practice centers and teachers.

A different kind of gender-related commentary also began to emerge, from the academic side of the American Buddhist community. This work by Buddhologists helped to deepen the commitment to gender equity by acquainting Americans with relevant developments in the great sweep of Asian Buddhist history. It resembled the kind of scholarship on gender that had begun to play an important political and religious role in Judaism and Christianity several decades earlier, one that eventually made an impact on religious communities at the grassroots. In a similar fashion, the effects of academic gender studies of the Buddhist tradition were first felt in college and university religion departments and in liberal divinity schools, but soon stimulated a lively discussion about gender, tradition, and innovation in many Buddhist practicing communities.

José Ignacio Cabezón, gay activist, former monk, and professor of Buddhist philosophy at the Iliff School of Theology in Denver, published a pioneering collection of edited essays, *Buddhism, Sexuality, and Gender*, in 1992. These were representative of the kind of historical and textual work done by scholars of religion to elucidate a wide range of gender-related issues. More important, the authors in the volume implicitly related historical questions about the bhikkhuni sangha in tenth-century Sri Lanka, homosexuality in Japanese monasticism, the complex gender symbolism of the bodhisattva Kuan Yin, and other topics to contemporary issues related to gender in the American Buddhist community. On one hand, this kind of writing encouraged innovation by giving American Buddhists a deep sense that Asian Buddhism was not only a timeless set of truths and practices but also a richly varied, politically constructed creation of human history. On the other hand, it also helped, in a way quite different from that of Japanese roshis or Tibetan lamas, to orient Americans to Asian traditions by suggesting that Old World flaws and shortcomings might be rectified in a New World setting.

Other academic studies more specifically designed to advocate innovation began to appear at about the same time. *Buddhism After Patriarchy* by Rita Gross, a student of Chogyam Trungpa, was published in 1993. It closely resembles early feminist work in Judaism and Christianity insofar as it is a sweeping interpretation of the history of a tradition in search of a usable past for contemporary women. On the down side, Gross found that Buddhism reflects the patriarchal values found in most Asian societies, a tendency expressed in the Buddha's reluctance to allow women to enter the original monastic sangha. Later monastic precepts and practices, particularly those concerned with the control of passions, created erotic stereotypes about women. The power of men in the sangha meant enduring social and institutional inequities for Asian women. On the positive side, Gross found many advantages for women in Buddhism. Its nontheistic character means that there is no creator, father, and judge as in Judaism and Christianity, a form of anthropomorphism often identified as a source of oppressive attitudes and practices toward western women. Gautama, the model for Buddhist practice, was not a divine son like Jesus, but a human teacher. There are, moreover, many powerful historical women and female bodhisattvas and dharma protectors in Buddhism whom Gross identified as models for the cultivation of women's spirituality, even though they were embedded in patriarchal social orders. Many Buddhists considered *Buddhism Beyond Patriarchy* highly controversial, but it helped to do for American Buddhism what Mary Daly's *Beyond God the Father* had done for American Christianity two decades before, which was to throw open the door to the critical and creative appropriation of religious history by American women.

The early work of Cabezón and Gross helped to set a precedent for a wide range of later studies by academics or those writing in an academic vein. Some of these address the historical and political situation of women in Buddhism, such as Susan Murcott's *The First Buddhist Women: Translations and Commentaries on the Therigatha*, Miranda Shaw's *Passionate Enlightenment: Women in Tantric Buddhism*, and Tessa J. Bartholomeusz's *Women Under the Bo Tree: Buddhist Nuns in Sri Lanka*. Others more directly explore the interpretive possibilities of Buddhism for contemporary American women, including Ann Klein's *Meeting the Great Bliss Queen: Buddhists, Feminists and the Art of the Self*.

Most of these developments can be traced more or less directly to the powerful reaction to the scandals in convert communities closely associated with the counterculture. But a similar concern with gender was no less important in another major convert community, Soka Gakkai International-USA, even though it emerged under less dramatic circumstances and drew less publicity.

In the early years of Nichiren Shoshu of America, Japanese women played a critical role in the success of shakubuku campaigns. The national organization was from the outset organized in Men's and Women's Divisions, which ensured that many women held important local and national leadership positions. But since the early 1990s and the schism, SGI has increased its efforts to eliminate patterns of deference inherited from Japan, such as Japanese women's tendency to defer to males as leaders of the chant. In the past decade or so, moreover, five women have joined 16 men as Vice General Directors. Gender parity is, like many other innovations in SGI-USA, a work in progress, cross-cut by issues related to race and ethnicity in unique ways. Given America's multicultural society, domestic race and ethnicity issues are major considerations in the advancement of women leaders. But the international Soka Gakkai movement has been historically dominated by the Japanese. At present, only one American Caucasian, a male, serves on the Board of Directors of SGI-USA, along with six Japanese men. In other countries, national SGI leaders are also often Japanese, but a number of them are women.

In any case, by the 1990s it was apparent that the ideal of gender equity was becoming one of the most important touchstones in the cross-cultural transmission of the dharma in convert communities. Some observers suggested that most serious convert Buddhists, in whatever school or tradition, were women. More important, the highly varied ways women were practicing and living the dharma—as monastics or lay teachers, intellectuals, institutional leaders, or cultural critics—was a main influence on the adaptation of Buddhism to the unique cultural climate of the United States.

A few examples suggest the widely varied roles played by women in convert communities. Ji Ko Linda Ruth Cutts began practicing zazen at the San Francisco Zen Center in 1971 and eventually became an ordained Zen priest in the Suzuki Roshi lineage. She has served as *tanto*, or leader of practice, at Green Gulch Farm, where she lives with her husband and two children. Jan Chozen Bays, a successor of Maezumi Roshi and a wife, mother, and pediatrician working with abused children, teaches in Oregon. She continues to study Zen with Shodo Harada Roshi, a Rinzai master and abbot of

Sogenji Monastery in Japan, and also leads two Oregon sanghas, a city zendo in Portland, and a country training center in the mountains to the east. Most members of these two sanghas are laity with families, so Bays devotes much of her teaching to practice issues related to work and family. But she is increasingly interested in establishing a center in the northwest for monastic-style, residential Zen training.

Yvonne Rand, a teacher and priest in the Soto Zen tradition for more than thirty years, now incorporates elements of vipassana and Tibetan Buddhism into her teaching. She is particularly known for her focus on reproductive issues and, like many Buddhist women, describes herself as anti-abortion and pro-choice. Inspired by the bodhisattva Jizo, a popular figure in Japan associated with the death of infants, she has developed a simple American Jizo ceremony as a way to cultivate awakening in the midst of the guilt, grief, and pain accompanying abortions, stillbirths, and miscarriages. Despite her own Buddhist convictions regarding taking life, she has written that "My experience as a Buddhist priest continues to teach me that looking into a situation in detail, without glossing over what is unpleasant or difficult, is what helps us to stay present and clear and to break through ignorance. This is certainly true in the potent realms of sexuality, fertility, and gestation."[6]

Women are among the leading creative intellectuals in the convert community, and the different ways they understand the dharma epitomize the increasingly diverse range of opinion found there by the end of the twentieth century. Joanna Macy is primarily known as a philosopher and social activist. She is a professor at the Graduate Theological Union in Berkeley and the California Institute of Integral Studies, and her *Mutual Causality in Buddhism and General Systems Theory* and *World as Lover, World as Self* are regarded by many as important works of American Buddhist philosophy. Over the decades, she has also worked with Tibetan refugees, in the Buddhist-inspired Sarvodaya Movement in Sri Lanka, and in "despair work," writings and workshops for disillusioned social activists. Her career is more fully profiled in the next chapter.

bell hooks, a long-time Zen practitioner and professor of English at the City College of New York, is widely known as a feminist theorist and cultural critic. She is also a commentator on the implicit racism in many convert circles, which tends to relegate both African Americans and ethnic Asian immigrants to the margins of the community. hooks is particularly inspired by Thich Nhat Hanh, whose Buddhism she sees as grounded in the anguish of the Vietnam War, rather than in Americans' restless quests for personal transformation. "In the United States there are many black people and people of color engaged with Buddhism who do not have visibility or voice," she noted in a *Tricycle* interview in 1994. "Surely it is often racism that allows white comrades to feel so comfortable with their 'control' and 'ownership' of Buddhist thought and practice in the United States. They have much to learn, then, from those people of color who embrace humility in practice and relinquished the ego's need to be recognized."[7]

Joan Halifax is among those working to integrate the dharma with the shamanic traditions of Native Americans and of other tribal peoples. During the 1990s, her primary dharma teaching was related to death and giving care to the dying. But over the course of several decades, she also developed an in-

Women have always been a creative force in American Buddhism and, since the early 1980s, have come to hold a wide range of prominent positions as leaders and teachers, whether as fully ordained nuns or as laypeople. Joan Halifax, founder of the Upaya Institute in New Mexico, has been ordained in three different Zen lineages and incorporates many New World themes in her Buddhist teaching and writing.
RON COOPER/COURTESY JOAN HALIFAX

terpretation of Buddhist ideas about the interdependence of all beings in light of the mythological studies of Joseph Campbell, the traditions of the Huichol Indians of Mexico, and the Buddhist teachings of Seung Sahn and Thich Nhat Hanh. "In Buddhism, the term sangha refers to the community that practices the Way together," she wrote in *The Fruitful Darkness: Reconnecting with the Body of the Earth* in 1993. "I ask, Where is the boundary of that community?"

> The frontier of the community, extending beyond the human being, includes the sacred mountains that surround our homeland, the rocks and springs that have given birth to civilizing ancestors. The eagle, bear, buffalo, and whale—wisdom beings of Sky and Earth. . . . And from a Buddhist perspective, this community is alive, all of it, and practices the Way together.[8]

The drive for gender equity in American Buddhism was also expressed with regard to gay and lesbian issues, the importance of which was magnified in the '90s as questions about how to relate alternative sexual identities to religious traditionalism became increasingly divisive. Residual homophobia continues to exist in dharma centers, but Buddhist gay men and lesbian women have been integrated into the social fabric of many different Buddhist communities as monks, nuns, and laypeople. The AIDS crisis served as the occasion for many Buddhists, both gay and straight, to become more frank and forthright about gay and lesbian perspectives on gender issues. This resulted in the creation of service organizations such as the White Plum Buddhist AIDS Network under the direction of Pat Enkyo O'Hara, sensei of the Village Zendo in New York City, and the Zen Hospice Project in San Francisco. It also fostered the creation of gay and lesbian practice groups such as New York's Maitre Dorje, and the Hartford Street Zen Center and the Gay Buddhist Fellowship in San Francisco.

The AIDS crisis also encouraged some Buddhists to use more traditional devotional expressions to address the religious needs of the gay community. At Kunzang Palyul Choling, a Nyingma Buddhist Temple in Poolesville, Maryland, resident monks and nuns performed *phowa* services in the late 1990s for those who died of AIDS. The goal of *phowa* is to merge consciousness at the time of death with the wisdom mind of the Buddha. It is a visualization technique used to attain enlightenment without a lifelong experience of meditation practice.

In June 1997, a meeting between gay and lesbian Buddhists and the Dalai Lama brought some of the institutional challenges of adapting tradition in the name of gender equity into unusually high relief. The meeting was held at the request of Buddhist activists, who asked for a clarification of remarks made by the Dalai Lama about sexual misconduct in two of his books, *The Way to Freedom* and *Beyond Dogma*. The activist delegation, which included Cabezón, Lourdes Arguelles of the Buddhist Peace Fellowship, and Steven Peskind, co-founder of the Buddhist AIDS Project, expressed two distinct concerns. The first was related to the Dalai Lama's stature as a Nobel Laureate and preeminent human rights leader, and how his views regarding gay rights issues might be interpreted by the public. The second was more strictly religious. How are gay and lesbian Buddhists to reconcile their personal identity with their religious identity if same-sex behavior is considered a violation of the Buddha's teachings?

The different responses of the Dalai Lama, first as a human rights advocate and then as a Buddhist monastic and leader, exemplify the complex challenges involved in balancing progressive American ideals with tradition-based religious orthodoxies. As far as human rights were concerned, the Dalai Lama took an unambiguously pro-gay position. "It is wrong for society to reject people on the basis of their sexual orientation," he is quoted as saying. "Your movement to gain full human rights is reasonable and logical."[9] According to the *San Francisco Chronicle*, he added, "From society's viewpoint, mutually agreeable homosexual relations can be of mutual benefit, enjoyable, and harmless."[10]

When he spoke as a leader of a religious tradition, however, the Dalai Lama's responses were a good deal more complex. He explained that questions about all Buddhist behavioral norms should be considered with reference to the aim of the tradition and practice, which is to eliminate emotional affliction and attachment. In general, sexual desire, one of the greatest sources of attachment, needs to be disciplined by all Buddhists, but especially by those who have taken monastic vows of celibacy, for whom all sexual behavior is considered misconduct. More specifically, Buddhist tradition provides ethical guidelines for all Buddhists in terms of four criteria—place, time, partner, and body organ involved. One place where sexual activity is prohibited is a temple precinct. Proscribed times include during daylight hours and during a woman's menstrual period. Buddhists should also avoid adultery, having sex with monks or nuns or a same-sex partner, or engaging in sex during late pregnancy. According to tradition, oral sex, anal sex, and masturbation are all sexual misconduct. The Dalai Lama underscored that none of these regulations are directed at gays and lesbians per se, but added that the authority of scripture and tradition were such that even he, head of the Gelugpa school and political and spiritual leader of the Tibetan people, had no power to alter them unilaterally.

By way of conclusion, however, His Holiness also noted that Buddhist traditions had taken shape in ancient India under very distinct cultural circumstances. Throughout Asian Buddhist history, the dharma has been open to interpretation in new settings. He suggested that the delegates begin to build a consensus among American Buddhists in different communities for a new understanding of ancient texts appropriate to a modern, American setting. This effort could be linked to the resolution of other important controversies related to gender, such as the status of nuns and women's ordination. Whatever the case, the Dalai Lama made it clear that gays and lesbians should rely on general Buddhist principles of tolerance and universalism as a foundation for their struggle for gender equity. Guidelines for conduct are not intended to exclude anyone from the Buddhist tradition and its practice communities.

Press releases and reports described the meetings as relaxed, warm, and cordial, with the Dalai Lama alternately chuckling and roaring with laughter as the delegates attempted to clarify some of the finer points regarding Buddhist ethics and gay and lesbian sexual practices. The delegates were reported to be pleased with both the tone and the outcome of the meetings. Tinku Ali Ishtiaq, co-chair of the International Gay and Lesbian Human Rights Commission, noted that "His Holiness the Dalai Lama's support for our rights is very significant." Lourdes Arguelles said, "It is always amazing to see how His Holiness rises beyond the culture-bound context of his own tradition and grapples with seemingly absurd proscriptions to focus on the complex needs and desires of human beings in the here and now." K. T. Shedrup Gyatso, spiritual director of the San Jose Buddhist temple, said, "I am very pleased with what His Holiness had to say. I can now go back to my temple and tell our gay, lesbian, and bisexual members that they are still Buddhists, that they are still welcome, and that they are as well-equipped for the Buddhist path as anyone else." The discussion, concluded Steve Peskind of the Buddhist AIDS Project, was "twentieth-century Buddhism at its best."[11] By the following spring, however, Peskind was more critical in an interview in the *Shambhala Sun*: "I was disappointed that he [the Dalai Lama] chose not to speak personally and directly," he recalled,

> beyond Buddhist tradition, to the real harm of some of these misconduct teachings, and their irrelevance for modern Buddhists and others. I wondered, does the Dalai Lama, whom many consider the embodiment of

Avalokiteshvara, who "hears the cries of all sentient beings and responds skillfully," really hear the cries of sexual minority Buddhists?[12]

The drive for gender equity effected the most conspicuous changes among lay-oriented Buddhist converts, but it also made an impact in formal monastic communities. The vast majority of American Buddhists have not chosen the monastic path. Among those who have, however, are a number of women who are helping to establish the monastic movement in the West and to underscore the importance of women's contributions to the dharma.

The term *nun* as descriptive of a woman Buddhist practitioner is, like a great deal of Buddhist terminology, highly ambiguous. To be used with any precision, it must be understood with reference to complex historical developments in Asia. There are three traditional forms of monastic ordination for women. Full ordination (bhikkhunis, or alternatively bhikshunis) became extinct in Theravada countries in the tenth century, was never introduced into Tibet, and has survived only in the Mahayana countries of China, Taiwan, Vietnam, and Korea. Efforts are being made, often in response to prompting by western women, to reestablish the Theravada lineage and to create a Tibetan one by building upon the bhikkhuni lineages that still exist in the Mahayana tradition. A second form, novice ordination, is found wherever bhikkhuni ordination is found, and it is also a part of the Tibetan tradition. Women who have taken it are called *sramanerika*. Where neither bhikkhuni nor sramanerika ordination exists, women who seek to live a monastic life are referred to by various terms, often as *precept-holding nuns* in English. Their status varies considerably from country to country, but they are, in a technical sense, neither fully laywomen nor fully monastics.

In the United States, American Buddhist women ordained in one or another lay-oriented lineage may choose to refer to themselves as nuns, on the model of the precept-holding women of Asia. This is more or less standard in American Zen, where, in keeping with the tradition of Japan, women can also be ordained as priests. However, very few American women have taken either bhikkhuni or sramanerika ordination. One of these is Pema Chodron, whose work with Shambhala International was briefly discussed in chapter 7. A mother of two children who recently became a grandmother, she received novice ordination in Scotland in the mid-1970s from the Sixteenth Gyalwa Karmapa and, at his request, received full ordination in a Chinese Mahayana lineage in Hong Kong in 1981.

Thubten Chodron is another woman who has received both ordinations. She is a senior teacher with the Foundation for the Preservation of

the Mahayana Tradition (FPMT), an organization in the Gelugpa tradition
of Tibet. She began practicing in 1975 with Zopa Rinpoche, one of FPMT's
founders, and received novice ordination in 1977 and full ordination in
1986. She teaches a range of Tibetan practices from the ngondros to Tara
sadhanas, Tara being a female bodhisattva of Tibet favored by many
American women in the Tibetan tradition. In the late 1990s, Thubten Chodron taught at Dharma Friendship Foundation in Seattle, Washington. She
writes: "Ordained life is not clear sailing. Disturbing attitudes follow us
wherever we go. They do not disappear simply because someone takes precepts, shaves their head, and wears robes. Monastic life is a commitment to
work with our garbage as well as our beauty. It puts us right in front of the
contradictory parts of ourselves." On the power of belonging to a monastic lineage, she writes,

> Buddhist teachers often talk about the importance of lineage. There is a
> certain energy or inspiration that is passed down from spiritual mentor
> to aspirant. Although previously I was not one to believe this, it has be-
> come evident through my experience in the years since my ordination.
> When my energy wanes, I remember the lineage of strong, resourceful
> monastics who have practiced and actualized the Buddha's teaching for
> 2,500 years. When I took ordination, I entered into their lineage, and
> the example of their lives renews my inspiration. No longer afloat in a
> sea of spiritual ambiguity or discouragement, I feel rooted in a practice
> that works and a goal that is attainable—even though one has to give up
> all grasping to attain it.[13]

Karma Lekshe Tsomo has combined an academic career in Asian studies
with a life as a fully ordained bhikkhuni and a commitment to Buddhist
women's issues. She received novice ordination from the Sixteenth Gyalwa
Karmapa in France in 1977, and five years later received full ordination.
During those years she also began to study Asian languages and Buddhist
philosophy both in American universities and in Dharamsala, India, the
headquarters of the Tibetan government in exile and the monastic residence
in exile of the Dalai Lama. In 1987, she helped to found Sakyadhita: International Association of Buddhist Women (*Sakyadhita* means "daughters of
the Buddha") in Bodhgaya, India, where the Buddha attained enlightenment, at the conclusion of the First International Conference on Buddhist
Women. Among its goals are to create a global network of practicing women, educate them to become dharma teachers, provide improved facilities

Buddhism provides the opportunity for women from many different traditions and countries to discover each other as they work together for the dharma in organizations such as Sakyadhita. Here Buddhist nuns from a variety of traditions are assembling at Hsi Lai temple in Los Angeles, a major center of the Fo Kuang Buddhist movement in Taiwan. DON FARBER

for their study and practice, and help establish communities of fully or-dained women where they do not currently exist.

Subsequent conferences were held in Bangkok, Thailand; Colombo, Sri Lanka; Leh, Ladakh in India; and Phnom Penh, Cambodia. In 1998, Sakyad-hita held its first North American conference at Pitser College in southern California. Its theme was "Unity and Diversity," and its goals were to en-courage dialogue between scholars and practicing Buddhists, provide a fo-rum for discussion of gender and women's spirituality, create a meeting place for women from different Buddhist traditions, and allow Asian and Asian American women to speak to a broad audience about their experiences in and out of North America.

Through Sakyadhita and other international connections, understanding of women's issues in America is being informed by the activities of Buddhist women overseas, where the women's movement has also become powerful. For example, Yifa, a nun in the monastic order of Fo Kuang Buddhism and Dean of Academic Affairs at Hsi Lai University in Rosemead, California, remarked upon the pivotal role played by women in the postwar Mahayana revival in Taiwan. "Why is Buddhism flowering so fragrantly in Taiwan?" she asked before an assembly of Christian and Buddhist monastics in 1996. "One reason is the significant contributions of Buddhist nuns who have also greatly benefited Taiwanese society." In Taiwan,

> Mahayana Buddhist nuns receive higher education, establish temples, give Buddhist lectures, conduct research, transmit Buddhist disciplinary precepts, manage temple economies, as well as manage and participate in various charitable programs. . . . These nuns have not only reformed the old traditional monastic system, but have also proved to be equal with the male Buddhist practitioner. . . . They have helped to propel Buddhism into people's daily lives and thereby to purify Taiwanese society.[14]

The contemporary gender revolution will continue to influence the creation of uniquely American forms of the dharma. As the liberation ethos that originated in the '60s developed through the '70s and '80s, convert Buddhists began to forge new paths across ancient terrain, not all of which followed the traditional contours of the Asian Buddhist landscape. And there is no reason to think they ought to have, because they are part of an effort to found a New World dharma. Thus, to focus on the drive for gender equity is also to acknowledge the diversity of American Buddhism, in which women and men, straight and gay, monastics and laity are all part of a community where innovation and tradition mingle in complex and often unexpected ways.

CHAPTER TWELVE

Socially Engaged Buddhism

The drive for gender equity among American Buddhists is in many respects a reflection of socially engaged Buddhism, a movement to apply Buddhist principles to issues in contemporary society. Buddhism has had a long history of engagement with social issues in Asia. The Buddha defied the caste system, a rigid social and religious hierarchy, when he formed the original sangha, and in the third century B.C.E., the emperor Ashoka embraced the principles of the dharma in running his empire. Throughout many centuries, the Buddhist emphasis on compassion for all sentient beings has been expressed in charitable activities, education, and caring for the sick and dying. The phrase "socially engaged Buddhism," however, is usually used to refer to the application of the dharma to social issues in a more comprehensive fashion than religious charity or philanthropy, one that seeks to redirect the personal quest for transcendence to the collective transformation of society.

One principle at work in much of socially engaged Buddhism is the Mahayana concept of nondualism, the conviction that at the most fundamental level of existence male and female, rich and poor, employer and employed, ruler and ruled are merely relative distinctions that fall away before universal Buddha mind or Buddha nature. Attachment to distinctions such as gender, economic class, and race is a hindrance to an individual's experience of liberation. Social inequities resulting from such ultimately illusory distinctions are to be remedied through compassionate action. Socially engaged Buddhism takes many different forms, from working for peace and reconciliation in regional conflicts in Asia to running hospices in New York City. But it is also expressed in Buddhists' cultivation of compassion and mindfulness in every aspect of their day-to-day lives.

There is some controversy about how best to understand socially engaged Buddhism at the level of practice and theory. Many Buddhists emphasize renouncing the world and cultivating enlightened awareness through meditation. The temple or dharma hall is the center of their religious life and the world is the arena for the expression of the Buddha's teachings about compassion, lovingkindness, and generosity. For others, however, a distinction between cultivating awareness and expressing compassion is a form of dualistic thinking, and socially engaged Buddhism requires that the two be thoroughly integrated. In this understanding, the Eightfold Path, with its emphasis on wisdom, ethics, and meditative consciousness, is followed by being present in the war zone, in the emergency room, or on the streets of the city. The world becomes, in effect, the temple or dharma hall. Compassion and lovingkindness are not extended to the world by those who have renounced it, but are actualized within the world by learning through social action the fundamental truth of the interdependence of all beings.

Socially engaged Buddhism in the United States draws upon at least three distinct sources for its inspiration. To a large degree, it is an expression of liberal-left social concerns inherited from the 1960s. Many activists first took up meditation as a complement to political work, and realized only in the 1970s that the dharma could be a powerful vehicle for social change. As a growing number of American Buddhists began to integrate activism with contemplation, they naturally focused on contemporary issues, from civil rights to nuclear weapons, environmentalism, and feminism.

Buddhist social movements in Asia are a second source of inspiration. In one form or another, socially engaged Buddhism has been a force in that part of the world since the middle of the nineteenth century, particularly in south Asia where Buddhists, Hindus, and Muslims alike were forced to respond to western colonialism. Throughout the twentieth century, traditional Buddhism has been recast by a number of Asian leaders in terms of western political liberalism, Marxism, socialism, and social Christianity. The single most important Asian source of inspiration in this country has been Thich Nhat Hanh, who began to develop Thein or Zen-based ideas about social action in southeast Asian during the war in Vietnam, when he coined the phrase "socially engaged Buddhism."

A third, more general source of inspiration is a reform-minded tradition in American religious history, particularly powerful in Protestantism. At least since the antebellum decades, Protestantism has given American religious culture a strong this-worldly, activist orientation. The impact of this activism on modern culture is sufficiently strong that socially engaged Buddhism, both overseas and in this country, is sometimes seen as a kind of Protestantization.

The main line of development in American socially engaged Buddhism is associated with two major groups, the first a cluster of organizations associated with Thich Nhat Hanh, the second the Buddhist Peace Fellowship. Generalizations about the differences between the two are difficult to make because of their shared history in this country and a substantial overlap between their constituencies. Both groups, moreover, make a point of emphasizing inspiration over doctrine and are nonsectarian and ecumenical in character. Each has a visionary dimension, although Thich Nhat Hanh's approach has a more thoroughly mystical quality that comes primarily from his Asian background and a strong poetic streak in his personality. The Thich Nhat Hanh group is also more cosmopolitan than the Buddhist Peace Fellowship, a fact that can be attributed in part to the more international scope of his movement.

Americans have been exposed to Thich Nhat Hanh's ideas about engaged Buddhism through his voluminous writings and the organizations with which he is involved, such as Plum Village in France, Parallax Press, and the Community of Mindful Living. But a particularly important expression of his approach is the Tiep Hien Order or Order of Interbeing. It was founded during the Vietnam War, but was not presented to Buddhists in the United States until Nhat Hanh's 1985 tour of this country. The order is a work in progress, as its charter, procedures, and guidelines are continually refined by the community, but its spirit is clearly expressed in *Being Peace*, a collection of talks made in the course of the 1985 tour, and in *Interbeing: Fourteen Guidelines for Engaged Buddhism*, which was first published in 1987 and revised in 1993.

Thich Nhat Hanh's ideas are grounded in the teachings of the Buddha, the bodhisattva ideal, and the expansive Mahayana worldview. His general approach can be sensed in his treatment of the First Noble Truth, that life is characterized by dukkha or suffering. It is typical of his upbeat outlook that he emphasizes "suffering is not enough" and that social peace begins with the cultivation of inner peace by individuals. Meditation, chanting the gathas, and other simple ritual practices are all means for the cultivation of love, harmony, and mindfulness, not in order to retreat from the world, but as preparation for a deep and thorough engagement with it. With the disarming simplicity that characterizes much of his writing, Thich Nhat Hanh insists that "Smiling is very important. If we are not able to smile, then the world will not have peace. It is not by going out for a demonstration against nuclear missiles that we can bring about peace. It is with our capacity of smiling, breathing, and being peace that we can make peace."[1]

The bodhisattva ideal and ideas about the interdependence of all beings are encapsulated in the two Vietnamese words *tiep* and *hien*. *Tiep* means "to be in touch," with oneself, all the buddhas and bodhisattvas, and the wisdom and compassion of universal Buddha nature. It also means "to continue," understood in the sense of continuing the movement of awakening first set in motion by the Buddha. *Hien* means "the present time," "to make real," and "to manifest." Practice is not undertaken for the future or for a future rebirth, but to embody wisdom, compassion, peace, and joy in the present. In the absence of adequate terms to translate *tiep hien*, Nhat Hanh coined the term *interbeing*. "Interbeing is a new word in English, and I hope it will be accepted," he wrote in *Being Peace*. "I am, therefore you are. You are, therefore I am. That is the meaning of the word 'interbeing.' We are interbeing."[2]

Nhat Hanh further grounds his vision of engaged Buddhism in the precepts, fourteen for those who are ordained in the Tiep Hien Order and five for lay practitioners, who are a vital part of the extended community. In keeping with the overall tenor of his thought, he recasts the precepts, which have traditionally been articulated as proscriptions, in a positive fashion, emphasizing what good can be done, not what actions should be avoided. For instance, one of the five precepts has often been translated as "I vow to abstain from taking things not given" or "I vow to refrain from stealing." In the Tiep Hien Order, however, many of its implications are drawn out to underscore the interconnectedness of social and natural life and applied to modern issues and daily living.

> Aware of the suffering caused by exploitation, social injustice, stealing, and oppression, I vow to cultivate lovingkindness and learn ways to work for the well-being of people, animals, plants, and minerals. I vow to practice generosity by sharing my time, energy, and material resources with those who are in need. I am determined not to steal and not to possess anything that should belong to others. I will respect the property of others, but I will prevent others from profiting from human suffering or the suffering of other species on Earth.[3]

Another precept that prohibits the use of alcohol has been expanded to encompass a comprehensive dietary program for mindful living. "Aware of

Thich Nhat Hanh, shown here with American students in Malibu, California in 1993, coined the phrase "engaged Buddhism" as a peace activist during the Vietnam War. His Mindful Living communities, together with the Buddhist Peace Fellowship, became major vehicles for Buddhist social activism in America in the 1990s. Don Farber

the suffering caused by unmindful consumption, I vow to cultivate good health, both physical and mental, for myself, my family, and my society. . . . I am determined not to use alcohol or any other intoxicants or to ingest foods or other items that contain toxins, such as certain TV programs, magazines, books, films, and conversations. . . . I understand that a proper diet is crucial for self-transformation and for the transformation of society."[4]

Nhat Hanh's program for engaged Buddhism is a seamless garment, to borrow a phrase from Roman Catholic ethical discourse, for personal and social responsibility. It provides guidelines for an individual's moral and spiritual life as well as a framework for the critical evaluation of social structures and vested interests that contribute to injustice and inequity. Consistent with Thich Nhat Hanh's views on compassionate action, his students emphasize acts of charity such as aiding education, assisting prisoners, and comforting the sick and dying. They see themselves as having a mission, not only to the politically and economically distressed but also to the emotionally and psychically wounded. The mystical quality of his approach to social engagement rests upon an unflinching conviction of the veracity of the law of cause and effect and the interconnectedness of all things. "Every action, every thought has an effect. Even if I clap my hands, the effect is everywhere, even in far away galaxies. Every sitting, every walking, every smile will have an effect on your own daily life, and the life of other people also, and practice must be based on that."[5]

The Buddhist Peace Fellowship (BPF) is more American in both origin and spirit, but has come to stand at the confluence of the three different sources that inspire engaged Buddhism in this country. It was founded in 1978 when a small group of Buddhists, among them Robert Aitken, Gary Snyder, and Joanna Macy, began to see the need to integrate their dual commitments to Buddhist meditation and 1960s-style social activism. "There was the peace movement and there was the sangha—and those were two distinct things," recalls Aitken, reflecting on his role in the founding of BPF. "I thought it was time to move out from under the bodhi tree, that our habitat and our life were in danger from nuclear weapons. The Buddhists were keeping silent and even cooperating."[6]

The tenor of BPF is suggested by Snyder's "Buddhism and the Coming Revolution," an essay first written in the early '60s in which he envisioned the West's emphasis on social revolution revitalized by the East's emphasis on morality, meditation, and personal wisdom. "Meditation is going into the mind to see this [wisdom] for yourself—over and over again, until it becomes the mind you live in. Morality is bringing it back out in the way you live, through personal example and responsible action, ultimately toward the true community (sangha) of 'all beings.' "[7] Another source of inspiration was the appeal to social conscience, which has played an important role in activist Christianity. In the early years, BPF allied itself with the Fellowship for Reconciliation, an old-line Protestant peace group founded at the onset of World War I that subsequently grew into an ecumenical social action movement.

Since its founding, BPF has also gone on to establish many contacts with engaged Buddhists in Asia. While still a fledgling organization, it launched its first social action campaigns in Bangladesh, Vietnam, and Cambodia. Through peace activists, BPF leaders met Thich Nhat Hanh, whose ideas about social engagement influenced the development of their ideas. BPF and the San Francisco Zen Center organized Nhat Hanh's first American retreat for western Buddhists and co-sponsored a series of his subsequent tours in the 1980s. For a time in the late '80s, BPF shared offices in Berkeley with two organizations closely associated with Thich Nhat Hanh, Parallax Press and the Community of Mindful Living. BPF also became affiliated with the International Network of Engaged Buddhists, an organization founded in 1989 under the direction of Sulak Sivarakasa, a prominent Thai leader of socially engaged Buddhism.

In the past twenty years, the Buddhist Peace Fellowship has grown into an organization with more than 4,000 members, some 15 local chapters nationwide, and a large number of national and international affiliates. It has undertaken medical missions on the Thai/Burma border, established meal programs and a revolving loan program for Tibetan refugees in Nepal and India, and worked with others to promote peace and reconciliation in Yugoslavia. In this country, BPF tends to focus on issues related to the promotion of nonviolence and weapons control, whether nuclear arms, land mines, or handguns. *Turning Wheel*, its nonsectarian quarterly, addresses a wide range of social and theoretical issues of concern to Buddhists and other activist communities.

The Buddhist Alliance for Social Engagement (BASE) is one of the most innovative BPF programs. BASE is meant to provide for lay American Buddhists the kind of institutional support for the cultivation of socially engaged Buddhism available to Asian monks and nuns who are a part of a monastic sangha. But it is also inspired by the BASE community movement in Latin America, which was founded in the 1970s as a vehicle for Catholic liberation theology. BPF ran its first pilot program in 1995. Volunteers were committed to combining socially relevant work with Buddhist practice, training, and reflection for six months. They had to work in San Francisco Bay area service organizations, attend twice-weekly practice sessions, and participate in retreats held monthly and at the opening and closing of the program. Training included the investigation of socially engaged Buddhist movements in Asia, the study of the dharma, and guided reflection on how Buddhist practice can be most effectively related to social action. By the end of the 1990s, BPF was beginning to expand its BASE programs to other parts of the country.

Like the Tiep Hien Order, BASE emphasizes social engagement as a path of Buddhist practice, not simply as a mode of Buddhist social service. Diana Winston, a BASE coordinator during the pilot program in 1995, recalls how her work at a San Francisco clinic for the homeless was a means of reflecting upon suffering and mindfulness in everyday life. "Why am I doing this?" she asked herself. "If it is just to be 'helpful' then I am missing the point. I need to remember the context. I am doing this in order not to let suffering out of my sight. . . . The more I can see suffering, in myself, in others, the more I can open to the possibility of freedom from suffering." As she neared the clinic each morning, she repeated her daily intention: "May this day of work be the cause and condition for the liberation of myself and all beings. May I be present. May my ego be removed from what I am doing."[8]

BASE also emphasizes group work to foster awareness of how the dharma can be realized in the personal and social dimensions of everyday living. Donald Rothberg, a long-time vipassana meditator and BPF board member, wrote of this experience in BASE, "We opened up to each other in ways that brought together, for example, my fears about intimacy and anger; your despair over continuing ecological devastation; her difficulties with working day in and day out with people with cancer; his joy about teaching composting to inner city youth; and their interpersonal friction in the group." BASE allows participants "to make connections between personal psychology, group dynamics, and social systems. Increasingly, we came to approach difficulties of any kind in the spirit of engaged Buddhism."[9]

In many respects, the BPF carries forward the best of the spirit of the 1960s—passionate dedication to social change, a commitment to personal spiritual growth, and high standards of self-criticism. Its rhetoric tends toward the visionary, as in Aitken's endorsement posted on its Internet homepage. "Buddhism is undergoing a profound change to a 'new Mahayana' whose delineations we don't yet see clearly. The monastery walls are down, which means that the Buddha's teaching of infinite compassion truly has no limits."[10] BPF politics remain grounded in the race, class, gender, ecology, antiwar, and pro-peace issues at the heart of the political consciousness of the '60s, but the organization is self-critical about its difficulties in expanding beyond its European American constituency. "What difficulties exist in opening to ethnic Buddhists and to people of color who take up Buddhism is an on-going discussion," wrote Alan Senauke, National Coordinator of BPF. "For me the critical matter is to recognize the priceless gift we have been given by Asian traditions and teachers, and to set aside any arrogance." Evoking the image of a weaver knitting together threads of international and interethnic friendship, Senauke notes: "Respectfully we extend ourselves and make connections with the different Asian sanghas. The full effect of our friendship and our work—completely apart from particular successes and failures—cannot be calculated. So we just keep on weaving."[11]

The Zen Peacemaker Order (ZPO), founded by Bernard Glassman and his wife, Sandra Jishu Holmes, is a more recently established group, but has the potential to rival Thich Nhat Hanh's groups and the Buddhist Peace Fellowship as a force in American activism. Glassman's work in the Greyston Mandala in Yonkers, New York, discussed in chapter 7, was at the cutting edge of Buddhist social activism in this country through much of the 1990s. But Glassman and Holmes's vision for the Zen Peacemaker Order is both more spiritual in tone and more ambitious.

As ZPO took shape in 1997, it began to resemble an alliance among people who were already Buddhists and a consortium of distinct groups, some of which already existed. The core of ZPO was seen as the Order itself, whose members included co-founders Glassman and Holmes, other teachers, and mentors, apprentices, and novices. Newly established organizations included an Interfaith Peacemaker Assembly, which is the administrative hub for a number of "villages" (socially engaged Buddhist affiliates around the country and overseas), and the House of One People, which Glassman and Holmes envisioned as an interfaith center. A fourth organization, the Upaya Peace Institute, was founded in 1990 by Joan Halifax, a well-known Buddhist teacher whose work was discussed in the previous chapter. All these were understood to be different but related ways to bear witness to suffering and joy and to heal both individuals and society, goals similar to those of Thich Nhat Hanh's Tien Hiep Order and Community of Mindful Living. For a time, ZPO was headquartered in Sante Fe, New Mexico, in a house that, after Holmes's death in 1998, was named Casa Jishu. At this writing, Glassman has taken a year-long sabbatical, is in Palo Alto, California, and plans to travel to Israel, while the work of the ZPO is continued by his assistants.

Socially engaged Buddhists address many concerns, but some observers have noted that environmentalism and ecology form the basis of a distinct-

Building on years of experience with social activism in the Greyston community in New York, Bernard Tetsugen Glassman founded the Zen Peacemaker Order in 1997. Shown here during a retreat on the Mall in Washington, D.C., members of the ZPO are dedicated to bearing witness to the joy and suffering in the world and to fostering personal and social healing. PETER CUNNINGHAM

ly American form of Buddhism-based social action, sometimes referred to as the "eco-centric sangha" or the "green dharma." A number of Buddhist groups run environmental programs. For instance, at Zen Mountain Monastery, Dogen's *Mountains and Rivers Sutra* is used as a touchstone for reflection on ecological issues. Others approach environmental concerns through research and public education. The Boston Research Center for the Twenty-first Century, an affiliate of SGI-USA, works to build grassroots support for the United Nations Earth Charter and has sponsored conferences on religion and ecology. Groups such as Metta Forest Monastery approach the wilderness in a more classically Buddhist way, as a place particularly well suited to practice in retreat from the distraction and attachments of urban society.

There is also a unique kind of Buddhist environmentalism that is more visionary and specifically American in tone. It is inspired partly by naturalists such as Henry David Thoreau, John Muir, and Aldo Leopold, and partly by Buddhist philosophy, in particular its ideas about the interdependence of all life. Gary Snyder was among the Americans to pioneer this synthesis of Buddhism and ecology. In 1975, he was awarded the Pulitzer Prize for *Turtle Island*, a collection of poetry that reflects Buddhist, ecological, and Native American themes and sensibilities. But since that time, Buddhist environmentalism has taken on many forms, especially on the West Coast, where experimentation with the dharma is pursued most avidly.

In 1990, in a collection of essays devoted to Buddhism and ecology, Alan Hunt Badiner referred to this emergent, Buddhist-inspired movement as "Dharma Gaia." Gaia, the Greek goddess of Earth, was first used in a modern, ecological sense in the 1970s by scientist James Lovelock, whose "Gaia Hypothesis" described Earth as a self-sustaining organism that adapts itself to environmental change without conscious guidance. While some scientists dismissed the argument, environmentalists concerned with the destruction of Earth's biodiversity quickly popularized it. The concept of Gaia soon fired the imaginations of others who associated it with a range of ideas from microbiological evolution to Earth as living mother, a popular notion in the New Age movement, and some forms of feminist spirituality. "Dharma," Badiner wrote, "comes from the Sanskrit root *dhr*, which means 'that which has been established in the mind,' 'the object of consciousness.' Dharma Gaia might therefore mean *Earth Consciousness*."[12]

In his introduction to the collection, Badiner drew out what he and others have seen as parallels between the Gaia Hypothesis and the interdependence of all beings. The Buddhist emphasis on awareness and mindful living "opens our perception to the interdependence and fragility of all life, and our indebtedness to countless beings, living and dead, past and future, near and far."

> If we have any real identity at all in Buddhism, it is the ecology itself—a massive, interdependent, self-causing dynamic energy-event against a background of ceaseless change. From Indra's Net of the Hua-yen school, to the Japanese teaching of *esho-funi* (life and environment are one), to the *interbeing* taught by Thich Nhat Hanh, Buddhist philosophy and practice constitute what scholar Francis Cook called a "cosmic ecology."[13]

Badiner also began to explore some of the social and political implications of this essentially religious worldview.

Buddhist practice can inspire the building of partnership societies with *need*-based, sustainable economies rather than *greed*-based, growth economies. . . . The arms industry among developed nations creates vast amounts of pollution, drains the planet's resources, and threatens the Earth's survival as a life-sustaining body. But Buddhism helps us realize that it is futile to blame others as solely responsible. We are encouraged to take a closer look at the unwholesome tendencies in our own behavior. Are we recycling? Are we consuming conscientiously? Right livelihood becomes the fruit of our awakening and the salvation of our form of life.[14]

This line of thinking has been further developed by Joanna Macy, an early leader of the Buddhist Peace Fellowship and a professor at Graduate Theological Union. Macy wrote on engaged Buddhism in Asia and American social activism before publishing *Mutual Causality in Buddhism and General Systems Theory: The Dharma of Natural Systems* in 1991. In this book, she created a dialogue between systems theory, a western philosophical and scientific view of reality as process, and early Buddhist ideas about the contingent nature of the self, interdependence, and the law of causality. With this as her foundation, she later wrote *World as Lover, World as Self*, a more popular presentation of her ideas. In *World as Lover*, Macy describes the emergence of what she calls "the eco-self" out of a confluence of three forces in late modernity. One is the ongoing erosion of the conventional ego-self by the psychological and spiritual suffering from threats of mass nuclear and environmental destruction. A second force is systems theory, with its view that life is best understood not in terms of discrete individualities but as patterns of relationship. A third force at work is a resurgence of nondualistic forms of spirituality, among which she counts the Creation Spirituality of Matthew Fox, a former Roman Catholic monastic, and westerners' new interest in Buddhist philosophy and practice. "These developments are impinging on the self in ways that are undermining it, or helping it to break out of its own boundaries and old definitions. Instead of ego-self, we witness the emergence of an eco-self!"[15]

Macy's presentation of world as lover and self is representative of a kind of American Buddhist literature whose substance and tone may owe as much to a long tradition of American romantic piety and scientism as to Buddhist philosophy. Some observers charge Macy with having moved beyond Buddhism into New Age religion, while others see in her the kind of creativity to be expected and applauded as the dharma comes west. Whatever the case, the energy of her vision of the "greening of the self" is evident in the following passage, where she retells the story of the entire evolutionary sweep of cosmic history and relates it to contemporary human living.

> We can reinhabit time and own our story as a species. We were present back there in the fireball and the rains that streamed down on this still molten planet, and in the primordial seas. We remember that in our mother's womb, where we wear vestigial gills and tail and fins for hands. We remember that. That information is in us and there is a deep, deep kinship in us, beneath the outer layer of our neocortex or what we learned in school. There is a deep wisdom, a bondedness with our creation, and an ingenuity far beyond what we think we have. And when we expand our notions of what we are to include in this story, we will have a wonderful time and we will survive.[16]

Another, quite different form of American socially engaged Buddhism is practiced by Jon Kabat-Zinn. For more than twenty years, Kabat-Zinn has been applying an eclectic mix of Zen and Theravada forms of meditation to medical concerns, under the heading of stress reduction and preventive medicine. Like many in his generation, he pursued higher education while beginning to explore Buddhist philosophy. He was first exposed to Zen Buddhism by reading Philip Kapleau's *The Three Pillars of Zen* and soon began to practice meditation. Within the next few years, he explored various forms of hatha yoga, a Hindu-based form of physical discipline, and Theravada meditation. During this time he was also working on a Ph.D. in molecular biology at the Massachusetts Institute of Technology and then a postdoctoral fellowship in anatomy at the University of Massachusetts Medical Center.

During a retreat, Kabat-Zinn began to contemplate the clinical and medical potential of meditation for treating pain and stress-related disorders. Back at the medical center, he shared his ideas with an orthopedic surgeon as they made rounds examining patients with a variety of pain-related ailments. He also began to develop a vocabulary—concepts such as wellness, mindfulness, relaxation, and stress reduction—to convey to wary patients and to a cautious medical establishment how Buddhist meditation could be used to mobilize people's inner resources in rehabilitation therapy.

In 1979, Kabat-Zinn and his colleagues established the Stress Reduction Clinic at the university, within the Medical Center's Division of Preventive and Behavioral Medicine. Since then, more than 7,000 people with a wide range of chronic medical problems, diseases, and pain conditions have par-

ticipated in the clinic's eight-week training program in mindfulness meditation, which is a model for others across the country. Kabat-Zinn has also
worked with groups of judges, educators, and Catholic priests and has uti-
lized mindfulness techniques in the training of Olympic athletes. He and his
colleagues later established a mindfulness-based stress-reduction program
with low-income minorities in the inner city. In the mid-1990s, they founded the Center for Mindfulness in Medicine, Health Care, and Society, also
under the auspices of the University of Massachusetts, to disseminate ideas
about how mindfulness practice can be applied in prisons, schools, corporations, factories, and other settings. Kabat-Zinn has written a number of
widely read and well-regarded books, including *Full Catastrophe Living:
Using the Wisdom of Your Body and Mind to Face Stress, Pain, and Illness*;
Wherever You Go, There You Are: Mindfulness Meditation in Everyday Life;
and *Everyday Blessings: The Inner Work of Mindful Parenting*, which he
wrote with his wife, Myla.

Kabat-Zinn's work represents the way in which the dharma in this country is being transformed in some quarters from a traditional religious philosophy and practice into a set of ideas and techniques for living, stream-
lined for a secular clientele but attempting to retain an essential core of
spirituality. As a keynote speaker at the Buddhism in America Conference in
Boston in 1997, Kabat-Zinn recalled, "There was a time that I considered
myself to be a Buddhist, but I actually don't consider myself a Buddhist
[now]. Although I teach Buddhist meditation, it's not with the aim of people becoming Buddhists, but with the aim of them realizing that they're
Buddhas. And there's a huge distinction." In the course of his address,
Kabat-Zinn likened Buddha mind to the western concept of genius. Imped-
iments to the experience of Buddha mind are largely self-imposed, he said.
To understand that is a "part of our work of liberation. . . . By practicing
non-doing, just non-harming, non-interfering, that genius can emerge."
Like many others who discovered the dharma in the 1960s, Kabat-Zinn sees
Henry David Thoreau as a paragon for American Buddhists, praising his
Walden as a "rhapsody of mindfulness."[17]

In a variety of forms, socially engaged Buddhism is an important strand
of American Buddhism. But Buddhists in this country are also bringing the
dharma to bear on social issues and human suffering in other, often more
unassuming, ways. Tibet support groups, where Buddhists join non-Buddhists to educate the public about the plight of the Tibetan people, are forms
of Buddhist social action, as are the medical charities of the Tzu Chi Foundation discussed in chapter 10. Theravada monks are at work in the inner

cities serving constituencies from youth gangs to aging and disabled refugees. Some of the larger dharma centers, temples, and monasteries sponsor hospice care and prison ministries, and the Naropa Institute has developed a degree program in which students combine a contemplative lifestyle with care for the aging. Nipponzan Myohoji, a group of Nichiren Buddhists unrelated to either Nichiren Shoshu Temple or SGI-USA, combines traditional Buddhist piety with social action by building Peace Pagodas worldwide (there are two in the United States, one near Albany, New York and another in western Massachusetts) and by leading international walks for peace to sites known for their inhumanity, such as Auschwitz, Hiroshima, and Nagasaki.

Moreover, many individual Buddhists undoubtedly express their convictions by engaging in small and large acts of kindness with no philosophical justification or rhetoric of world transformation. Given the secular, this worldliness of American society, however, it is very likely that the more visionary forms of socially engaged Buddhism will continue to appeal to many Buddhists. Socially engaged Buddhism, particularly in its "eco-centric sangha" phase, may well emerge as a distinctly American expression of the dharma in the twenty-first century.

CHAPTER THIRTEEN

Intra-Buddhist and Interreligious Dialogue

The presence in the United States of many forms of Buddhism has provided unprecedented opportunities for practitioners from a wide range of schools and traditions to engage in the creative exchange of ideas. Sometimes intra-Buddhist dialogue results in greater mutual understanding and cooperative ventures. But it also has led to the development of new and eclectic forms of philosophy and practice that are uniquely American. At the same time, interfaith dialogue has been proceeding among Buddhists, Christians, and Jews. These conversations are introducing elements of the dharma to people in America's churches and synagogues and have inspired some Christians and Jews to draw selectively upon them as a source of religious renewal.

Intra-Buddhist Dialogue

One kind of intra-Buddhist dialogue occurs in regional or metropolitan associations formed by Buddhists, both immigrants and converts, from a variety of traditions and ethnic groups. These include organizations such as the Buddhist Association of Southwest Michigan, the Texas Buddhist Council, and the Buddhist Council of the Midwest that promote Buddhism through education, mediate local disputes, or organize celebrations of the Buddha's birthday. Buddhists often come to a greater degree of understanding and respect for each other's traditions as an indirect consequence of such practical efforts at local and regional cooperation.

In another, more formal kind of intra-Buddhist dialogue, representatives of different traditions meet in an effort to formulate doctrines and convictions to which they can collectively assent. The Buddhist Sangha Council of Southern California and the American Buddhist Congress were at the forefront of this kind of dialogue in the 1990s. Under their sponsorship, Theravada, Mahayana, and Vajrayana Buddhists from a wide range of ethnic and national groups, both converts and immigrants, met at Hsi Lai Temple in 1997. Their goal was to articulate a vision of the "unity in diversity of Buddhism as a world religion" and to lay out "a set of principles which would reflect our common stand and mission."[1]

In a document resulting from the meeting, representatives reviewed major steps in a process of intra-Buddhist dialogue that began in Asia in 1891, when Henry Steel Olcott, the American Theosophist, drafted a "Common Platform Upon Which All Buddhists Can Agree." By gaining the approval of Theravada and Mahayana Buddhists from Sri Lanka, Burma, and Japan, Olcott helped to set in motion a pan-Asian Buddhist ecumenical movement. This movement was advanced in 1945 when Christmas Humphries, a Buddhist convert in Britain, drafted a similar document that was approved by the Supreme Patriarch of Buddhism in Thailand, prominent Buddhists in Sri Lanka, Burma, China, and Tibet, and leaders from a wide range of Japanese traditions. Subsequent meetings advancing this process were held in Sri Lanka in 1950 by the World Fellowship of Buddhists and at the Conference on World Buddhism in North America in Ann Arbor, Michigan in 1987.

The Hsi Lai meeting established guidelines for intra-Buddhist consensus in the United States, while underscoring the importance of respecting communities' differences. For instance, the delegates collectively recognized Gautama as the historical source of the dharma, an important point for Theravada Buddhists. But in keeping with the less historical perspective of the Mahayana tradition, they affirmed there have been in the past and will be in the future many other arhats, buddhas, and bodhisattvas. They acknowledged their common aspiration to attain liberation for themselves and for all beings, as well as their shared commitment to the Triple Gem, and they reaffirmed key doctrines such as karma and samsara, which many modern, particularly western, Buddhists have openly called into question. However, the representatives emphasized the continuing importance of "deferring to inter-traditional differences," recognizing doctrinal, institutional, and ritual distinctiveness, as well as what they called the Buddha's "guidelines for an open-minded and tolerant quest for Ultimate Truth."[2]

More informal kinds of dialogue are ongoing at the grassroots level, particularly in convert communities, resulting in what Jack Kornfield has called "shared practice," a process in which Zen leaders might investigate Theravada sutras or Insight meditation teachers study with Tibetan Buddhists.[3] This kind of exchange has also fostered the emergence of what Don Morreale has called "non-sectarian" and "mixed tradition" Buddhism, innovative forms of the dharma that defy categorization in terms of Asian precedents.[4] Such sharing and mixing of traditions suits many American centers, where Buddhists with long-term commitments to specific traditions often practice together in an ecumenical setting on a daily basis. It is also well suited to the fluidity that characterizes many Americans' practice commitments. Quite often, converts spend years cultivating Zen, vipassana, or Tibetan meditation only to change their practice and their institutional affiliation. This eclectic and pragmatic approach comes naturally to Americans who, as a general rule, value personal religious experience highly but have little use for doctrinal consistency or patience with traditional orthodoxy.

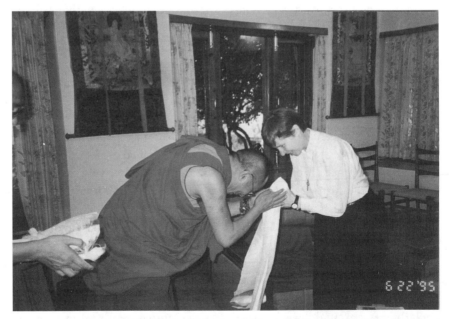

As the many traditions of Buddhism set down roots in the United States, religious dialogue is proceeding both among Buddhists and with those in other religions, particularly Christians and Jews. Here the Dalai Lama and Mary Margaret Funk, a Benedictine nun, express their mutual respect during a 1996 gathering at the Abbey of Gethsemani in Kentucky, part of an extended dialogue between Buddhist and Christian monastics.
OUR LADY OF GRACE MONASTERY

Shared-practice and mixed-tradition Buddhism tends to be developed in an ad hoc fashion in response to particular communities' needs or as converts begin to create new rites and ceremonies. In some cases, traditions are more formally integrated, such as in Shambhala International, where Tibetan Buddhism and Zen are combined as an expression of the diverse interests of Chogyam Trungpa Rinpoche.

A British teacher, Sangharakshita, the founder of Friends of the Western Buddhist Order (FWBO), has developed a nonsectarian form of the dharma on a more systematic basis. FWBO is among the most important Buddhist movements in the United Kingdom and Australia, but it also has centers in Europe and in the United States in Boston, Seattle, San Francisco, Montana, New Hampshire, and Maine. Sangharakshita founded the FWBO in 1967 after returning from a lengthy sojourn in Asia. His goal was to establish a new Buddhist path suited to the needs of western Buddhists, drawing inspiration from traditions across Asia. FWBO practice currently includes elements drawn from Zen and vipassana meditation, Tibetan-style visualizations, and physical disciplines such as yoga, ta'i chi, and massage therapy.

The creation of new forms of western Buddhism is a complex undertaking, and during the 1990s, Buddhist teachers held a number of consultations in an effort to develop a common understanding of the challenges they faced. In 1993, more than twenty Zen, Vajrayana, and vipassana teachers from America and Europe met with the Dalai Lama at his monastery in Dharamsala, India. Participants included Americans Thubten Chodron, Surya Das, Robert Thurman, and Jack Kornfield, and Britain's Stephen and Martine Batchelor and Ajahn Amaro. During preliminary meetings, a number of issues emerged as central concerns, including the integration of the dharma with western psychology, gender equity, the future of monasticism in the West, the relationship between the dharma and Asian culture, and ethical norms for students and teachers.

In the course of the meetings, the Dalai Lama maintained his reputation for unimpeachable integrity and orthodoxy, which he balanced with a call for western teachers to proceed with the adaptation of Buddhism to the West. "The past is past," Batchelor reported him saying on the last day. "What is important? The future. We are the creators. The future is in our hands. Even if we fail, no regrets—we have to make the effort."[5] Surya Das wrote that "One hour after the final meeting, while discussing the conference with two observers, His Holiness himself slapped his knee and exclaimed happily, 'We have started a revolution.' "[6]

Western teachers took the opportunity to express their personal frustrations, including problems they had experienced with their own Asian teachers. For instance, one American Zen teacher recalled that after completing koan study and receiving dharma transmission and authority to teach, he remained unsatisfied and unhappy. He eventually parted company with his roshi, who could not tolerate his going into psychotherapy. Others raised questions about the ethics of Buddhist teachers. What was to be done about alcohol abuse, sexual harassment, egotism, and arrogance in teachers who claimed to be enlightened beings? Are realized teachers above ethical norms? How are legitimate limits to be established for American Buddhist communities, many of which came into being during the free-wheeling decades of the 1960s and '70s?

Western teachers also explored the possibility of creating new Buddhist institutions. Some expressed the need for teacher training courses that amounted to more than years of sitting meditation under the direction of teachers. Others advocated the formation of a Sangha Council of Buddhist Elders to nurture monastics, redress inequities, and field questions about adapting the dharma to western lifestyles. There was consensus about the need for greater attention to the precepts, to ground Buddhist meditative practice in tradition-based morality and ethics to avoid the kind of scandals that erupted in the 1980s. According to Batchelor, the Dalai Lama had few concerns about whether or not westerners adapt Asian dharma names, wear clerical dress, or perform traditional ceremonies. He is also reported to have expressed a willingness to abandon Buddhist beliefs rooted in cosmological ideas that have been invalidated by scientific inquiry. He remained adamant, however, about the importance of observing the precepts and following the guidelines for monastic ordination as outlined in the vinaya.

Commentators recall the meeting as a transforming experience. One participant said it "had a bone-deep sense of rightness."[7] Another likened his encounter with the Dalai Lama to a Vajrayana empowerment, one that renewed his confidence in the mission to transmit the dharma to the West. Surya Das hit a visionary note often heard among Americans:

> I myself felt that there was an incredible, instantaneous synergy which all the participants definitely experienced; a spontaneous energy now being felt all over the world, both within and beyond the Buddhist community—perhaps best summed up as an emerging American Buddhism, or a Western Buddhism, or perhaps even a New World Buddhism.[8]

Stephen Batchelor was more guarded and somewhat amused:

> For the Americans, the Buddhist future unfolded as a kind of hi-tech Walden Pond peopled by dharma-intoxicated bodhisattvas. The disquieting features—institutions, sectarianism, scandal (the things we were here to talk about)—had conveniently evaporated. The Europeans were more cautious.[9]

Afterward, many western teachers signed an "Open Letter to the Buddhist Community," in which they summed up lessons they took from the meeting. In the name of adapting the dharma, western Buddhists should freely draw upon the insights of other religious traditions and secular forms of thought and practice such as psychotherapy. To guard the integrity of the dharma, however, the student-teacher relationship must be understood to be one of mutual responsibility and respect. Teachers cannot stand above ethical norms; students must be encouraged to take care in selecting teachers. Sectarianism can be countered by dialogue, study, and shared practice, but teachers must learn to discern the difference between the dharma and its cultural expression. Their first priority is not to establish Buddhism per se in the West, but to cultivate a way of life in keeping with the essentials of the Buddha's teachings.

> Our first responsibility as Buddhists is to work towards creating a better world for all forms of life. The promotion of Buddhism as a religion is a secondary concern. Kindness and compassion, the furthering of peace and harmony, as well as tolerance and respect for other religions, should be the three guiding principles of our actions.[10]

Christians and Buddhists

The mood of the dialogue among Christians and Buddhists was captured in a review of Thich Nhat Hanh's book *Living Buddha, Living Christ* in 1996 in *Christian Century*, a leading publication of American Protestantism. "A Zen Buddhist teacher sets a statue of Jesus on an altar alongside the Buddha and lights incense to both. A Catholic priest sits cross-legged in meditation and attends to his breathing as he has been instructed by Zen teachers." The reviewer further observed that "Increasingly Buddhists and Christians are

borrowing from each other's traditions, and the results present new opportunities and new questions for both religions."[11]

For many decades, Buddhist-Christian dialogue tended to focus on doctrinal and philosophical difficulties. Christians proclaim faith in God, while
Buddhists are nontheistic. Christian theology is cast in terms of sin and re-
demption, while Buddhism teaches liberation from ignorance. Most Christian practice takes the form of prayer to a supreme being, while Buddhists
who meditate do so to realize Buddha mind or Buddha nature. Christians
consider Jesus a uniquely divine son of God, while Gautama was a mortal
teacher. A great deal of effort has been devoted to exploring the consequences of these and other differences, a process of subtle theological and
philosophical study and deep reflection by both Christians and Buddhists
over the course of several generations.

During the past few decades, however, greater emphasis has been given
to the new opportunities presented by interreligious dialogue. Many Christians have worked to move past problems in the dialogue process, but few
are as well known as the late Thomas Merton, a Catholic monk and priest
who played a key role in introducing Buddhism to American Christians.
Born in France in 1915, Merton was the son of a New Zealander father and
an American mother. Raised by them in a secular household, he underwent
conversion in 1938 while studying in America, entered the Roman Catholic
Church, and several years later joined the Trappist monastic community in
Kentucky at the Abbey of Gethsemani. While in his early thirties, Merton
wrote his autobiography, *The Seven Storey Mountain*, which was published
in 1948. It became a best-seller and helped to establish Merton as one of the
most influential American writers on spiritual issues in the decades after the
Second World War.

Over the next twenty years, Merton developed an unusually high public
profile for a religious contemplative. While submitting to the rigorous
monastic regime of Gethsemani, he also published on a wide range of topics from prayer and contemplation to literature and poetry. He strove to balance his life as a monk, hermit, and priest with his commitment to social justice, developing ideas about Christian responsibility as he reflected on
nuclear arms, ecumenism, race issues, and the war in southeast Asia. When
he died in Bangkok in 1968 at the age of fifty-three, Merton had a complex
reputation as a public personality; a partner in dialogue with artists, poets,
existential philosophers, and secular atheists; and a solitary mystic.

Merton was drawn to the religions of Asia in the late 1950s, but developed a particular interest in the similarities between Zen and Christian mys-

ticism. He stood in a long line of Christian mystics who emphasized that God transcended all human concepts and language. They characterized knowledge of God as poverty of mind, a wilderness, the dissolution of self, and a state of unknowing, emphases Merton found echoed in the enigmatic wisdom of Zen koans and, above all, in the Mahayana idea of shunyata or emptiness. Merton's interest in Zen led to a correspondence with D. T. Suzuki, the results of which were published in Merton's *Zen and the Birds of Appetite* in 1968.

In that same year, Merton was granted permission by his abbot to make a journey to Bangkok, Thailand to participate in a meeting among Benedictines heading Catholic monasteries in Asia. But he took the opportunity to meet a range of Buddhist leaders such as Walpola Rahula, a leading authority on Theravada doctrine, Chogyam Trungpa, and Chatral Rinpoche, a highly respected lama in exile. Merton also journeyed to Dharamsala to meet with the Dalai Lama, with whom he established such cordial relations that their interview, during which they discussed their respective monastic traditions, was extended for three days.

Merton was not interested in conflating Buddhism and Christianity but in furthering conversations between practitioners of each faith, which led him to emphasize the importance of tradition. Speaking at the Spiritual Summit Conference sponsored by the Temple of Understanding, an international group of religious liberals, he made a passionate plea for Asian monks and nuns to maintain their traditions, even as they became more engaged with the western world and its complexities. Referring to the confusion that swept through the Catholic Church in the wake of the Second Vatican Council, Merton noted that "much that is of undying value is being thrown away irresponsibly, foolishly, in favor of things that are superficial and showy, that have no ultimate value. . . . I say as a brother from the West to Eastern monks, be a little careful. The time is coming when you may face the same situation and your fidelity to your ancient traditions will stand you in good stead. Do not be afraid of that fidelity."[12]

Merton gave his last public address in Bangkok, a controversial one in which he explored the possibilities for dialogue between Christians and Marxists. Back in his room a short time later, he stepped from the shower, turned on a room fan with faulty wiring, and died by electrocution. His death occurred at about the time Buddhism was becoming a broadly popular religious movement in America, but his life and writing inspired numerous Christians to begin to explore Asian religions while remaining faithful to their own heritage.

In 1996, Merton's memory was honored at an event that brought Christian and Buddhist monastics and lay practitioners together at the Abbey of Gethsemani. At the 1993 centennial of the World's Parliament of Religions, the Dalai Lama had suggested a dialogue in a setting where he would be able to speak as a monk to other monastics. His suggestion was taken up by the Monastic Interreligious Dialogue, a Benedictine group established in 1978 to spearhead conversations between Christians and practitioners of Asian religions. Abbot Timothy Kelly and the monastic community in Kentucky quickly offered to host such an event, and in June 1996, more than 200 people gathered for "the Gethsemani Encounter."

Participants included monks and nuns from thirty-nine Catholic monasteries worldwide; Tibetan, Zen, and Theravada monks, nuns, and teachers; heads of Catholic religious orders from Rome; and representatives of other Christian traditions. American Buddhists included Joseph Goldstein and Sharon Salzberg of IMS, Judith Simmer-Brown of the Naropa Institute, and Zoketsu Norman Fischer and Zenkai Blanche Hartman of the San Francisco Zen Center. Havanpola Ratanasara, Samu Sunim, and Yifa, a nun associated with Hsi Lai temple, were among the Asian teachers working in American Buddhist communities who attended. Prominent Christians included Margaret Mary Funk, a leading figure in the Christian "centering prayer" movement; David Steindl-Rast, a long-time Zen practitioner and senior member of the Benedictine Monastery of Mount Savior in New York; and Basil Pennington, a leading author on Christian mysticism serving at Our Lady of Joy Monastery in Hong Kong.

Participants delivered brief papers, but the heart of the meeting was personal and experiential rather than formal and academic. People engaged in sitting meditation on a daily basis, experienced each others' religious rituals, and explored what was distinct to each particular tradition and what they shared. They discussed the relation between contemplation and social action and the significance of Christ and Buddha in a cross-traditional frame of reference. In the course of the proceedings, Maha Ghosananda, a Cambodian monk and peace activist, led a spontaneous walking meditation to Merton's grave. Pierre François de Béthune, a Belgian Benedictine, later wrote that the Gethsemani Encounter marked "a new climate of openness" and a "profound change in thinking." Buddhists and Christians could now see themselves together "as forerunners of a spiritual unity that is prophetic of all humankind."[13]

Many Buddhists have also been working independently to further the conversation between the two traditions. Zen Master Soeng Hyang (Barbara

Rhodes) and other senior teachers are engaged in various facets of Buddhist-Christian dialogue led by the Kwan Um School of Zen. Ruben Habito, a dharma heir of Yasutani Koun Roshi and student of Yasutani Roshi before his death, leads the Maria Kannon Zen Center in Dallas, formed in 1991 as a place for people of various faiths to practice Zen. Like most others engaged in Buddhist-Christian dialogue, Habito sees no conflict between Christian faith and Buddhist practice, and in a 1997 interview addressed what for many Christians remains an important question. "I would like to assure everyone concerned that Zen does not threaten a healthy faith in the ultimate as expressed in the Christian tradition," Habito noted. Zen is "an invitation to a direct experience, and the only thing that is required is a willingness to engage in that journey of self-discovery." Whether one is Christian, Jew, or Muslim, Zen can "affect their own faith understanding creatively or positively."[14]

Robert E. Kennedy, a Jesuit priest, a professor of theology, a Japanese language instructor, and a psychotherapist with a private practice, began to study in Japan in the mid-1970s but received dharma transmission from Bernard Glassman in 1991, becoming one of the first American Catholic priests authorized to teach Zen. In his book *Zen Spirit, Christian Spirit: The Place of Zen in Christian Life*, Kennedy demonstrates how Buddhist and Christian scripture, practice, and concepts illuminate each other, while remaining distinct. But by way of introduction, he makes it clear that "I never have thought of myself as anything but Catholic and I certainly have never thought of myself as a Buddhist. . . . What I looked for in Zen was not a new faith, but a new way of being Catholic that grew out of my own lived experience." Recalling his first teacher, Kennedy writes:

> Yamada Roshi told me several times he did not want to make me a Buddhist but rather he wanted to empty me in imitation of "Christ your Lord" who emptied himself, poured himself out, and clung to nothing. Whenever Yamada Roshi instructed me in this way, I thought that this Buddhist might make a Christian of me yet.[15]

Jews, Buddhists, and Jewish Buddhists

The dialogue between Jews and Buddhists has taken on its own distinct character, due in part to the important role played by Jewish Buddhists in the introduction and adaptation of the Buddha's teachings to America. American Jews have a long history of exploring the dharma. Charles Strauss, among the earliest American Buddhists, took refuge following the World's Parliament of 1893. Allen Ginsberg, one of the most passionate and powerful voices of the Beat generation, drew much of the force for his poetry from being both Buddhist and Jewish. But other issues have also strengthened this connection, including the similarities and differences between traditional Jewish mysticism and Tibetan Buddhism and the experience shared by Jews and Tibetans of living in diaspora communities.

The publication of Rodger Kamenetz's *The Jew in the Lotus: A Poet's Rediscovery of Jewish Identity in Buddhist India* in 1994 drew attention to the growth of the Jewish-Buddhist dialogue movement. Kamenetz explored the phenomenon of Jewish Buddhists, which many people had noted but few had directly addressed. He cited surveys that indicated the proportion of Jews in Buddhist groups was up to twelve times that of Jews in the population of the United States. Moreover, many Jews held prominent positions in American Buddhist communities. Joseph Goldstein, Jack Kornfield, Jacqueline Schwartz, and Sharon Salzberg co-founded the Insight Meditation Society in Barre, Massachusetts. Sam Bercholz, founder of Shambhala Publications, and Rick Fields, a chronicler of American Buddhism, both studied under Chogyam Trungpa at the Naropa Institute. Bernard Glassman of the Zen Peacemaker Order and Norman Fischer of the San Francisco Zen Center are two of a number of leaders from Jewish backgrounds in the Zen community. Kamenetz also popularized the term *Jubu*, which since the 1960s had gained a degree of currency among Jews in American Buddhism communities.

In *The Jew in the Lotus*, Kamenetz also familiarized general readers with a process of exchange between Jews and Buddhists that had been set in motion at the instigation of the Dalai Lama. During the 1980s, the American Jewish World Service gave assistance to Tibetan exiles in south Asia. Grateful for aid and aware that many Buddhists in America came from Jewish backgrounds, the Dalai Lama told agency leaders of his desire to learn more about Jews and Judaism. This request eventually led to a meeting between Jewish rabbis and scholars and the Dalai Lama in the course of his 1989 America tour, which in turn led to a more ambitious meeting in Dharamsala in 1990, recorded in Kamenetz's illuminating and engaging book.

The delegates to Dharamsala represented a wide range of positions in Judaism, but tended to be liberals in their respective communities. Among them was Zalman Schachter-Shalomi, a charismatic rabbi known for his upbeat interpretation of Kabbalistic mysticism, and Irving and Blu Greenberg, a couple well known as representing the progressive wing of Orthodoxy.

Also present were Reform Rabbi Joy Levitt, Jonathan Omer-Man, founder and president of a Jewish religious center in Los Angeles, and Moshe Waldoks, a spiritual renewal leader well known for his *Big Book of Jewish Humor*. Nathan Katz represented Jewish scholars in Buddhist Studies and Paul Mendes-Flohr, secular academics in Jewish Studies. A portion of *The Jew in the Lotus* is devoted to their debates about the religious protocol appropriate to their meeting with the Dalai Lama, which makes the book an intimate introduction to religious sensibilities in contemporary Judaism.

Kamenetz focuses much of his account on a comparison of Jewish mysticism and Tibetan Buddhism. The discussion of mysticism arose one afternoon when Schachter, who had come to Dharamsala with charts outlining the similarities and differences between Kabbalistic and tantric mysticism, fell into a one-on-one conversation with the Dalai Lama, who became fascinated by the way Kabbalists correlate levels of creation with the Hebrew alphabet and emotional states. He soon was asking Schachter probing questions about angels in the Kabbalah and how they compared to Tibetan dharma protectors and bodhisattvas. Their conversation then turned to a comparison of what Kabbalists term *ain sof* and Mahayana Buddhists call shunyata, both of which convey ideas about the boundless quality of ultimate reality.

The Dalai Lama then initiated a discussion about strategies used by Jews to keep their tradition alive in the two thousand years of the diaspora. Levitt spoke of how the synagogue became a community and cultural center, a place of prayer and learning, and a source of communal values. Blu Greenberg talked about how the family was the center of Jewish religious life for many centuries. Kamenetz reports that this was new information to the Dalai Lama who, despite the fact that he was the leader of the Tibetan people, was most familiar with life among celibate clergy. He also tended to view religion as distinct from culture, so he found it of particular interest that one could be both secular and Jewish. Waldoks and others were frank in expressing their pain at losing Jews to Buddhism, so the Dalai Lama's views on conversion were met with general approval. "In my public teaching I always tell people who are interested that changing religions is not an easy task. So therefore it's better not to change, better to follow one's own traditional religion, since basically the same message, the same potential is there."[16]

The Dalai Lama also offered the delegates insights he had gained as the leader of a society thrust into the modern world almost overnight. He urged Jews to revive mystical teachings that, much like tantra, had been kept in secrecy for many centuries. He had also learned that there was nothing to be gained by attempting to limit people's right to choose. Tibetans were also exploring other traditions and he found it best to be prepared to find something of value in every religion. Finally, he had learned to be realistic about the challenges to tradition posed by modernity. "If we try to isolate ourselves from modernity, this is self-destruction," he noted. "You have to face reality. If you have reason, sufficient reason to practice a religion, sufficient value in that religion, there is no need to fear. If you have no sufficient reason, no value—then there's no reason to hold on to it. Really. I feel that."

> So you see, the time is changing. Nobody can stop it. Whether God created it—or nature is behind it, nobody knows. It is a fact. It is reality. So we have to follow the time, and live according to reality. What we need, ourselves, as religious leaders, is to do more research, find more practices to make tradition something more beneficial in today's life.[17]

Several years later, Kamenetz was instrumental in starting another Jewish-Buddhist collaboration called Seders for Tibet. Seder, the Passover meal commemorating the ancient Hebrews' release from slavery in Egypt, has been important in maintaining Jewish intergenerational memory and collective identity. The idea to recast the ritual to include the plight of Tibet in exile came to Kamenetz in 1996 upon his return from another trip to Dharamsala, when he sought to find a way to foster Jewish-Tibetan solidarity. Sponsorship of Seders for Tibet was soon taken up by The International Campaign for Tibet, leaders in different Jewish denominations, and Jewish students on campus. In a surprise move, the Dalai Lama expressed his desire to attend a seder during a visit to Washington, D.C. in 1997.

As he recalls in *Stalking Elijah: Adventures With Today's Jewish Mystical Masters*, Kamenetz found himself in April of that year gathered with Supreme Court Justice Stephen Breyer, Adam Yauch of the Beastie Boys, and the Dalai Lama at a seder hosted by Rabbi David Saperstein of Washington's Religious Action Center. "At one point," he writes, "the fifty of us crowded in a small room grew silent as we listened to a recording smuggled out of Tibet."

> We heard the quavering voice of Phuntsok Nyidron, a nineteen-year-old nun serving seventeen years in Drapchi prison. From far away, she sang to our seder about the meaning of freedom. Together we read the translation of her lyric, "We the captured friends in spirit . . . no matter how hard we are beaten/Our linked arms cannot be separated."[18]

At the closing of the seder, they recited the traditional Passover prayer of hope—"L'Shana Haba-ah B'Yerushalayim, next year in Jerusalem"— but added, "L'Shana Haba-ah B'Lhasa. Next year in Lhasa."[19]

The Dharamsala meeting in 1990 and Seders for Tibet in 1997 are only two landmarks in a broader process of dialogue among Jews and Buddhists. *Tikkun*, a progressive journal of contemporary Judaism, noted in 1998 that "for more than a generation Jewish seekers have hit the enlightenment road and have traveled every path. Now we are hitting middle age and are producing a literature, a Jewish literature, describing our peregrinations. . . . Of particular interest is the eruption of new material dealing with Judaism and Eastern religions." Among the books cited were Kamenetz's *The Jew in the Lotus*, Norman Fischer's *Jerusalem Moonlight*, Judith Linzer's *Torah and Dharma: Jewish Seekers in Eastern Religions*, and Sylvia Boorstein's *That's Funny, You Don't Look Buddhist: On Being a Faithful Jew and a Passionate Buddhist*.

Boorstein's book is an intimate and accessible account of her successful attempt to reconcile a dual religious identity. She was raised in Brooklyn, New York, but eventually drifted away from a strong sense of Jewish religious identity. After earning a Master's of Social Work at the University of California and a Ph.D. in psychology from the Saybrook Institute, she practiced as a psychotherapist. In the mid-1970s, she took up vipassana meditation and later became a teacher at Insight Meditation Society. In the 1980s, she was among the Buddhist representatives at a major Buddhist-Christian dialogue hosted by the Naropa Institute. By about the mid-1990s, however, she also began to describe herself as an observant and prayerful Jew.

In *That's Funny, You Don't Look Buddhist*, Boorstein recalls the discomfort she once experienced trying to be both Jewish and Buddhist. When teaching Jews meditation, she feared but did not experience disapproval. Among Buddhists, she was reluctant to identify herself as Jewish. The issue came to a head at the meeting of western Buddhist teachers with the Dalai Lama in 1993, after a question was asked in a preliminary meeting: What is the greatest current spiritual challenge in your practice and teaching? Boorstein recalls thinking to herself, " 'Okay, this is it! These are major teachers in all lineages, these are people I respect and who I hope will respect me.' And I said my truth":

I am a Jew. These days I spend a lot of my time teaching Buddhist meditation to Jews. It gives me special pleasure to teach Jews, and sometimes special problems. I feel it's my calling, though, something I'm supposed

to do. And I'm worried that someone here will think I'm doing something wrong. Someone will say, "You're not a real Buddhist."

Posing the question in an atmosphere charged with such creative potential,
however, provided the solution. "I never did ask the Dalai Lama if what I
am doing is okay," she later wrote. "It had become, for me, a nonquestion
by the time we got to our meeting."[20]

As Boorstein describes it, she came to understand that she is a Jew because her parents provided her with a loving upbringing and being Jewish is
a fundamental part of her personal identity. Yet she became a religious Jew
once again because of her experience with Buddhism. From the first day of
her first Buddhist retreat, she recalls being captivated by the Buddha's teaching on the cessation of suffering, which gave her a way to pursue a life devoted to cultivating compassion and contentment. This happiness with herself, in turn, led her back to Judaism. "I am a prayerful Jew because I am a
Buddhist," she wrote. "As the meditation practice that I learned from my
Buddhist teachers made me less fearful and allowed me to fall in love with
life, I discovered the prayer language of 'thank you' that I knew from my
childhood returned, spontaneously and to my great delight."[21]

Boorstein devotes much of her book to teasing out parallels between the
traditions of Judaism and Buddhism. She identifies the V'ahavta prayer in
Judaism—"And you shall love the Lord Your God with all your heart, with
all your soul, and with all your strength"—as Judaism's form of metta, or
lovingkindness, practice. She sees Abraham's saying "Hineyni" or "Here I
am" to God in the Book of Genesis as an expression of the mindfulness
Buddhists cultivate in meditation. The author of the Book of Job who spoke
of the Voice from the Whirlwind was alluding to an experience of God she
understands in terms of emptiness. Boorstein conveys how she has come to
think religiously on a number of levels when she discusses her understanding of Buddhist ideas about karma and the interdependence of all being.

> To myself, I say, "God reigns, God reigned. God will reign forever."
> To my grandchildren, I say, "Everything, no matter what, is okay.
> And we'll try as hard as we can to fix anything that is broken."
> To Buddhist students, I say: "The cosmos is lawful. Karma is true.
> Everything evolves from a single interconnected source. Nothing is dis-
> connected from anything else. Future events are dependent on our ac-
> tions now. Virtue is mandated; we are responsible for one another.
> Everything matters."[22]

Intra- and interreligious dialogue is a complex, multifaceted undertaking with great philosophical and theological implications that lie beyond the scope of this book. But these selected developments suggest how the dharma is being reshaped in new and challenging ways as it sets down roots in this country. There are both problems and creative possibilities in this process. On one hand, many view religious traditions as having developed internal consistency over centuries, with scripture, doctrine, and ritual practices working together to shape a path that enables practitioners and communities to cultivate both spirituality and personal and collective identities. On the other hand, all living traditions are more or less in a constant state of change, even if only very cautious, and the movement of the dharma to America will require significant adaptations and innovations.

Buddhism in America is in a state of creative ferment, in which the forces of tradition and innovation are at work both within and among a wide range of religious traditions. The fundamental teachings of the Buddha, which are themselves subject to a variety of traditional interpretations, have been introduced into a new cultural environment, setting in motion processes of revitalization and re-creation. Scholars routinely use a kind of shorthand to describe comparable processes that took place in Buddhist Asia. Ancient Theravada Buddhism absorbed the animistic traditions of rural Sri Lanka, for instance, and Indian Tantric Buddhism fused with the shamanic religion of central Asia. In the United States there is as yet no comparable shorthand; however, it is clear that intra-Buddhist dialogue and interreligious dialogue among Buddhists, Christians, and Jews is helping to develop distinct forms of Buddhism that reflect the uniqueness of a new, North American setting.

Thus it is no surprise that some leaders of particular traditions, schools, and lineages stand guard over boundaries that give them their coherence and consistency. Some may dismiss this as sectarian rivalry, as no doubt it sometimes is, but the instinct to defend tradition can be healthy and deserves to be encouraged. On the other hand, there is no question that the United States presents a perhaps unprecedented opportunity for creative interaction. Cross-fertilization among different traditions is occurring in many different quarters and in a wide variety of ways. That some of this will, in the long term, help to shape uniquely American forms of the dharma can be considered inevitable.

CHAPTER FOURTEEN

Making Some Sense of Americanization

During the last forty years, Buddhism in the United States has been transformed from the religion of a relatively small number of Asian Americans and an esoteric preoccupation of a much smaller European American avant-garde into what amounts to a mass movement. Shaped by immigration, conversion, schism, and exile, Buddhism is now thriving to such a degree that it is impossible to exhaustively catalogue its variations and combinations in this country. Perhaps as many as three quarters of America's Buddhists are in new immigrant communities, whose contributions to the long-term development of the dharma remain particularly difficult to assess and are often overlooked—and, I think, highly underrated. The American Buddhist community as a whole encompasses an extremely wide spectrum of opinions about the nature and practice of Buddhism. Within it, traditionalist and innovative impulses coexist, sometimes comfortably, sometimes not. Tolerance is generally valued highly and the idea that all expressions of the dharma are in essence one is widely accepted.

However, there are few pressures on Buddhists to foster unity. In my travels and many conversations, I have often been struck by the degree to which many communities are more or less out of communication with one another. Despite intra-Buddhist dialogue on national, regional, and local levels, and phenomena like shared and mixed practices, many groups continue to develop quite independently. Some, most notably SGI-USA and Jodo Shinshu, have taken on forms that resemble the sectarian model familiar in the West. Others are organized more as schools within traditions, like Tibetan Nyingmas and Kagyus or Theravada Mahanikayas and Dhammayuts, that resemble Catholic religious orders but without the larger institution of the Church and the centralizing office of the papacy. Theravada and Tibetan forms of Buddhism both emphasize the student-teacher lineage, a mode of organization that is also prominent and operates powerfully in the Zen community.

As a result, American Buddhism resembles an extensive web or network of monasteries, temples, and centers cross-cut by lines of affiliation that are often difficult to trace clearly. I was surprised to discover that people in the Kagyu community in Woodstock, New York were generally uninformed about developments among Gelugpas in Ithaca, a few hours' drive away. My incorrect assumption was that the two groups would make communication between them a high priority because they were both in the Tibetan tradition. Instead, they were primarily preoccupied with far-flung developments related to their own communities. One informed observer of American Zen suggested that as many as 80 percent of the Zen teachers in this country are associated with the Soto school. This struck me as a reasonable if surprisingly high estimate. But the point is that when looking at the numerous Zen groups in this country from outside the community, one would not readily guess that this organizational principle was at work.

The lack of strong pan-Buddhist national organizations may simply reflect the current stage of development in American Buddhism. Judaism and Catholicism, both of which were present in the colonial period, only developed strong national institutions over the course of the nineteenth century. But Buddhists may forego the development of comparable national organizations; the current decentralization could become a permanent condition. This approach to the dharma may be a strength rather than a weakness. It has so far meant that American Buddhism is characterized by variety and complexity at a time when the nation's ideals are increasingly being recast in terms of multiplicity and autonomy at the local and regional levels. Some observers have speculated that Buddhism in the United States may come to resemble Buddhism in China where, despite the eventual emergence of characteristic Chinese forms, the dharma remained fluid, eclectic, and regionally inflected over the course of many centuries.

The most prominent feature of American Buddhism for the last three or so decades has been the gulf between immigrants and converts, created by a range of deep cultural, linguistic, and social differences. A less obvious but extremely important dimension of this gulf is more strictly religious; here the contrast between tradition and innovation often appears in particularly high relief.

The transmission of the dharma from Asia to the United States is an epoch-making event, the full consequences of which will only become apparent in the next century. Here a group of Buddhists, both Asian and American-born and from several traditions, parade in the streets of Los Angeles in 1994 in an ecumenical celebration of the Buddha's birthday. DON FARBER

The Buddhism of immigrants tends to remain informed by the rich cosmological worldviews of Buddhist Asia. Rebirth and karma are often treated as existential facts, bodhisattvas as dynamic, personalized forces or cosmic entities. Liberation and awakening are essentially religious aspirations and rituals often retain an unambiguous sense of being efficacious. For many converts, however, the dharma is becoming integrated with a more secular outlook on life. Many have implicitly or explicitly abandoned the idea of rebirth. Cosmic bodhisattvas tend to be regarded as metaphors, rituals as personal and collective means of expression. Traditional doctrine and philosophy often take a back seat to inspiration and creativity. The transcendental goal of practice is itself often psychologized or reoriented to social transformation. Stephen Batchelor, a British Buddhist influential in convert circles in this country, has argued that the dharma in the West ought to become a "Buddhism without beliefs," which he characterizes in his book by that title as an "existential, therapeutic, and liberating agnosticism," a very different kind of Buddhism than that found within most immigrant communities.[1]

The numerous ways in which traditionalism and innovation are being worked out in American Buddhism, among both immigrants and converts, are not subject to easy generalization because they are related to complex processes of cross-cultural translation that need to be closely examined on a case-by-case basis. But the separation between the immigrant and convert communities does reflect a different orientation to the cultural and social uses of the dharma. "If you look at the history of the Asian groups coming here, especially the recent ones, religion is at the center of their lives," *Tricycle*'s Helen Tworkov told an interviewer from the Harvard Pluralism Project.

> It's used as a way of conserving their history, of conserving their traditions, their rituals, what they want to pass on to their children. So the whole nature of it is to conserve. For the Euro-American, the impulse to convert was very, very different. We didn't want to conserve, especially for my generation coming to Buddhism in the 60s. We didn't want to conserve anything from our culture. We wanted to do exactly the opposite. We wanted everything that was new.[2]

During the 1980s, some observers began to use the phrase "American Buddhism" to denote expressions of the dharma that developed among converts in and around the 1960s counterculture and were shaped by subsequent events in the 1970s and '80s. The phrase was meant to convey the idea that converts' innovations were giving rise to uniquely American forms of Buddhism that could claim normative status and be understood as the wave of the future. At about the same time, others deliberately began to use the phrase "Buddhism in America" to convey the idea that there are many expressions of the dharma in this country, some associated with immigrants, others with converts, but none that can be characterized as normative. This difference in emphasis reflects a running debate over which group can legitimately claim to carry the standard for the dharma in the United States, a question that refers to the distinctly different claims of Americanness converts and immigrants can make. Converts often believe that their experience as native-born gives them a uniquely American perspective from which to interpret the dharma. Advocates for the immigrants tend to point to the centrality of the immigrant experience and its importance to the nation's religious history as a different, but no less valid, claim to Americanness.

Given the extraordinary diversity in the worldwide Buddhist community and the amount of time needed for any religion to take root in a new culture, I think that it is premature to announce the establishment of a unique, authentic form of American Buddhism. Writing as a historian rather than a partisan in current debates, I am most interested in the long-term challenges involved in building viable forms of Buddhism, whether among converts or immigrants. Observing the current vitality of the American Buddhist landscape, I often wonder how it will change, even within the next thirty years or so, as some forms continue to thrive and others fall by the wayside. All the groups under consideration in this book have successfully negotiated the problems of becoming established. But they now face new challenges to their survival over the long haul, be these rooted in economic considerations, leadership and succession issues, or in keeping and replenishing their membership. The definition of American Buddhism will be determined by those forms that survive the winnowing process that can be expected during the early decades of the twenty-first century.

I am convinced, however, that for many years to come, Buddhists in a number of schools and traditions will look back on the years between 1960 and 2000 as an era in which the foundations were laid for their sanghas. But given the current situation, the challenges Buddhists face need to be assessed in terms of immigrants and converts and the kind of issues the two groups face at the opening of a new century.

Immigrant Buddhism

Barring unforeseen calamities like the Second World War or the conflict in Vietnam, most large immigrant Buddhist communities are likely to follow general patterns familiar from the histories of other immigrant groups in this country, but with variations unique to our rapidly globalizing society and to particular traditions. If the example of other immigrant groups holds true, it can be expected that there will be recurrent waves of innovation and traditionalism with each successive generation, in tandem with a deeply running and thorough adaptation to the values of mainstream America.

But most Buddhist immigrant groups are now roughly at the same stage as Japanese Americans in the Jodo Shinshu tradition in the 1920s or '30s, although many, such as Thais, Sri Lankans, and Chinese, are substantially larger communities. They are also establishing themselves in America at a time when the country as a whole, despite some anti-Asian sentiments and persistent racism, is more multicultural in outlook and more racially and religiously pluralistic than it was in the early part of the twentieth century. Most Buddhist immigrant groups now have well-established networks of temples and other institutions and have begun the process of retaining, adjusting, and abandoning elements of their received traditions as part of the adaptation to this country. A second and in many cases a third generation is on the rise, whose attitude toward tradition will largely determine the shape of immigrant Buddhism in the twenty-first century.

Asian immigration remains open, however, which means that a "first generation" is being constantly replenished. At this writing, as a financial crisis deepens in Asia, a new, unanticipated wave of Asian Buddhist immigration may be in the making. Such continued immigration has had important consequences for religious traditions in the past. Among German Lutherans, for instance, ongoing migration in the nineteenth century contributed to institutional differentiation as newly arriving Germans, appalled at the Americanization of Lutheranism by an earlier generation of immigrants, formed their own networks of churches. Splits between some of these groups began to be healed only a century later, at a time when older theological and liturgical controversies ceased being divisive issues. At present, a similar kind of differentiation is likely to occur in Buddhist immigrant communities.

Paul Numrich has observed a few additional, familiar patterns among Thai and Sri Lankan Buddhist immigrants in the mid-1990s. Given the power of lay-based religious movements in the United States, modern trends toward the laicization of Buddhism in Asia seem especially important. Many temples were originally founded by laypeople, who continue to exert a good deal of influence, both financial and religious. This trend is likely to increase as immigrants become more experienced with administering democratic forms of religious polity. At the same time, Theravada monks play an essential role in the religious life of the temple. Their monastic orders remain important parts of many congregations' religious identities, a factor that may lead to Theravada denominationalism.

Numrich has also observed what he calls "a double-barreled 'gap' " between the older, immigrant generation and their children. One part of this is the generation gap, which in this country is virtually institutionalized as a rite of passage for American teens. But the other, more important, gap is cultural and linguistic. One informant told Numrich that Thai American teenagers in Chicago often "shift gears" when they leave their parents' homes to be with their friends. Others reported that teens tend to disappear from temple life in response to peer pressure. But many of Numrich's young informants suggest that the temple plays an important role in their social life, even if the religious aspect is often lost on them—a phenomenon hardly unique to Buddhist immigrants or, for that matter, teenagers. "I learned who I am and about the people in my country at this temple," one wrote in response to Numrich's survey. "I really like this Wat." Another fifteen-year-old reported that "This place is very important for all of us kids for it lets us know and be proud of who we are and where we come from." Still another noted: "We're not trying to escape from Thai [culture]; we study Thai dancing, we learned Buddhism, we speak Thai."[3]

I encountered a twenty-something Thai American woman at Wat Metta in southern California whose take on her relationship to Buddhism might be considered anomalous. I suspect, however, it may also be characteristic of the ways in which tradition will become important for many of America's Buddhist immigrants. In response to my question about whether she was a practicing Buddhist, she said something to the effect that "as a kid I did the whole American thing." But during a recent trip to Thailand, she had seen that Buddhists were gatekeepers to business in what at the time was one of Asia's booming economies. Wanting to get into the action overseas, she had come to Wat Metta, while completing business school, to brush up on her Buddhist protocol and etiquette. There was nothing disingenuous in her remarks, but her sentiments did not seem particularly religious. A similar relation to tradition was common among Catholic and Jewish immigrants for whom strictly religious concerns were often less important than the pragmatic opportunities presented by networks established within and around ethnic communities.

It is likely that some of the finest expressions of American Buddhist philosophy and exemplars of practice and piety will emerge from these communities by virtue of the fact that people within them will quite naturally straddle Asian tradition and American innovation. But when considering the potential contribution of these immigrants to the United States, it is important not to focus exclusively on notions of religion as a quest for transcendence while discounting the political and social consequences of ethnic identity. Observers have long noted that in the deep but unstable relationship between culture and religion in immigrant communities, it is often not the church, synagogue, or temple that ultimately claims primacy. Religion, along with political, commercial, and other social concerns, becomes one element in a powerful, if somewhat amorphous, sense of ethnic identity. Much of American immigration history concentrates on shifting patterns of Americans' ethnic self-understanding as they bear on a wide range of questions from intermarriage to urban, regional, national, and international political activity.

One can already pick up a sense of this Buddhist ethnoreligious identity formation at work in the 1990s. The Hsi Lai temple–Democratic National Committee funding controversy sent shock waves through the Chinese American community that reverberated back to Taiwan, the full consequences of which, in both religious and political terms, remain to be seen. A crackdown by Hanoi on a Buddhist revival in Vietnam spurred the formation of a political action coalition among religious, community, and business leaders in southern California's Vietnamese American community. An integral part of the contribution Buddhist immigrants make to America in the long term will be the establishment of living links to many nations across the Pacific, which will have a range of consequences over the course of the twenty-first century.

It is also important to keep in mind that the distance between converts and immigrants does not imply that immigrant Buddhists from Tibet, Sri Lanka, China, Korea, Japan, and a number of other Asian countries are, or even care to be, a united force in this country. Alliances among ethnic coreligionists are remarkably unstable. It took Roman Catholicism several generations to forge an American institution uniting immigrants who, at the turn of the twentieth century, represented over twenty different linguistic communities. The formation of separate German, Polish, and other national Catholic churches was averted only by papal intervention. But no comparable central administration exists for immigrant Buddhists, so diversity is likely to remain a primary feature of the community. The idea of an Asian American or Asian Pacific American political coalition has been favored by many activists since the 1970s, but has been difficult to sustain as a viable ethnic-political force on the American scene. Prominent, highly respected Buddhist leaders like Thich Nhat Hanh and the Dalai Lama are well known in a number of different immigrant groups, but they have had little effect in creating a sense of a common Buddhist identity. It is hard to imagine an external force, such as the rise of anti-Semitism in Europe that fostered the formation of an American Jewish identity, that could galvanize disparate Buddhist immigrant groups to forge a shared Asian American and Buddhist identity.

Nevertheless, it is safe to suggest that major Asian Buddhist groups will play a vital part in the creation of American forms of Buddhism in the twenty-first century. I disagree with those converts who see ethnicity-based sectarianism as an obstacle to the development of the dharma in this country. Most people who are religious are so in particular ways and in particular communities that often have an ethnic basis. The real issue is whether these communities will remain self-contained or, as leaders like Havanpola Ratanasara of the American Buddhist Congress hope, reach out to the broader Buddhist and American communities. As with so many issues in immigrant communities, a good deal rests on choices yet to be made by the second and third generations. A few observers have suggested that some children of immigrants are beginning to express an interest in convert Buddhism, where they can explore their own heritage in the American idiom that is their first cultural language, without the intervention of their parents. This may well be so. But it seems likely that the main line of immigrant Buddhism will be firmly tied to developments within, rather than outside, the immigrant communities.

American historians of religion have for a long time directed most of their attention to the Protestant churches and their immense impact on religious institutions and discourse in this country. As a result, they have been slow to give attention to current Buddhist immigration. On occasion, I have heard a number of the most prominent dismiss its importance, noting that Buddhist immigrants amount to less than two percent of the American population. This has always surprised me given that Jews, who have never numbered more than three percent of the population, have made an immense contribution to American religion and culture. It may well be the case that Asian Buddhists will make a comparable mark in the coming century.

At this juncture, however, it is worthwhile noting that the phenomenon of large-scale Buddhist immigration is a part of a new era in American immigration history in which Buddhists, Hindus, Muslims, and others are arriving in very substantial numbers. Fifty years ago, historians routinely referred to the "old immigration," by which they meant Irish and German Catholics and western European Jews who arrived in the antebellum period, and the "new immigration," Jews and Catholics arriving from southern and eastern Europe around the turn of the century. Many of the religious and political implications of this history helped form the Protestant, Catholic, and Jewish "triple melting pot" in the post–World War II era, a form of American self-identity that was a long time in the making. The nation has since moved on to understand itself in more multiracial and multicultural terms. But seen in this historical perspective, the importance of the large-scale Buddhist immigration from points across Asia is far too early to call. It is part of a broad reorientation in American history that, barring a reactionary movement to cut off Asian immigration, is only beginning.

Convert Buddhism

Converts face new challenges unique to their status as native-born Americans, most of which are also related to a range of second-generation issues. To the extent that these Buddhists have raised their children in the dharma, the community is developing its own "birth-right" Buddhists, to borrow a Quaker term, who will surely influence the future of American Buddhism. But I have seen very little hard evidence of a substantial rising generation within these communities. Many members of Soka Gakkai have integrated chanting daimoku into their family life. Highly organized communities such as Shambhala International and the Dharma Realm Buddhist Association have formal school programs for their children. I have on occasion witnessed Buddhist "rites of passage" ceremonies for teens who spent their childhood in and around convert dharma communities.

But I also recall a conversation with a prominent figure in the Buddhist publishing world that made a lasting impression, although it provides only anecdotal information. In response to my question about how converts educate their children to be Buddhists, he replied that, as far as he could see, many were reluctant to "lay their Buddhism" on their children. At the very least, this provides a suggestive point of contrast with immigrants who, throughout American history, have deemed it a natural right, if not an absolute imperative, to pass on their religion to their offspring.

The second-generation issue, however, is important in the convert community in several additional ways. One key aspect has to do with the recruitment and retention of a new generation of practitioners. Although I have spoken with young SGI-USA members whose commitment is based on their parents' involvement in the movement, I have no clear sense of whether and how new recruiting is proceeding since SGI abandoned the shakubuku campaigns that accounted for its rapid growth in the 1960s and '70s. In regard to Zen and other forms of contemplative Buddhism, recent statistics indicate that sitting meditation continues to have a broad appeal for Americans. Don Morreale, in his *Complete Guide to Buddhism*, puts these statistics into a historical perspective that suggests this may be a long-term trend. Between 1900 and 1964 there were twenty-one meditation centers founded in this country. The number increased substantially between 1965 and 1974, with the establishment of 117 new centers. An additional 308 were founded between 1975 and 1984, and 616 between 1985 and 1997. Morreale lists more than 1,000 meditation centers in existence in this country as of 1997. A good number are Asian American Zen, Vajrayana, or Theravada groups that teach meditation, but most are associated with the convert community. It should be recalled, however, that estimates of the number of convert Buddhists range from 100,000 to 800,000, an extremely wide margin of error. This makes it very difficult to assess how the burgeoning of meditation centers might translate into new and committed membership.

Despite optimism about the future that can border on the visionary, there is concern about the "graying" of American Buddhism, a reminder that most developments in convert communities remain tied to the baby-boom generation that turned to the dharma in the 1960s. When the teachers in this generation began to come of age in the 1980s, commentators emphasized their innovations—family-centered lay practice, gender equity, the integration of Buddhism with psychology, and so forth. There is every reason to think that these kinds of innovations will have enduring effects on American Buddhism. But many prominent converts are only in their fifties; they have twenty or more years to be communities' teachers and leaders, plenty of time for new situations and unexpected issues to arise. In Colorado, I saw advertisements offering Buddhists the opportunity to buy early into dharma-centered retirement communities. What old age might mean for convert Buddhism is impossible to predict, but such advertisements are a reminder that the fate of many adaptations made in the last few decades will ultimately be in the hands of another generation.

This aspect of the generational issue also directs attention to the importance of creating new leaders for the convert communities. SGI-USA, whose vitality in this country owes so much to the work and example of Daisaku Ikeda, will eventually face important leadership and succession issues that will undoubtedly have an impact on the entire organization. Within the community, however, SGI-USA has well-developed youth divisions that will presumably provide a new generation of leaders and administrators. In the Tibetan Buddhist community, a great deal depends on the formidable task of training new lamas who have a strong, in-depth sense of the practice traditions in a range of lineages, whether they are Tibetans in exile or Americans.

In the Zen community and the Insight Meditation movement, where a constant influx of Asian teachers is not taken for granted, the creation of new leaders is directly related to the maintenance of teaching lineages. A number of lineages are well positioned with a second, third, and sometimes a fourth generation of teachers likely to function as leaders. The continued development of all forms of convert Buddhism, however, will require the differentiation of roles and the ongoing development of members who function in more mundane capacities as fund-raisers, board members, and administrators.

One key issue for convert Buddhists is maintaining the authenticity of the dharma for future generations. On the one hand, most Buddhists celebrate the diversity of expression found among converts. It is generally considered all to the good that Buddhists undertake practice for a wide range of reasons—peace of mind, self-empowerment, the deepening of personal relations, building character, social transformation, and so on. On the other hand, some commentators have asked whether the premium placed on innovation will not, in the long term, distort the central teachings of the Buddha and rob the dharma of its depth and integrity, a question that is framed differently by different convert communities.

In Soka Gakkai International-USA, questions about the integrity of teachings, doctrinal orthodoxy, institutional continuity, and the like have tended to cluster around the growing tensions and eventual break with the Nichiren Shoshu priesthood. Since 1991, SGI has been free to plumb the depth of Nichiren's teachings, draw upon the examples of Makaguchi, Toda, and Ikeda, and develop its practice and philosophy in line with the needs of its members. Within the movement, there seems to be a remarkable tolerance about the needs and aspirations members bring to their practice: One can chant the daimoku to cultivate enlightened consciousness, strengthen character, or better one's position financially. SGI also emerged from the schism unambiguous in its lay orientation. Its main practice centers are found in people's homes, and SGI members have taken up the sacramental roles once filled by the priesthood on a rotating, voluntary basis. Informed SGI members are quick to point out that this lay orientation is quite in keeping with the spirit of Nichiren's revolt against the monastic establishment in thirteenth-century Japan and that in this regard it is the Nichiren Shoshu priesthood that is aberrant. This tolerant, lay-oriented practice does not itself ensure the survival of SGI-USA over the long term, but it does place the movement well within American norms, in tune with the demands of the secular workplace and the nuclear family.

The situation is somewhat different among converts whose main practice is sitting meditation, particularly in Zen and the Theravada-based Insight Meditation movement. The membership of both these groups is overwhelmingly comprised of laypeople who have taken up a rigorous form of practice formerly reserved for monastics, which they must balance with the demands of secular life. But both groups depend on dharma transmission from teacher to student and the formation of lineages to perpetuate the movement and to ensure the ongoing integrity of the teachings. This has led in-house observers to question the consequences of the ambiguous status of American meditators who are not quite monastics, yet more than typical laity. Can these practitioners preserve and transmit the dharma in its most authentic expression? Will contemplative Buddhism survive in the long term without a strong monastic sangha? Should the dharma be recast in order to reflect the needs, aspirations, and capacities of laypeople?

The debate over these questions is too complex to be reduced to a simple conflict between monastics and laity, conservatives and liberals, or even traditionalists and innovators. On the level of theory, it is being addressed in a growing body of literature exploring the relationship between Buddhist philosophy and practice and a range of humanistic psychologies. But at its most basic level, the debate amounts to differences in opinion about the current challenges and opportunities for Buddhism in America and the West and the strategic responses converts ought to make to them.

The unconflicted view expressed by Don Morreale in his *Complete Guide* might be taken as representative of those whose priority has been to adapt the dharma to fit the needs of the American middle class, the demands of work and family. "Everything has changed in Buddhist America. The wildness of the early days is over and meditation is no longer the province of a handful of visionaries and poets. Buddhism has gone mainstream," he writes. "At retreats one is likely to find oneself sitting next to a stock broker or a therapist or a retired social worker who may or may not claim to be a Buddhist. It is an older crowd as well: fewer and fewer people in their twenties and more and more in their forties, fifties, and sixties."

> The teaching situation has changed. . . . The strict, almost martial, spirit that was once the norm in many Zen centers has given way to a lighter approach. Day care is frequently available, as well as flexible schedules to accommodate work and family. . . . Time at retreat alternates with work in the world, giving the participants an opportunity to earn money, to spend time with their families, to integrate what they've learned in seclusion. . . . The distinctly Asian flavor that once permeated Western dharma centers has given way to something that feels very familiarly North American.[4]

Important substantive shifts in emphasis have accompanied these American-izing trends: the abandonment of hierarchical models in teacher-student re-lations, the autonomy of local sanghas, and the emergence of consensus-based decision making.

Other commentators, while supporting such adaptations, ask at what point innovation ceases to do justice to the spirit and substance of the Bud-dha's teachings. For instance, Helen Tworkov, in a 1994 article, "Zen in Balance: Can It Survive America?" noted that "It is not simply an histor-ical accident that Buddhism begins with a person walking away from a life of luxury, from a palace, a family, art, from security and every comfort. Nor is it an accident that Zen was nourished in a monastic setting, by stu-dents and teachers who chose to abandon worldly existence." These ob-servations led her to ask "whether what we have confidently called 'Amer-icanization' has become a justification for the co-optation of Zen by sec-ular materialism."[5]

In a similar vein, John Daido Loori, a highly regarded roshi, noted that "Most of the lay practice that goes on among new converts in America is a slightly watered-down version of monastic practice, and most of the monas-tic practice is a slightly glorified version of lay practice. . . . To me, this hy-brid path—halfway between monasticism and lay practice—reflects our cul-tural spirit of greediness and consumerism. With all the possibilities, why give up anything? 'We want it all.' Why not do it all?"[6]

The debate over the quality of American Buddhism in the long term is important, but in the absence of rigorous, universally held standards, is un-likely to be resolved anytime soon. Not having taken up the devotionalism and ritualism of Asian laity, most Buddhists in these communities will no doubt continue to meditate as a form of lay practice, whether at a Zen cen-ter, on a vipassana retreat, or on a more explicitly therapeutic model like that of Jon Kabat-Zinn. Such a pluralistic approach to practice is in keeping with the overall tenor of American Buddhism, where the accent is on flexibility, pragmatism, individualism, and diversity.

The popularity of such approaches, however, is not in itself an answer to the question of whether something vital will be lost in the absence of a strong, convert monastic community. In colloquial terms, Pema Chodron contrasts the different social and emotional environments of monastics and laity and suggests their consequences. "In the monastic life, you can't do your usual number of blaming others and justifying yourself. You can't get away with that," she is quoted as saying in *Tricycle*.

You can get away with it with your husband, or your wife, or your lover, or your children. Within the monastic community, the relationships are equally fraught with confusion and difficulty, but you can't get away from the realization that your own neurosis plays a big part in the fact that you want to lay the blame on the situation or on somebody else. You're brought back to yourself in a very profound and inescapable way. . . . Monastic life isn't tough because you have to work hard all day long. It isn't tough because you don't have time to yourself. It isn't tough because there is no time to practice, it's tough because there are no exits and you come up so close to yourself. When I mentioned this to the abbot of Gampo Abbey, Thrangu Rinpoche, he said, "Well isn't that the point, that you see yourself."[7]

Thanissaro Bhikkhu, abbot of Metta Forest Monastery, expressed a similar view in more traditional language. When asked by an interviewer about the use of Buddhist meditation for therapeutic ends, he replied: "That's fine. That's called domesticated Buddhism and it's always going to be there."

Thais like ceremonies where they can make merit for their dead relatives. Americans like retreats where they can feel connected to the world. They're coming from the same impulse. But please don't present just that much as the whole of Buddhism. There are books that will tell you that the sign of successful spiritual practice is the ability to have meaningful relations—nothing about nirvana. But there will always be people who want more, and Buddhism should be there for them.[8]

There is at present no single answer to these questions, and it is important to underscore the fact that the Buddhist meditation movement has been substantial only since the 1960s. Current configurations were shaped by a rapid succession of events that unfolded over the course of the next three decades. It may be that in time clear distinctions will be made among different kinds of practitioners—"weekend sitters," "high-performance householders," "full-bore monastics," and the like—in a way analogous to Buddhism in ancient India, which distinguished "stream-winners" from "once-returners." Categories of this kind, based on practice styles and degrees of commitment rather than levels of attainment, seem to be the common intent behind the development of parallel practice paths in such different organizations as Shambhala International and Zen Mountain Monastery.

In light of these and other issues, I have reflected many times on the question of how much historical perspective is needed on current events in order to make some sense of Americanization. When Rick Fields first published *How the Swans Came to the Lake*, a book that played an important role in fostering self-conscious Americanization among converts, he was a part of a community still closely associated with the revolutionary idealism of the counterculture. At that time, few commentators, Buddhist or otherwise, paid much attention to trends that are now seen as helping to define the late twentieth century—the rising migration from Asia, cultural and economic globalization, and the increased power of Pacific Rim nations. In later editions of *Swans*, Fields directed his attention to the coming of age of American-born teachers in light of precedents from Thoreau and Emerson to the Beats, perpetuating a highly selective view of American Buddhist communities.

By the end of the century, however, there is distance enough from the 1960s to see that the American Buddhist landscape has become very complex—part converts, part old-line Chinese and Japanese Americans, part new immigrants who, as rough as the relevant statistics are, appear to have a significant demographic edge. There are, moreover, complicated relations among these groups in parallel congregations; international academic, political, and women's groups; trans-Atlantic and trans-Pacific practice communities; and intra-Buddhist dialogue networks. This more complex view suggests that American Buddhism is a massive, multifaceted, collaborative effort. I have attempted to suggest this by highlighting when possible some of the different, ongoing interactions between converts and immigrants. But to bring out this collaboration more clearly, the history of Buddhism in America must be revisioned at least since the early twentieth century when, as Fields so admirably describes, networks began to develop among Asian, Asian American, and European American seekers in ways that suggested this eventual complexity.

My own view is that most American Buddhists, immigrants and converts, are still in what might be thought of as the "heroic age" of the founding of their communities. Thus, questions about the emergence of mature expressions of Americanized Buddhism are less immediate than those about the ongoing process of community formation. In this context, immigration remains the single most important force at work. This is not meant to privilege the immigrant experience over that of converts, but to highlight the fact that even the most ardent Americanizing convert stands only a step, perhaps two, removed from an Asian teacher, who probably arrived here as an immigrant. In the theorizing about American Buddhism in the wake of the scandals of the 1980s, there may have been a version of the well-known second-generation phenomenon in immigrant communities, when a native-born generation attempts to radically differentiate itself from its elders by a zealous embrace of all things American. In the past, this has usually been corrected by a third generation's return to tradition. It will be no great surprise if converts, having established their Americanness as Buddhists, return to Asian sources and teachers for many decades, even generations.

Given the continuing importance of immigration, I think that American Buddhists, both immigrants and converts, might do well to pay more attention to the progress of older groups like the Buddhist Churches of America, in which tensions between tradition and innovation, sectarianism and universalism, Anglicization and language maintenance, and ethnic identity and Americanization have played themselves out over many generations. Despite the challenges the BCA currently faces, it has the most substantial Buddhist track record of any large group in this country. In its history are embedded a good many lessons about the kinds of tolls that Buddhists can expect to be charged on the road to mainstream America.

Sylvia Boorstein

is a well-known teacher in the Insight Meditation movement. She was raised in Brooklyn, New York in a strongly Jewish home, but later drifted away from a sense of Jewish religious identity. She graduated from Barnard College, received a Master's of Social Work from the University of California at Berkeley, and later earned a Ph.D. in psychology from the Saybrook Institute. She practiced psychotherapy for a number of years before beginning to study vipassana meditation in the mid- to late 1970s. By the mid-1980s, she was a senior teacher at the Insight Meditation Society in Barre, Massachusetts. She later cofounded Spirit Rock Meditation Center outside San Francisco. She is probably best known for her popular presentation of Buddhism in *Don't Just Do Something, Sit There: A Mindfulness Meditation Manual* and *It's Easier Than You Think: The Buddhist Way to Happiness*.

Boorstein is a pioneer in dealing with the complex questions of interreligious dialogue and of dual religious identity, both of which are important issues in the adaptation of Buddhism to the United States. In the 1980s, she was a representative of American Buddhism in a Buddhist-Christian dialogue at the Naropa Institute in Boulder, Colorado. She was among the western Buddhist teachers who met with the Dalai Lama in 1993 to discuss the challenge of transmitting the dharma to the West. However, she is also among the American dharma teachers who have most directly addressed the combination of Jewish and Buddhist religious commitments and identities, which she explores in her book, *That's Funny, You Don't Look Buddhist: On Being a Faithful Jew and a Passionate Buddhist.*

Boorstein now thinks of herself as a devout Jew and Buddhist; she continues to teach Buddhist meditation and to practice psychotherapy. Over the course of the 1990s, she also became a well-known figure in the Jewish renewal movement. She served as a panelist with other noted Jewish spiritual leaders at the "Jew in the Lotus" conference in Philadelphia in 1995, which was an outgrowth of a meeting between Jewish leaders and the Dalai Lama in Dharamsala in 1990. She is on the Advisory Board of Chochmat HaLev, a San Francisco Bay area meditation and spirituality training center, and on the faculty at Elat Chayyim, a family-based Jewish education center in the Catskill Mountains of New York State.

Chogyam Trungpa,

a Kagyu lama and rinpoche, was among the first major wave of Tibetan teachers to work in the West. He was head of the Surmang monasteries in eastern Tibet until the age of twenty, when he fled his homeland. He then served at the Young Lamas Home in Dalhousie, India, but moved to England in 1963 to study comparative religion at Oxford University. In 1967, he relocated to Scotland where he founded Samye Ling, among the first Tibetan Buddhist practice centers in the West. Shortly thereafter, he gave up his monastic vows, married, and moved to the United States, where he emerged as one of the most brilliant and popular teachers working in and around the countercultural movements of the 1960s. The first center he established in the United States was Tail of the Tiger in Barnet, Vermont, now known as Karme Choling.

During the 1970s, Chogyam Trungpa relocated to Boulder, Colorado, where he founded Vajradhatu, an organization that served for a time as an umbrella organization for his many teaching activities. He also gained a reputation for his ability to present the essence of traditional Buddhist teachings in a way that addressed the needs and aspirations of western students. To this end, he developed a path of contemplative study and practice called Shambhala Training. During the 1980s, he continued to develop his unique teaching style, drawing inspiration from other forms of Buddhism, particularly Zen, and from the arts and psychotherapy. During these years, the organization he founded flourished, with some hundred city-based meditation centers, several rural retreats, and a Buddhist monastery on Cape Breton Island in Nova Scotia, which is now called Gampo Abbey. In 1986, he moved to Halifax, Nova Scotia, where he reestablished his headquarters. He died the following year and was cremated at Karme Choling in Vermont.

After a period of turmoil after his death, Trungpa's eldest son, Osel Rangdrol Mukpo, took over the leadership of the movement, which he reorganized into a cluster of organizations collectively called Shambhala International. These now include Gampo Abbey; several different teaching lineages; a range of centers in Canada, the United States, and Europe; Naropa Institute in Boulder, Colorado; and Rocky Mountain Shambhala Center, an international retreat center about two hours from Boulder. Under the direction of his son, now known as Sakyong Mipham Rinpoche, Chogyam Trungpa's unique combination of traditionalism and innovation continues as a major influence in the American Buddhist community.

Ruth Denison

is among the pioneers who introduced vipassana meditation into the United States. She was born in a village in eastern Germany and raised a Christian. As a child, she had a strong mystical streak; she recalls being influenced by the life of Theresa of Avila, a Catholic mystic, as a teen. Prior to World War II, Denison was an elementary school teacher. With the defeat of Germany and the ensuing chaos, she lost track of her family and was incarcerated for a time in a forced labor camp run by the Russian occupying forces. During this harrowing period, her religious beliefs remained a source of solace.

After her escape, she secured a teaching position in West Berlin and then immigrated to the United States, where she settled in Los Angeles, began to attend college, and in 1958 met her future husband. Before their marriage, he had been a monk in the Vedanta Society, a well-established Hindu group in the United States, and traveled in circles that included Alan Watts, the psychologist Fritz Perls, and others in what was then the spiritual avant-garde. Through them, Denison was introduced to Asian religions.

In 1960, she and her husband traveled to Asia to study meditation. They spent time in Zen monasteries in Japan, but eventually went to Burma where they practiced at a center of Mahasi Sayadaw, where Denison was first exposed to vipassana meditation. They then moved on to study for three months with U Ba Khin, who became Denison's teacher. Once back in Los Angeles, she took up Zen practice because at that time there were no vipassana teachers in America, but continued to return to Burma to study with U Ba Khin, who eventually gave her permission to teach. In the early 1970s, Denison began to lead retreats in Europe and the United States, developing vipassana-based techniques that incorporate various psychological approaches to meditation. In 1977, she purchased a cabin in the desert near Joshua Tree, California, which would grow into Dhamma Dena, an important vipassana retreat center, in the 1980s. Denison became a teacher at the Insight Meditation Society after its founding in Barre, Massachusetts in 1975. Throughout the 1990s, she was held in high esteem as one of America's most popular meditation teachers.

Joan Halifax

has followed a path over the last four decades that epitomizes the questing spirit of her generation. She was born in 1942 and raised a Christian. She went to college in New Orleans in the 1960s and became involved in the civil rights movement, then moved to New York where she worked with Alan Lomax, an anthropologist at Columbia University. Several years later, she traveled to Tibet and then Africa, eventually studying the African Dogon people. Upon her return, she married Stanislav Grof, a Czech psychiatrist, with whom she explored the use of LSD in therapy for people facing terminal cancer, eventually earning a Ph.D. in medical anthropology. After her marriage with Grof ended, Halifax worked with Joseph Campbell, the popular interpreter of mythology. She then began to study shamanism as practiced by the Huichol Indians in Mexico, while settling in southern California and co-founding the Ojai Foundation, an organization devoted to alternative forms of community and spirituality.

Halifax developed an early interest in Buddhism from reading the works of D. T. Suzuki and Alan Watts, but she formally took refuge only after being introduced to Seung Sahn, the head of the Kwan Um school of Zen. After studying with him for ten years, she received ordination in 1976. In the mid-1980s, she met Thich Nhat Hanh at Plum Village in southern France; she studied with him and was ordained as a teacher in the Tiep Hien order in 1990. In that year she founded the Upaya, a Buddhist center in Santa Fe, where she continues to teach today. Since 1994, Upaya has provided spiritual counseling to the terminally ill; by the end of the 1990s, Halifax was best known in the Buddhist community for her work on death and dying.

Halifax recently became interested in the kind of socially engaged Buddhism taught by Bernard Glassman, founder of the Zen Community of New York. In the late 1990s, when Glassman and his wife, Sandra Jishu Holmes, began the Zen Peacemaker Order, Halifax joined them as a Founding Teacher. She is now a priest and teacher in the Soto Zen tradition.

Upaya was renamed the Upaya Peace Institute and is now one of the teaching paths in the Zen Peacemaker Order. Halifax is the author of a number of books, including *The Human Encounter With Death*, which she wrote with Grof; *Shamanic Voices: A Survey of Visionary Narratives*; *Shaman: The Wounded Healer*; and *The Fruitful Darkness: Reconnecting With the Body of the Earth*.

Asayo Horibe

is a sansei, a third-generation Japanese American. She was born in the Rohwer Relocation Camp in McGehee, Arkansas, one of the camps where Japanese Americans were interned during World War II. She was raised in Michigan and then in the Chicago area, where her parents belonged to the Midwest Buddhist Temple, a Jodo Shinshu temple that is part of the Buddhist Churches of America. For fifty years, however, Horibe has been a member of the Buddhist Temple of Chicago (BTC), an independent institution founded in 1944 by Gyomay M. Kubose, a prominent area Buddhist, and others of Japanese descent. Kubose's goal was to use elements from Shin, Zen, and other Buddhist traditions to forge a nonsectarian approach to the dharma that would appeal to all Americans.

During her years at the BTC, Horibe has served as Sunday school teacher, youth group adviser, Board member, and Vice President of Public Relations. In 1989, she also became the first President of the Heartland Sangha in Evanston, Illinois where she now lives. The Heartland Sangha is affiliated with the American Buddhist Association, an umbrella group for a number of organizations devoted to disseminating the dharma in the nonsectarian spirit of Gyomay Kubose. In 1994, she co-chaired the Temple's fiftieth anniversary celebration. She continues to be active in Heartland Sangha today and serves as its secretary.

Horibe has been a member of the Buddhist Council of the Midwest, the largest intra-Buddhist group in the United States, since 1992. Members of the Council represent a wide range of Buddhist schools and national traditions from more than forty-five temples and dharma centers in Illinois, Indiana, Wisconsin, and Michigan. In 1997, she was elected to serve a two-year term as its president. In that capacity, she helps to mediate disputes and misunderstandings and to strengthen relations among different groups. She also works to educate the general public about Buddhism in an effort to correct popular misconceptions. Most recently, she and other Chicagoland Buddhists have been providing dharma-related information to the Illinois State

Chaplaincy, an agency that oversees religious ministries in state mental institutions, hospitals, and prisons.

Horibe is also active in the broader interfaith community, having organized symposia on social issues such as interracial and interfaith marriages. She continues to serve the Japanese community in the Japanese American Service Committee and the Japanese American Citizens' League and is involved in a number of Asian American programs and activities. She is the single mother of three girls and a grandmother of three, and has worked as a Registered Professional Nurse for more than thirty years.

Jon Kabat-Zinn

is a widely read advocate for the therapeutic value of Buddhist meditation in health maintenance and preventive medicine. He graduated from Haverford College with majors in chemistry and comparative literature, and later completed a Ph.D. in molecular biology at the Massachusetts Institute of Technology. During these years, he became involved in the movement to end the Vietnam War and helped found the Union of Concerned Scientists, an association of academics and professionals trying to raise consciousness about environmental issues and the arms race. He was exposed to Buddhism by reading Philip Kapleau's *The Three Pillars of Zen* and soon began to practice zazen. Within the next few years, he also explored various forms of Theravada meditation.

In 1976, Kabat-Zinn accepted a postdoctoral fellowship in anatomy at the University of Massachusetts Medical Center. As he moved between Buddhist practice and the world of medicine, he began to contemplate the clinical and medical potential of meditation to alleviate pain and stress-related disorders. In 1979, he and several colleagues established the Stress Reduction Clinic at the University Medical Center within its Division of Preventive and Behavioral Medicine. Since then, well over 7,000 people with chronic medical problems and pain conditions have participated in the clinic's eight-week training program in mindfulness meditation, which has become a model for others across the country. He and his colleagues also started similar community-based programs for low-income minorities in inner cities. In the mid-1990s, they established the Center for Mindfulness in Medicine, Health Care, and Society at the University of Massachusetts Medical Center to encourage the use of meditation in prisons, schools, corporations, factories, and other settings.

Kabat-Zinn continues to conduct research related to these issues, but has also become a popular public lecturer and workshop leader. He has appeared on the Oprah Winfrey Show and was featured in the 1993 PBS series *Healing and the Mind*, hosted by Bill Moyers. He has written a number of books, including *Full Catastrophe Living: Using the Wisdom of Your Body and Mind to Face Stress, Pain, and Illness* and *Wherever You Go, There You Are: Mindfulness Meditation in Everyday Life*. More recently, he published *Everyday Blessings: The Inner Work of Mindful Parenting*, written with his wife, Myla.

Karma Lekshe Tsomo (Patricia Jean Zenn)

has combined an academic career in Asian studies and a life as a fully ordained bhikkhuni in a way that has few parallels among European American Buddhists. Her scholarly work began with her B.A. in Oriental languages at the University of California in 1969. She later received two Master's degrees from the University of Hawaii, one in Buddhist philosophy, another in the study of Asian religions. In 1993, she began a Ph.D. program, also at the University of Hawaii, in the comparative study of Asian philosophy. Throughout these years, she often pursued her studies abroad, particularly at the Buddhist Institute of Dialectics and the Library of Tibetan Works and Archives, both in Dharamsala, India. She is fluent in Tibetan and Japanese and has studied Mandarin Chinese, German, Hindi, Pali, and Sanskrit in order to better pursue her studies.

Lekshe was born and raised in southern California, where she was exposed to Buddhism in the bohemian atmosphere of Malibu. She became more deeply involved, however, only while traveling in Asia in the 1960s. In 1977, she received novice ordination from the Sixteenth Gyalwa Karmapa, head of the Karma Kagyus, in France. Five years later, she was fully ordained as a bhikkhuni in Taiwan and Korea. She has since written widely on issues related to women monastics and the challenges involved in transplanting Asian monastic traditions to the West. In 1987, she helped to found Sakyadhita: International Association of Buddhist Women and has coordinated a series of international conferences devoted to issues of concern to Buddhist women. She has also worked to establish seven Buddhist educational programs for women in remote districts in the Indian Himalayas under the auspices of Jamyang Choling, a nonprofit, nonsectarian organization registered in California.

Karma Lekshe Tsomo's work with Sakyadhita and her writing are at the forefront of efforts by and for Buddhist women, where issues such as the status of women, the relations between laity and monastics, and the interaction between Asians and European Americans are under a great deal of discussion. Her major publications include *Sakyadhita: Daughters of the Buddha*, *Buddhism Through American Women's Eyes*, and *Sisters in Solitude: Two Traditions of Monastic Ethics for Women*.

Masao Kodani

is a sansei, a third-generation Japanese American, raised in the Jodo Shinshu tradition of the Buddhist Churches of America. He was born in Los Angeles in 1940 and spent his early childhood years in the internment camp at Poston, Arizona. After the war, he was raised first in East Los Angeles and then in Watts. He received his undergraduate education at the University of California at Santa Barbara, where he majored in east Asian studies. Upon completing his bachelor's degree, he contemplated graduate school on the East Coast, but at the instigation of a BCA priest he entered Ryukoku University in Kyoto, Japan instead, where he earned a degree in Buddhist studies.

During these years, Kodani decided to enter the BCA priesthood, and he graduated from Ryukoku prepared to start a career in the ministry back in the United States. After traveling throughout Asia for a year, he took a post as a junior minister at Senshin Buddhist temple in Los Angeles in 1968, where he has remained for thirty years. In 1978, he became Senshin's senior minister. He has been active in Los Angeles-area interreligious affairs, first in the Los Angeles Interreligious Council and more recently in the Buddhist Sangha Council of Southern California. He has also promoted taiko, a form of Japanese drumming, as an expression of Japanese American cultural identity. Taiko was originally performed during Bon Odori, a traditional BCA dance festival, but in the late 1960s, Senshin took the lead in developing a taiko group that performs year-round on many different occasions, an example soon followed by other area temples.

Like other leaders in the Buddhist Churches of America, Kodani is concerned about developing strategies to ensure the future of the community. He has long been an advocate for progressive change within an institution that has tended to emphasize traditionalism and sectarian orthodoxy. At Senshin temple, he has developed a form of ministry suited to the needs of a congregation spanning three or four generations, balancing the maintenance of Japanese linguistic and cultural traditions with a contemporary form of dharma-centered spirituality. Kodani sees the experience of Jodo Shinshu Buddhists in this country as valuable to other Buddhists who have only recently arrived. Newcomers now face many of the challenges the Buddhist Churches of America confronted in adapting the dharma over the course of several generations, but at a time when the pace of adaptation is highly accelerated.

John Daido Loori

is Abbot of Zen Mountain Monastery (ZMM), the founder and leader of the Mountains and Rivers Order (MRO), and the CEO of Dharma Communications. He began to practice Zen meditation in 1968, having served in the navy, worked in the natural products industry, and led arts organizations in New York State. From 1972 to 1976, he studied with Soen Nakagawa and then with Taizan Maezumi, founder of the Zen Center of Los Angeles. He received *denkai* (priestly transmission) from Maezumi in 1983 and *shiho* (dharma transmission) from him in 1986. In 1994, he received Dendokyoshi Certification, formal recognition by the Japanese Soto school of his status as a foreign-born Zen master and teacher. In 1997, Loori also received dharma transmission in the Harada-Yasutani and Inzan lineages of Rinzai Zen, making him one of three Western dharma-holders in both the Soto and Rinzai schools. Loori has transmitted the dharma to two students—Bonnie Myotai Treace Sensei in October 1996 and Geoffrey Shugen Arnold Sensei in July 1997.

In ZMM and the MRO, Loori has created institutions highly respected for their careful yet creative adaptation of Asian Buddhism to the American context. In ZMM, he trains and teaches monastics and several thousand lay students through a network of temples, practice centers, and sitting groups both in this country and in New Zealand. As CEO of Dharma Communications, he has established one of the leading vehicles for Buddhist education and outreach in the United States. He is the author of a dozen books related to Zen practice, including well-known titles such as *Still Point: A Beginner's Guide to Zen Meditation* and *The Eight Gates of Zen: Spiritual Training in an American Zen Monastery*. Dharma Communications also produces *Mountain Record*, a Buddhist quarterly, and Buddhist audio-visual materials.

The social services and arts are major elements of study and practice at ZMM. Community members engage in social work ranging from wilderness preservation to Buddhist prison missions. Loori continues to teach creative photography, based on the traditional Zen arts and aesthetics, at colleges and universities in week-long and month-long workshops. Over the past thirty years, he has exhibited his photography in more than thirty one-person shows and some fifty group shows both in the United States and overseas. His work has been published in *Aperture* and *Time-Life* magazines. Loori and Zen Mountain Monastery have been featured by leading media such as

ABC Nightly News and *Newsweek*, *Tricycle*, and *Utne Reader* magazines; and in publications and television productions in Russia, Japan, and Korea.

Hakuyu Taizan Maezumi

was a Zen roshi who, along with Shunryu Suzuki, played a key role in the emergence of the Soto tradition as one of the most importance forces in American Buddhism. He was born in Japan in 1931 and ordained as a Soto Zen monk at the age of eleven. He later received degrees in Oriental literature and philosophy from Komazawa University and studied at Sojiji, one of the two main Soto monasteries in Japan. He first received dharma transmission from Hakujun Kuroda in 1955 and later was approved to teach by Koryu Osaka, a lay Rinzai teacher, and Hakuun Yasutani, the founder of the Sanbo Kyodan, or Three Treasures Association, an independent lineage drawing upon both the Rinzai and Soto traditions. Maezumi was thus a dharma successor in three Zen lineages, which served his community well in developing practice styles suited to the United States.

Maezumi came to Los Angeles in 1956 to serve as a priest for the Japanese American community at Zenshuji Temple, the Soto headquarters in the United States. He soon began to teach zazen to Caucasians and other Americans, and in 1967 established the Zen Center of Los Angeles. At about this time, Maezumi married an American woman and began to raise a family. ZCLA eventually became the basis for a network of Soto teachers and practitioners that, with a similar network based at the San Francisco Zen Center, became prominent during the 1980s.

Maezumi established a number of temples in the United States and Europe that are formally registered with Soto Headquarters in Japan. In addition to ZCLA, these include the Zen Community of New York in Yonkers; Zen Mountain Monastery in Mount Tremper, New York; Kanzeon Zen Centers of Salt Lake City, Utah and Europe; and Zen Mountain Center in Mountain Center, California. Zen communities are located in Oregon, San Diego, and Mexico City, and there are more than fifty additional groups in Europe and the United States. Maezumi had twelve students who are seen as his successors. They formally incorporated in 1995 into the White Plum Sangha, a loose affiliation of teachers that can be likened to an extended dharma family. The Sangha now includes a second and third generation of teachers and the beginning of a fourth. It is estimated that Maezumi ordained 68 Zen priests and gave the lay Buddhist precepts to more than 500 people before his unexpected death in Tokyo in 1995.

Havanpola Ratanasara

was born in Sri Lanka and entered the monastic order at the age of eleven. He received a B.A. in Pali and Buddhist philosophy at the University of Ceylon. He later attended Columbia University in New York and the University of London, where he earned a Ph.D. in education. For a number of years, he was senior lecturer in the departments of Education and Buddhist Studies at the University of Keliniya in Sri Lanka, before being appointed delegate to the twelfth General Assembly of the United Nations in 1957. He immigrated to the United States in 1980 and helped to found Dharma Vijaya Buddhist Vihara, one of the first Theravada temples to be established in the Buddhist immigrant community in Los Angeles.

Ratanasara has helped found and served in a number of Buddhist and interreligious groups in the Los Angeles area. He cofounded and was vice president of the Interreligious Council of Southern California, an organization that pioneered interfaith dialogue in the region. He has served as president of the Buddhist Sangha Council of Southern California, an organization founded in 1980 that sponsors inter-Buddhist celebrations of Vesak and participates in a wide range of interreligious initiatives. Ratanasara later played a key role in the formation of the American Buddhist Congress, which is devoted to fostering inter-Buddhist understanding on a national scale.

Ratanasara has also been president of the College of Buddhist Studies in Los Angeles, which was instituted by the Sangha Council in 1983. It provides opportunities to study Buddhism from a nonsectarian point of view and promotes understanding among different schools and traditions. Ratanasara sees an important role for monastics in the future of American Buddhism, and he has worked with other ordained monks in Los Angeles to further the cause of full ordination for women. In addition to his work in this country, Ratanasara guides four temples in Sri Lanka and recently opened the International Institute of Buddhist Studies at a temple outside Colombo. He is the author of a number of books, most recently *The Path to Perfection: A Buddhist Psychological View of Personality, Growth and Development.*

Michael Roach

is a fully ordained monk in the Gelugpa lineage of Tibetan Buddhism. In 1995, he became the first American to complete the *geshe* degree, the Tibetan equivalent of a doctorate in Buddhist philosophy, after twenty-two years of study at Sera Mey Monastery in India and in the United States under Khen

Rinpoche Geshe Lobsang Tharchin of Howell, New Jersey. Roach is a scholar of Sanskrit, Tibetan, and Russian, and has translated and published numerous scholarly works. But he is also a leading popular teacher who gives classes, workshops, and lectures at Buddhist centers across the country. He has been teaching Buddhism to Americans since 1981.

For many years, following his graduation from Princeton University, Roach helped to run the New York operations of an international diamond purchasing firm, a difficult, high-stakes business but one that enabled him to support his various projects related to Tibetan Buddhism. He is now best known as the founder of the Asian Classics Institute, a public Buddhist meditation and education center under the direction of Lobsang Tharchin, in Greenwich Village; Diamond Abbey, a residential community for monks and nuns outside New York; and Godstow Retreat Center in Redding, Connecticut. Roach also plays an active, ongoing role in the restoration of Sera Mey Monastery, a Lhasa-based Gelugpa monastery relocated in south India in the wake of the Chinese occupation of Tibet. At this writing, Geshe Roach and his assistants were preparing for a three-year meditation retreat, scheduled to begin in March 2000.

Roach is highly regarded by scholars for his direction of the Asian Classics Input Project (ACIP). ACIP searches for copies of important and endangered Tibetan- and Sanskrit-language Buddhist manuscripts and inputs them onto computer for publication and distribution. Thus far, some 100,000 manuscript pages of sutras, commentaries, and monastic textbooks have been transcribed from woodblock prints and published in digital form both on the Internet and on CD-ROM. The work of transcription has been largely accomplished by the Sera Mey Computer Center and other input centers, located in monasteries and refugee communities in India, Mongolia, and Russia, where exiled monks, nuns, and laypeople learn new skills for supporting themselves while helping to save the great literary heritage of the Tibetan tradition.

Chia Theng (C. T.) Shen,

a retired shipping executive who lives in New York, is an influential lay Buddhist leader, scholar, and philanthropist. He was born in China in 1913 and received a B.S. in electrical engineering from the National Chiao Tung University in Shanghai in 1937. He began his career in the shipping industry in Shanghai, then moved to Hong Kong before emigrating to the United States in 1949. Once in America, he and his wife, Woo Ju, became deeply involved in the study and practice of Buddhism; over the course of several decades, they have made major contributions to the Chinese American and other Buddhist communities.

The Shens began their philanthropic activity in 1964 with the founding of the Buddhist Association of the United States in the Bronx, an organization that is now the largest Chinese Buddhist association in metropolitan New York. In 1970, they founded Bodhi House, an international gathering place for Buddhists from a wide range of traditions, on Long Island. They also donated land and support for Chuang Yen Monastery, a complex of temples, residences, and study centers north of New York City in Putnam County, which is among the largest Buddhist centers in this country. Their interest in ecumenical Buddhism led them to support the American work of the Sixteenth Gyalwa Karmapa, the head of the Karma Kagyu order. They donated land on which the Karmapa established the North American seat of the Karma Kagyus at Karma Triyana Dharmachakra Monastery in Woodstock, New York.

The Shens have also contributed a great deal to projects devoted to translating Buddhist texts into western languages. In 1968, they donated land in the San Francisco area to Hsuan Hua, the founder of the Dharma Realm Buddhist Association, to establish the Buddhist Text Translation Society. Three years later, they helped found the Institute for the Translation of the Chinese Tripitaka, the Chinese Buddhist canon, in Taiwan. They also established the Institute for Advanced Studies of World Religions, which is currently located on the grounds of the Chuang Yen monastery. C. T. Shen is himself considered an authority on the *Diamond Sutra* and has published studies and lectured on a number of other sutras important to the Mahayana tradition of east Asia. Most recently, he has been involved in one of a number of efforts to create a computer database of Buddhist scriptures in CD-ROM format.

Gary Snyder

is the most prominent Buddhist practitioner and poet to emerge from the Beat generation. He was born in San Francisco and raised in Washington State. He received his B.A. from Reed College, where he cultivated interests in Buddhism, haiku, and Chinese poetry. In 1952, he returned to San Francisco to study Asian languages at the University of California at Berkeley. In 1955, Snyder participated in the "Six Poets at the Gallery Six" poetry reading, a San Francisco event that brought East and West Coast poets together and helped to inaugurate the Beat movement. He was the inspiration for the character Japhy Ryder in Jack Kerouac's *The Dharma Bums*, a book that played a major role in popularizing the connection between Buddhism and the Beats. Snyder moved to Japan in 1956 to study and practice Zen at Daitokuji, a Rinzai monastery in Kyoto, where he remained for most of the 1960s. During these years, he published his first two books of poetry, *Riprap* and *Myths and Texts*.

Snyder returned to the United States in 1970 and settled in the foothills of the Sierra Nevada mountains in northern California with his wife and family. Since that time, his writing, both poetry and critical essays, has increasingly addressed ecological issues and has been widely influential in the environmental movement. In 1975, he was awarded the Pulitzer Prize for *Turtle Island*, a collection of poetry that reflects Buddhist, ecological, and Native American themes and sensibilities. Over the decades, he has published eighteen books that have been translated into more than twenty languages. In 1997, he received both the Bollingen Prize for Poetry and the John Hay Award for Nature Writing.

For his contribution to Buddhism in the United States, Snyder received the Buddhism Transmission Award from the Japan-based Bukkyo Dendo Kyokai Foundation (Buddhist Awareness Foundation) in 1998. The first American literary figure to receive the award, he was honored for his longstanding interest in relating Zen thought and practice to modern ideas about the natural world. His most recent major work is *Mountains and Rivers Without End*, inspired in part by Dogen's *Mountains and Rivers* sutra and by Chinese landscape painting. Since 1985, Snyder has taught at the University of California at Davis in the Creative Writing Program and in the Department of English. He founded "The Art of the Wild," an annual conference devoted to the wilderness and creative writing, and helped to establish the Nature and Culture Program, an undergraduate academic major devoted to social and environmental concerns at UC-Davis.

Virginia Straus

has combined her religious convictions and professional interests in her work in Soka Gakkai International. Born in 1948 in Walpole, Massachusetts, Straus was raised in the Episcopalian church, but by the time she went away to Smith College she considered herself an agnostic. At Smith and then later at Stanford University, her fundamental questions raised by Christianity were sharpened as she explored French existentialism and modern English literature, but she found satisfying answers only later, in Nichiren's Buddhist philosophy. Straus also began to develop a professional life devoted to social issues. She eventually moved to Washington, D.C., where she worked on public policy, first for Congressman John Anderson and later in the White House under Jimmy Carter. During this period, she learned a great deal about national, state, and local policy issues. At the end of the Carter administration, Straus moved to New York and took a position in the publishing industry.

At about this time, a friend introduced her to Nichiren Buddhism at a meeting in Greenwich Village, where she met performers and other artists chanting daimoku. Dubious at first, she was given a sutra book, began to chant at home, and soon felt her outlook on life begin to change. She explored Nichiren's philosophy and the writings of Daisaku Ikeda, and in 1983 received a gohonzon. From the start, Straus found the diversity of people practicing Nichiren Buddhism to be a source of inspiration; as she became more involved in the organization, it provided many opportunities for bonding with women from a wide range of backgrounds. Later in the 1980s, she traveled to Japan where she viewed first hand the controversies over the SGI movement. She came away from this experience more impressed with the leaders of the movement than with their critics.

Once back in this country, Straus relocated to Massachusetts and became involved in the movement's shakubuku campaigns and culture festivals. She renewed her commitment to working on social issues and helped to found the Pioneer Institute for Public Policy Research, an independent think tank addressing state and local policy questions. In 1993, when Daisaku Ikeda founded the Boston Research Center for the Twenty-first Century, a Soka Gakkai International affiliate organization devoted to peace, ecology, and other progressive social issues, Straus served as its first Executive Director. She now sees her work at the Center as a natural expression of a long-standing aspiration to unite philosophy and social action in her professional life.

Thanissaro Bhikkhu (Geoffrey DeGraff)

was first exposed to Buddhist meditation at Oberlin College, when he participated in a Winter Term project with a Thai monk and a Zen monk. After graduation in 1971, he won a two-year fellowship to teach in Chieng Mai, Thailand, and toward the end of that time he began studying meditation under Ajaan Fuang Jotiko, a member of the Thai Forest Tradition. During a brief return to the States, Thanissaro weighed the relative merits of academic and monastic life. While attending a panel on Buddhist studies, he realized that he aspired to more than the householder's path. He returned to Thailand for ordination in 1976 and studied with Ajaan Fuang until the latter's death in 1986.

In 1991, Ajaan Suwat Suvaco, another member of the Forest Tradition, invited him to help start Metta Forest Monastery, or Wat Metta, in a hilltop avocado grove in the mountains of northern San Diego County. Thanissaro was named its abbot in 1993. In 1995, he became the first westerner authorized to be a preceptor or teacher by the Dhammayut Order in Thailand. He currently serves on the governing board of the Dhammayut Order in the United States.

Thanissaro is also well known as a scholar and translator of Buddhist texts and teachings from both Pali and Thai. While with Ajaan Fuang, he translated the complete writings of Ajaan Lee Dhammadharo, Ajaan Fuang's teacher; in the years since, he has translated the writings of other members of the Forest Tradition, such as Ajaan Mun, Ajaan Maha Boowa, and Ajaan Thate. He has also translated the *Dhammapada* and an anthology of Pali sutras for the website "Access to Insight." He is the author of *The Buddhist Monastic Code*, *The Mind Like Fire Unbound*, *The Wings to Awakening*, and *Refuge*, and coauthor of the fourth edition of *The Buddhist Religion*. A regular teacher at the Barre Center for Buddhist Studies, Thanissaro was instrumental in setting up the center's Dhamma Dana Publication Fund, which is dedicated to the free distribution of Buddhist texts in the United States.

Thich Thien-An

is among the pioneering Asian teachers who brought Buddhism to this country in the 1960s. He was born in Hue, Vietnam in 1926 and grew up in a Buddhist family. He entered the monastery at the age of fourteen, where he continued his education. He eventually earned a Doctor of Literature degree from Waseda University in Japan, where he also received training in the Rinzai Zen tradition; he then returned to Vietnam. The escalation of the war had an immense impact on his life. His father, Tieu-Dieu, was among the monks who immolated themselves in order to draw the world's attention to the Vietnam War and helped precipitate the downfall of South Vietnam's Ngo Dinh Diem government.

Thien-An arrived in southern California in 1966 as an exchange professor at the University of California at Los Angeles, where his students en-

couraged him to teach Buddhist meditation in addition to his academic sub-
jects. Several years later, he applied for permanent residence and founded
the International Buddhist Meditation Center, a residential practice community in inner-city Los Angeles. For a number of years, Thien-An was devoted to teaching nonsectarian Buddhism to his American students, which
required the adaptation of Asian traditions to American values and mores.
Like many Asian teachers, he looked forward to the day when western Buddhism would help to revive the dharma in Asia.

When Saigon fell and the American troops were evacuated, Thien-An
was faced with a very different kind of responsibility. Over the next few
years, Vietnamese began to arrive in this country in increasing numbers,
often in dire straits after years as refugees. In response, Thien-An turned the
Center into a residence for refugees. His American monks and students joined
newly arrived Vietnamese monastics to provide badly needed religious and
social services. Thien-An soon established the first Vietnamese temple in this
country, Chua Vietnam, in an apartment building in central Los Angeles that
also served as a refugee residential facility. He was later appointed the first
Supreme Patriarch of Vietnamese Buddhism in America. Before his early
death from cancer in 1980, he established a considerable legacy that continues
in the work of the Center today and includes rigorous practice, higher education, social service, and the example of cooperative interaction among Buddhists from a variety of national backgrounds and traditions.

CHRONOLOGY

1844   Henry David Thoreau publishes an excerpt from the *Lotus Sutra* in the *Dial*, journal of the New England Transcendentalists, marking the inauguration of American romantics' fascination with Buddhism.

1853   The first Buddhist temple in San Francisco is founded by the Sze Yap Company, and housed on the top floor of the company's headquarters.

1875   Helena Petrovna Blavatsky and Henry Steel Olcott form the Theosophical Society in New York City, an organization that will be one of the most important links between India and the West for the next century.

1882   Congress passes the Chinese Exclusion Act, one of a number of pieces of legislation aimed at curtailing east Asian immigration.

1893   The World's Parliament of Religions, the largest interreligious forum in the nineteenth century, is held in Chicago, marking the formal arrival of leading Asian missionaries in the West.

1899   The Buddhist Mission to North America, the forerunner of the Buddhist Churches of America, is formally inaugurated with the arrival of the first permanent Jodo Shinshu missionaries.

1927   Zenshuji Soto Zen temple is founded in Los Angeles to serve the needs of Japanese Americans, but along with Sokoji temple, founded in San Francisco in the next decade, it will become an important base for convert Buddhists.

1931   Nyogen Senzaki and Sokei-an, two Rinzai Zen monks and col-

leagues of Shaku Soyen, begin teaching in Los Angeles and
New York City, respectively.

1932　Dwight Goddard publishes *The Buddhist Bible*, an anthology of
both Theravada and Mahayana material, which several decades later
introduces Jack Kerouac and others in the Beat generation to important Buddhist sutras.

1945　The Jodo Shinshu Buddhist Mission to North America reincorpo-
rates as the Buddhist Churches of America, a shift in identity pre-
cipitated by the devastating wartime experience of Japanese
Americans.

1950s　The Zen boom takes off, led by D. T. Suzuki, teaching at Columbia
University, and Alan Watts, among the most prominent popularizers
of Buddhism and other Asian religions.

1959　Alan Watts publishes *Beat Zen, Square Zen, and Zen*, which charts
ways Americans are beginning to embrace Buddhism on the eve of
the 1960s.
Robert and Anne Aitken cofound a Zen sitting group in Hawaii,
later known as the Diamond Sangha.

1960　Daisaku Ikeda, third president of Soka Gakkai, makes his first trip
to the United States to encourage the fledgling movement in this
country, which then primarily consisted of Japanese immigrants.

1962　Shunryu Suzuki and his students incorporate as the San Francisco
Zen Center.
Hsuan Hua arrives in San Francisco, where he will eventually found
the Dharma Realm Buddhist Association.

1964　Eido Shimano revitalizes the Zen Studies Society, an organization
originally founded to support the work of D. T. Suzuki.
The Buddhist Association of the United States establishes its headquarters in the Bronx in New York City.

1965　The Immigration and Nationality Act is passed, ending an older
quota system that effectively barred Asian immigration. Immigration from Buddhist countries soars.

1966　Philip Kapleau founds the Rochester Zen Center.
The Washington Buddhist Vihara, the first Theravada temple in the
United States, is founded in Washington, D.C.

1967　Taizan Maezumi and his students establish the Zen Center of
Los Angeles, among the pioneering Zen communities in this country.

1969　Shambhala Publications is formed as an outgrowth of a Berkeley,
California-based metaphysical bookstore.

1970   Tail of the Tiger (later Karme Choling) is founded by Chogyam
       Trungpa in Barnet, Vermont, as Tibetan Buddhism becomes an
       important element in countercultural Buddhism.

1972   Seung Sahn, a Korean monk and master teacher, arrives in the
       Providence, Rhode Island area, where he will later establish the
       Kwan Um School of Zen.

1973   The Dalai Lama makes his first trip to the West, setting a precedent
       for his later travels, which will be instrumental in publicizing the
       plight of the Tibetan people and popularizing Tibetan Buddhism in
       the West.

1974   Naropa Institute is founded in Boulder, Colorado; it will become
       the first fully accredited Buddhist-inspired liberal arts college in
       this country.

1975   The fall of Saigon triggers a massive Vietnamese migration to the
       United States over the next decade, leading to the establishment of
       many Vietnamese temples.
       The Insight Meditation Society is founded in Barre, Massachusetts.

1976   The City of Ten Thousand Buddhas is founded in Talmadge,
       California under the auspices of the Dharma Realm Buddhist
       Association.

1978   The Buddhist Peace Fellowship is founded to promote linking
       Buddhist contemplation to social action, a trend that will later be
       known as socially engaged Buddhism.

1979   The Cambodian Buddhist Society, the first of many temples founded
       by Cambodian refugees, is established in Silver Spring, Maryland.
       Jon Kabat-Zinn and his colleagues start the Stress Reduction Clinic
       at the Medical Center at the University of Massachusetts.

1980   Friends of the Western Buddhist Order establishes a community in
       New Hampshire, the first of a number across the country.
       The Buddhist Sangha Council of Southern California is formed in
       Los Angeles.

1983   Richard Baker resigns as abbot of San Francisco Zen Center, after
       which SFZC begins to experiment with new forms of elected com-
       munity leadership.

1985   Sandy Boucher publishes *Turning the Wheel: American Women
       Creating the New Buddhism.*
       Thich Nhat Hanh presents the Order of Interbeing to Americans
       during his tour of this country.

1987   Sakyadhita: The International Association of Buddhist Women is

founded in Bodhgaya, India, marking the increasing importance
of international networks among Buddhist women.
The Conference on World Buddhism in North America is held in
Ann Arbor, Michigan.

1988　Hsi Lai Temple, in the Taiwan-based Fo Kuang Buddhist movement, opens in Hacienda Heights, California, becoming the largest
Buddhist monastic complex in the western hemisphere.

1989　Tenzin Gyatso, the Fourteenth Dalai Lama, is awarded the Nobel
Peace Prize.

1990　American Jewish leaders travel to Dharamsala to discuss Judaism
and Buddhism with the Dalai Lama.

1991　Nichiren Shoshu and Soka Gakkai International formally separate.
Tricycle: The Buddhist Review, an independent journal of opinion in
the Buddhist community, begins publication.

1993　Western Buddhist teachers travel to Dharamsala to discuss teaching
the dharma in the West with the Dalai Lama.
The World's Parliament of Religions, a centennial celebration of
the first Parliament, is held in Chicago.

1995　Buddhist Peace Fellowship runs its first Buddhist Alliance for Social
Engagement, or BASE, program.
Zenkai Blanche Hartman joins Zoketsu Norman Fischer as co-abbot
of San Francisco Zen Center.

1996　Christian and Buddhist monastics and lay practitioners gather at the
Abbey of Gethsemani in Kentucky as a part of an ongoing
Buddhist-Christian dialogue movement.

1997　Theravada, Mahayana, and Vajrayana Buddhists from a range of
ethnic and national groups meet at Hsi Lai Temple to develop an
ecumenical platform for Buddhists.
Gay and lesbian activists meet with the Dalai Lama to discuss issues
related to Buddhist teachings and sexuality.

1999　The Buddhist Churches of America, the oldest institutional form
of Buddhism in the United States, celebrates its centennial.

NOTES

1. The American Buddhist Landscape

1. Field Notes, Senshin Buddhist Temple, Los Angeles, July 6, 1997.

2. Lawrence Shainberg, *Ambivalent Zen: A Memoir* (New York: Pantheon, 1995), 129–30.

3. Quoted in Jack Kornfield, *Living Dharma: Teachings of Twelve Buddhist Masters* (Boston: Shambhala, 1996), 61.

4. Martin Baumann, "The Dharma Has Come West: A Survey of Recent Studies and Sources," *Journal of Buddhist Ethics* [online] 4 (1997), http://jbe.la.psu.edu/ (11/6/98).

5. David Van Biema, "America's Fascination with Buddhism," *Time* (Oct. 13, 1997), 75.

4. The American Setting

1. Quoted in Rick Fields, *How the Swans Came to the Lake: A Narrative History of Buddhism in America*, 3rd rev. ed. (Boston: Shambhala, 1992), 194.

2. Quoted in ibid., 184–85.

3. *Time* (Feb. 4 , 1954), 65–66.

4. *Time* (July 21, 1958), 49.

5. Quoted in Carole Tonkinson, ed., *Big Sky Mind: Buddhism and the Beat Generation* (New York: Riverhead, 1995), 31.

6. Ibid., 178–79.

7. Rick Fields, "Results from the Tricycle Poll: Help or Hindrance, A High History of Buddhism," *Tricycle: The Buddhist Review* (Fall 1996):44–58.

5. Jodo Shinshu: America's Old-Line Buddhists

1. Quoted in Nyogen Senzaki, *Like a Dream, Like a Fantasy: The Zen Writings*

and Translations of Nyogen Senzaki, ed. Eido Shimano (Tokyo and New York: Japan Publications, 1978), 22–23.

2. "A Shin Buddhist Stance on School Prayer" (San Francisco: Buddhist Churches of America, n.d.).

3. Quoted in Tetsuden Kashima, *Buddhism in America: The Social Organization of an Ethnic Religious Institution* (Westport, Conn.: Greenwood, 1977), 122–23.

4. Evelyn Yoshimura, "The Point of Being Buddhist, Christian or Whatever in America," *Rafu Shimpo*, May 12, 1995. See also at *Hou—u: Dharma Rain* [online] 1:1 (Jan. 1997), http://www.geocities.com/Athens/5443/dr11_pnt.htm (11/1/98).

5. Originally published in full in *Prajna: Light of Compassion* 41 (4) (April 1995). Quoted at Rev. Masao Kodani, "The History of the Buddhist Churches of America: Problems of Propagation and Projections for the Future," *Hou—u: Dharma Rain* [online] 1:1 (Jan. 1997), http://www.geocities.com/Athens/5443/dr11_hst.htm (11/1/98).

6. Quoted in Kenneth K. Tanaka, *Ocean: An Introduction to Jodo Shinshu Buddhism in America* (Berkeley: Wisdom Ocean Publications, 1997), 73.

7. Masao Kodani, "Horafuki (Blowing One's Own Horn)," (Jan. 1984) in Masao Kodani, *Dharma Chatter* (n.p., n.d. Senshin Buddhist Temple Commemorative volume).

8. Masao Kodani, "Positive Self-Image and All of That" (July 1991) in Masao Kodani, *Dharma Chatter* (n.p., n.d. Senshin Buddhist Temple Commemorative volume).

9. Quoted on *Becoming the Buddha in L.A.* (video). WGBH Educational Foundation, 1998.

6. Soka Gakkai and Its Nichiren Humanism

1. Quoted in Dayle M. Bethel, *Makaguchi the Value Creator: Revolutionary Japanese Educator and Founder of Soka Gakkai* (New York: Weatherhill, 1973; pbk. ed., 1994), 105.

2. Ibid.

3. Quoted in Jane D. Hurst, *Nichiren Shoshu Buddhism and the Soka Gakkai in America: The Ethos of a New Religious Movement* (New York: Garland, 1992), 140–41.

4. For statistics on membership and ethnic breakdown, see ibid., 141, 143.

5. Craig Bratcher, "One of My Experiences, Part I, Tozan: 4–4–97–4–11–97" [online], http://www.cebunet.com/nst/cb.html (11/1/98).

6. Telephone interview with Linda Johnson, May 3, 1998.

7. Zen and Its Flagship Institutions

1. "On Transmission and Teaching: Excerpt from a Question and Answer Session with Toni Packer at the Buddhism in America Conference, Boston, January, 1997," edited and expanded for the Springwater Center newsletter by Toni Packer [online], http://www.servtech.com/spwtrctr/bostonQA.html (10/6/98).

2. Quoted in Helen Tworkov, *Zen in America: Five Teachers and the Search for an American Buddhism* (New York: Kodansha International, 1989), 41.

3. Quoted in Louis Nordstrom, ed., *Namu Dai Bosa: A Transmission of Zen Buddhism to America* (New York: The Zen Studies Society, 1976), 214.

4. Quoted in Tworkov, *Zen in America*, 217.

5. Erik Fraser Storlie, *Nothing on My Mind: Berkeley, LSD, Two Zen Masters, and a Life on the Dharma Trail* (Boston: Shambhala, 1996), 67–69.

6. Quoted in Tworkov, *Zen in America*, 231.

7. "Buddhism at Millennium's Edge" [online], http://bodhi.zendo.com/sfzc/Pages/millennium/index.html (10/6/98).

8. Dennis Genpo Merzel Roshi, "A Message From the President of White Plum Sangha" [online], http://www.neis.net/kanzeon/Plum.html (1/12/98).

9. Telephone conversation with John Daido Loori Roshi, September 17, 1998.

10. Quoted on *Mountain Seat Ceremony: Abbot Installation of Reverend John Daido Loori, October 14, 1989, Zen Mountain Monastery, Mount Tremper, New York* (video). Zen Mountain Monastery, Dharma Communications, 1989.

11. Quoted at "Peacemaker Community" [online], http://www.zpo.org/peace_community.htm (10/6/98).

8. The Tibetan Milieu

1. Quoted in "Beastie Boys: The Big Show, On the Road with Adam Yauch," *Tricycle: The Buddhist Review* (Winter 1994):89.

2. Will Blythe, "Mr. Popular," *Outside Magazine* (Nov. 1997) [online], http://outside.starwave.com/magazine/1197/9711pop.html (11/4/98).

3. "Statement by H.H. Penor Rinpoche Regarding the Recognition of Steven Seagal as a Reincarnation of the Treasure Revealer Chungdrag Dorje of Palyul Monastery" [online], http://www.palyul.org/statement.html (11/4/98).

4. William Ellison, "From the Himalaya to Hollywood: The Legacy of *Lost Horizon*," *Tricycle: The Buddhist Review* (Winter 1997):62.

5. Kennedy Fraser, "A Private Eye; Buddhism's Flowering in America: An Inside View," *New York Times* (Nov. 3, 1997).

6. Phone conversation with Larry Gerstein, November 14, 1997.

7. Quoted at Erik Davis, "Digital Dharma," *Wired* (Aug. 20, 1997) [online], http://www.wired.com/wired/2.08/departments/electrosphere/dharma.html (1/8/98).

8. Layne Russell, "Kalu: Kalu Rinpoche arrives in Vancouver, 1972," [online], http://www.sonic.net/layne/kalu.html (9/10/98).

9. "Medicine Buddha Sadhana by Thubten Gyatso," [online], http://www.ism.net/osel/meditate/medicine.html (11/4/98).

10. Joshua Glenn, "The Nitty-Gritty of Nirvana: An Interview with Robert Thurman," *Utne Online* (1997), http://www.utne.com/lens/bms/12bmsthurman.html (9/10/98).

11. Robert Thurman, *Inner Revolution: Life, Liberty, and the Pursuit of Real Happiness* (New York: Riverhead, 1998), 286.

12. Ibid., 287–88.

9. The Theravada Spectrum

1. Walpola Piyananda, "The Difficulties of a Monk." *On Common Ground: World Religion in America*, Diana L. Eck and The Harvard Pluralism Project (CD-ROM) (New York: Columbia University Press, 1997).

2. Letter from Robert W. Fodde, Investigative and Protective Service, Florissant, Missouri to Phravisuddi Sombodhi, Wat Vajiradhammapadip, Mount Vernon, New York, October 23, 1990. Copy in possession of the author.

3. *Blue Collar and Buddha*, produced by Taggart Siegel. (Filmmakers Library, 1989). 57 minutes.

4. "Nine Loving Memory," Wat Promkunaram, Phoenix, Ariz. (Temple brochure, 1993), n.p.

5. Eric Kaplan, "Arizona Killing Fields: Monks from the East Meet Death in the West," *Tricycle: The Buddhist Review* (Spring 1992):46–50.

6. "Bowing To Life Deeply : An Interview with Ruth" *Insight Magazine Online* (Spring 1997), http://www.dharma.org/insight/ruth.htm (8/16/98).

7. Jack Kornfield, "American Buddhism." In Don Morreale, ed., *The Complete Guide to Buddhist America* (Boston: Shambhala, 1998), xxix.

8. Ibid., xxix–xxx.

9. Don Morreale, "Everything Has Changed in Buddhist America." In *The Complete Guide to Buddhist America*, xvi–xvii.

10. "Empty Phenomena Rolling On: An Interview with Joseph Goldstein," *Tricycle: The Buddhist Review* (Winter 1993):13–18.

11. Paul David Numrich, *Old Wisdom in the New World: Americanization in Two Immigrant Theravada Buddhist Temples* (Knoxville: University of Tennessee Press, 1996), 63–74.

12. "Going Upstream: An Interview with Bhante Henepola Gunaratana," *Tricycle: The Buddhist Review* (Spring 1995):38.

13. Thanissaro Bhikkhu, "The Economy of Gifts: An American Monk Looks at Traditional Buddhist Economy," *Tricycle: The Buddhist Review* (Winter 1996):58.

14. Letter from Thanissaro Bhikkhu to the author, August 19, 1998.

10. Other Pacific Rim Migrations

1. Rone Tempest, "Furor Over Donations to Democrats Bewilders Asian Contributors," *Los Angeles Times*, Oct. 28, 1996.

2. C. T. Shen, "Mayflower II: On the Buddhist Voyage to Liberation" (New York: Institute for Advanced Studies of World Religions, 1983), iv–vi.

3. Katherine Kim, "From Elation to Shame: Korean Americans Riding an Emotional Roller Coaster," *Jinn: The Online Magazine of the Pacific News Service*

(Dec. 30, 1997), http://www.pacificnews.org/jinn/stories/3.26/971230-kore-ans.html (10/6/98).

4. All quoted material from Samu Sunim is found in *World Buddhism in North America: A Documentary*, produced by the Zen Lotus Society, Ann Arbor, Michigan, 1989.

5. Seung Sahn, "Roots of American Buddhism." *Primary Point* 1:4 (Fall 1984) [online], http://www.kwanumzen.com/primarypoint/v01n4–1984-fall-DSSN-RootsOfAmericanBuddhism.html (10/6/98).

6. Seung Sahn, "Wearing a Kasa, Carrying the World: Uncovering the Mystery of Form." *Primary Point* 6:2 (Oct. 1989) [online], http://www.kwanumzen.com/primarypoint/v06n2–1989-fall-DSSN-WearingAKasaCarryingTheWorld.html (10/6/98).

7. Andrew Lam, "Vietnam After Normalization: Vietnamese in America Bid Farewell to Exile Identity," *Jinn: The Online Magazine of the Pacific News Service* (July 11, 1995), http://www.pacificnews.org/jinn/stories/columns/pacific-pulse/950711-normal.html (10/6/98).

8. Quoted in Andrew Lam, "A Vietnamese Temple On The Edge Of Cyber-Space." *Jinn: The Online Magazine of the Pacific News Service* (Feb. 9, 1996), http://www.pacificnews.org/jinn/stories/2.03/960209-temple.html (3/16/98).

9. Quoted in Bert Elger, "Big Plans for Little Saigon." *Asian Week* (May 17–23, 1996) [online], http://www.asianweek.com/051796/LittleSaigon.html (9/10/98).

10. Ibid.

11. Quoted in Jeffrey Brody, "Homage to a Buddha, Temple, Garden Grove Comes to Terms," *Orange County Register*, Jan. 15, 1990.

12. Lynn Smith, "Prayer to Buddha: Faithful Celebrate Families, Values," *Los Angeles Times*, Orange County Edition (Aug. 26, 1991).

13. Quoted in Nam Nguyen, as told to Andrew Lam, "In Their Own Words—Viet Magazine's Nam Nguyen." *Jinn: The Online Magazine of the Pacific News Service* (Jan. 2, 1997), http://www.pacificnews.org/jinn/stories/3.22/971028-viet.html (10/6/98).

14. Quoted in Sallie B. King, "Thich Nhat Hanh and the Unified Buddhist Church," in Christopher S. Queen and Sallie B. King, eds., *Engaged Buddhism: Buddhist Liberation Movements in Asia* (Albany: State University of New York Press, 1996), 338–39.

11. Gender Equity

1. Kathy Butler, "Encountering the Shadow in Buddhist America," *Common Ground* (May/June 1990):16.

2. Ibid., 16–17.

3. "Authority and Exploitation: Three Voices," *Tricycle: The Buddhist Review* (Fall 1991):67.

4. Ibid., 68–69.

5. Helen Tworkov, "Zen in the Balance: Can It Survive America?" *Tricycle: The Buddhist Review* (Spring 1994):52.

6. Yvonne Rand, "Abortion: A Respectful Meeting Ground." Quoted in Karma Lekshe Tsomo, ed., *Buddhism Through American Women's Eyes* (Ithaca: Snow Lion, 1995), 89.

7. bell hooks, "Waking Up to Racism," *Tricycle: The Buddhist Review* (Fall 1994):44.

8. Joan Halifax, *The Fruitful Darkness: Reconnecting with the Body of the Earth* (San Francisco: HarperSanFrancisco, 1993), 139–40.

9. "Minutes of Meeting Between His Holiness the Dalai Lama and Gay and Lesbian Leaders, San Francisco, June 11, 1997," Maitre Dorje Gay and Lesbian Buddhist Society [online], http://www.geocities.com/WestHollywood/9033/minutesf.html (9/10/98).

10. Don Lattin, "Dalai Lama Speaks on Gay Sex," *San Francisco Chronicle* (June 11, 1997).

11. "The Dalai Lama Meets with Lesbian and Gay Leaders." Press release (June 11, 1997), International Gay and Lesbian Human Rights Commission [online], http://www.iglhrc.org/press/pr_970611.html (10/9/98).

12. Steve Peskind, " 'According to Buddhist Tradition': Gays, Lesbians, and the Definition of Sexual Misconduct." *Shambhala Sun* (March 1998) [online], http://www.shambhalasun.com/PESKIND.htm (3/14/99)

13. Thubten Chodron, "You're Becoming a What? Living as a Western Buddhist Nun." In Marianne Dresser, ed., *Buddhist Women on the Edge: Contemporary Perspectives from the Dharma Frontier* (Berkeley: North Atlantic, 1996), 226–27.

14. Yifa, "The Women's Sangha in Taiwan." Quoted in Donald W. Mitchell and James Wiseman, eds., *The Gethsemani Encounter: A Dialogue on the Spiritual Life by Buddhist and Christian Monastics* (New York: Continuum, 1998).

12. Socially Engaged Buddhism

1. Thich Nhat Hanh, *Being Peace*, ed. Arnold Kotler (Berkeley: Parallax, 1987), 9.

2. Ibid., 85–87.

3. Thich Nhat Hanh, *Interbeing: Fourteen Guidelines for Engaged Buddhism*, rev. ed. (Berkeley: Parallax, 1993), 57.

4. Ibid., 58–59.

5. Nhat Hanh, *Being Peace*, 56.

6. Quoted in Susan Davis, "Working with Compassion: The Evolution of the Buddhist Peace Fellowship," *Tricycle: The Buddhist Review* (Spring 1993):59.

7. Gary Snyder, "Buddhism and the Coming Revolution," Quoted in Carole Tonkinson, ed., *Big Sky Mind: Buddhism and the Beat Generation* (New York: Riverhead, 1995), 178–79.

8. Diana Winston, "Making a Dent?" Excerpted from *Turning Wheel* (Winter

1996) and quoted at "Immediate Family, Extended Family, Expanded Family by members of BPF's BASE Program" [online], http://www.igc.org/bpf/baseart.html (10/11/98).

9. Donald Rothberg, "I Experienced the BASE Program as Temporary Family." Excerpted from *Turning Wheel* (Winter 1996) and quoted at "Immediate Family, Extended Family, Expanded Family by members of BPF's BASE Program" [online], http://www.igc.org/bpf/baseart.html (10/11/98).

10. Quoted at "Buddhist Peace Fellowship" [online], http://www.igc.org/bpf/index.html (10/11/98).

11. Alan Senauke, "History of the Buddhist Peace Fellowship: the Work of Engaged Buddhism" [online], http://www.igc.org/bpf/engaged.html (10/11/98).

12. Alan Hunt Badiner, *Dharma Gaia: A Harvest of Essays in Buddhism and Ecology* (Berkeley: Parallax, 1990), xvii.

13. Ibid., xiv–xv.

14. Ibid., xvii–xviii.

15. Joanna Macy, "The Greening of the Self." In Arnold Kotler, ed., *Engaged Buddhist Reader: Ten Years of Engaged Buddhist Publishing* (Berkeley: Parallax, 1996), 173–74.

16. Ibid., 180.

17. Jon Kabat-Zinn, "Toward the Mainstreaming of American Dharma Practice: A Case Study." *Buddhism in America: A Landmark Conference on the Future of Buddhist Meditative Practices in the West*, January 17–19, 1997, Boston, Mass. (audio recording) (Boulder, Colo.: Sounds True Recordings, 1997).

13. Intra-Buddhist and Interreligious Dialogue

1. Buddhist Sangha Council of Southern California Buddhists and the American Buddhist Congress, "Buddhist Inter-traditions: Consensus on Commitment and Practice." Hsi Lai Temple, Hacienda Heights, Calif. (Mar. 15, 1997), 2.

2. Ibid., 11–12.

3. Jack Kornfield, "American Buddhism." In Don Morreale, ed. *The Complete Guide to Buddhist America* (Boston: Shambhala, 1998), xxii.

4. Ibid., xviii, 323–79.

5. Stephen Batchelor, "The Future is in Our Hands," Dzogchen Foundation [online], http://www.dzogchen.org/wbtc/sbatchelor.html (5/8/98).

6. Surya Das, "Inquire, Find Out & Speak Out," Dzogchen Foundation [online], http://www.dzogchen.org/wbtc/speakout.html (5/8/98).

7. Batchelor, "The Future is in Our Hands" (5/8/98).

8. Surya Das, "Inquire, Find Out & Speak Out," Dzogchen Foundation [online], http://www.dzogchen.org/wbtc/speakout.html (10/14/98)

9. Stephen Batchelor, "The Future is in Our Hands," Dzogchen Foundation [online], http://www.dzogchen.org/wbtc/sbatchelor.html (10/14/98).

10. "Open Letter to the Buddhist Community," Dzogchen Foundation [online], http://www.dzogchen.org/wbtc/openletter.html (10/14/98).

11. Leo D. Lefebure, review of *Living Buddha, Living Christ* by Thich Nhat Hanh. *Christian Century* 113 (Oct. 16, 1996): 964.

12. Quoted in Michael Mott, *The Seven Mountains of Thomas Merton* (Boston: Houghton Mifflin, 1984), 544.

13. Quoted in Donald W. Mitchell and James A. Wiseman, eds., *The Gethsemani Encounter: A Dialogue on the Spiritual Life by Buddhist and Christian Monastics* (New York: Continuum, 1998), xii.

14. "Interview: Envisioning the Future With Ruben Habito," Maria Kannon Zen Center [online], http://www.mkzc.org/intervie.html (11/8/98).

15. Robert E. Kennedy, *Zen Spirit, Christian Spirit: The Place of Zen in Christian Life* (New York: Continuum, 1996), 13–14.

16. Rodger Kamenetz, *The Jew in the Lotus: A Poet's Rediscovery of Jewish Identity in Buddhist India* (San Francisco: HarperSanFrancisco, 1994), 228–29.

17. Ibid., 231.

18. Rodger Kamenetz, *Stalking Elijah: Adventures With Today's Jewish Mystical Masters* (San Francisco: HarperSanFrancisco, 1997), 327–29.

19. "A Complete Seder For Tibet Haggadah," International Campaign for Tibet (online), http://www.savetibet.org/action/seder/hagg.htm (11/8/98).

20. Sylvia Boorstein, *That's Funny, You Don't Look Buddhist: On Being a Faithful Jew and a Passionate Buddhist* (San Francisco: HarperSanFrancisco, 1996), 3.

21. Ibid., 5.

22. Ibid., 58–59.

14. Making Some Sense of Americanization

1. Stephen Batchelor, *Buddhism Without Beliefs: A Contemporary Guide to Awakening* (New York: Riverhead, 1997), 15.

2. Helen Tworkov, "Buddhist Voices: Two Buddhisms." In *On Common Ground: World Religion in America*, Diana L. Eck and The Harvard Pluralism Project (CD-ROM) (New York: Columbia University Press, 1997).

3. Paul David Numrich, *Old Wisdom in the New World: Americanization in Two Immigrant Theravada Buddhist Temples* (Knoxville: University of Tennessee Press, 1996), 100, 105.

4. Don Morreale, "Everthing Has Changed in Buddhist America." In Don Morreale, ed., *The Complete Guide to Buddhist America*, edited by Don Morreale (Boston: Shambhala, 1998), xv.

5. Helen Tworkov, "Zen in the Balance: Can It Survive America?" *Tricycle: The Buddhist Review* (Spring 1994):56.

6. John Daido Loori, "Clouds and Water: The Monastic Imperative," *Tricycle: The Buddhist Review* (Winter 1995):70.

7. Ane Pema Chodron, "No Place to Hide: A Talk by the Director of Gampo Abbey," *Tricycle: The Buddhist Review* (Winter 1995):43–45.

8. Thanissaro Bhikkhu, "Survival Tactics for the Mind," *Tricycle: The Buddhist Review* (Winter 1998):66.

GLOSSARY

abhisheka "empowerment." An initiatory process in which a lama introduces students to a particular cycle of teachings and empowers them to practice those teachings.

Amida (var. **Amitabha**) A great cosmic Buddha of particular importance in the Pure Land traditions of east Asia.

ango "dwelling in peace." A three-month-long period of intensive practice in the Zen tradition.

arhat (var. **arahat**) "worthy one." In the Theravada tradition, one who is certain of attaining nirvana in this life.

bhikkhu (var. **bhikshu**) Fully ordained monk.

bhikkhuni (var. **bhikshuni**) Fully ordained nun.

bodhisattva "wisdom body." In the Mahayana tradition, one dedicated to cultivating wisdom and compassion with the goal of liberating all beings.

bodhi puja Ritual expressing respect and veneration for the bodhi tree under which the Buddha gained enlightenment.

Buddha puja Ritual expressing respect and veneration for the Buddha in Theravada temples.

bujizen Self-styled Zen practice.

Ch'an "dhyana." State of deep mental absorption in the Chinese tradition, used to denote a major tradition of Mahayana Buddhism.

cyber-sangha Virtual community sustained by websites, Buddhist list servers, and dharma chat groups.

dai-gohonzon A camphor wood, mandalalike object of worship inscribed by Nichiren and housed in the Nichiren Shoshu temple at Taiseki-ji.

daimoku The chant "*Nam-Myoho-Renge-Kyo*," which literally means "hail to the wonderful dharma *Lotus Sutra*" and is of central importance in Nichiren Buddhism.

deva puja Ritual expressing respect and veneration for a range of animistic deities in Theravada temples.

dharma (var. **dhamma**) Natural law or doctrine, often used to refer to Buddhism or the path taught by the Buddha.

dharma-vinaya "the law and the discipline." The term the Buddha used to denote the path he discovered under the bodhi tree.

dhyana State of deep mental absorption, used to denote the quality of consciousness cultivated through meditation.

dokusan "going alone to a high place." A private meeting or interview between a Zen teacher and a student.

dukkha Suffering, dissatisfaction, stress, or more colloquially "being out of joint," the First Noble Truth.

Dzogchen "the great perfection." A meditation considered the highest form of practice in the Nyingma tradition of Tibet.

gathas Hymnlike, often poetic Buddhist prayers chanted in both convert dharma halls and immigrant temples.

gohonzon A scroll that is a key element in Nichiren Buddhist practice, a conse-crated replica of one originally inscribed by Nichiren (see **dai-gohonzon**).

gongyo "assiduous practice." The recitation of selected passages from the *Lotus Sutra* in Nichiren Buddhism.

gosho The letters of Nichiren, an important element of Nichiren scripture.

Hinayana "little vehicle." Refers to the oldest schools of Buddhism to emerge in ancient India.

jiriki "one's own efforts." In the Japanese tradition, contrasted with *tariki* or "other power" as one of the means by which one strives for enlightenment.

jukai "receiving or granting the precepts." A formal rite of passage that marks entrance into some Buddhist communities.

kaidan "ordination platform." Where a Buddhist formally takes the precepts; used to refer to the high sanctuary in Nichiren Buddhism.

karma "act," "action." Refers to mental or physical actions and their consequences.

Kathin A major festival in Theravada during which the laity replenish the monas-tic community's stores by making gifts to the sangha.

kensho A breakthrough insight into the nature of Buddha mind in the Zen tradi-tion, particularly associated with the teaching style of Hakuun Yasutani.

khenpo Abbot of a monastery in the Tibetan tradition.

kinhin A form of walking meditation practiced in Zen centers and monasteries between periods of zazen.

koan A story about or remarks made by earlier roshis, used to instruct Zen students in the dharma.

kosen-rufu The establishment of true Buddhism, peace, and harmony throughout the world as understood in Nichiren Buddhism.

lama "teacher" in the Tibetan tradition.

Mahamudra "the great seal." A meditation considered the highest form of practice in the Kagyu tradition of Tibet.

Mahayana "great vehicle." The broad tradition that emerged out of the older Hinayana schools of India, stressing not only individual liberation but also a commitment to help others gain freedom from suffering (see **bodhisattva**).

mantra Chanted syllable or phrase.

mandala Symbolic representation of the forces of the universe in graphic form.

mudra Ritual gesture used to express the qualities of a particular bodhisattva or buddha.

Nembutsu The phrase *Namo Amida Butsu* (var. *Namu Amida Butsu*), or "Name of Amida Buddha," a chant of particular importance in Pure Land Buddhism. Japanese pronunciation of the Chinese term **nien-fo**.

ngondro "something that precedes." Practice used to clear away negativity in preparation for Vajrayana practice.

nien-fo In the Chinese tradition, the devotional recitation of the names and attributes of the buddhas and bodhisattvas, especially Amitabha.

nirvana (var. **nibbana**) "unbinding." The liberation taught by the Buddha— freedom from attachments and illusions.

oryoki "that which contains just enough." Refers to bowls used during meals in some Zen monasteries and training centers.

panca sila The five basic precepts: to refrain from killing, stealing, engaging in sexual misconduct, lying, and taking intoxicants.

pophoe Religious service in the Korean tradition, consisting of scripture reading, ceremonies, chanting, and a sermon.

Pure Land A broad tradition in Mahayana that emphasizes the transcendental abode or pure land of Amida.

rimed A nonsectarian, ecumenical movement that arose in Tibet in the nineteenth century and has had major influence on the transmission of the Tibetan dharma to the West.

rinpoche "precious one." Honorific used to refer to a Tibetan teacher who has completed a long course of study.

Rinzai School of Japanese Zen typically associated with an emphasis on the use of koans.

roshi "old or venerable master." A title conferred upon a person in the Zen tradition who has realized the dharma.

sadhana "means of accomplishing." A basic Vajrayana meditative practice based on visualizations.

Shakyamuni "sage of the Shakya clan." One of the names of the Buddha Gautama.

samu Work service or work practice in a Zen center or monastery.

sangha The Buddhist community, understood in a variety of ways in different schools and traditions.

sangha dana See **sanghika dana**.

sanghika dana "offering or gift to the sangha." A basic element of lay practice in Theravada temples in which meals are prepared or gifts given to support the monastic community.

sensei Teacher, one who has undergone sufficient training to teach Zen in a serious fashion.

sesshin "collecting the heart-mind." A period of three or seven days of intense meditation and practice in the Zen tradition.

shakubuku Form of proselytizing, preaching, and teaching, associated with Nichiren Buddhism.

shamatha-vipashyana See **shamatha**.

shamatha Tranquility meditation, a basic form of sitting meditation in the Tibetan tradition.

shikantaza "just sitting." A method of meditation associated with Soto Zen, in which the mind is to rest in a state of brightly alert attention.

shinjin In the Jodo Shinshu tradition, refers to a spiritual transformation that involves understanding, insight, and awareness, sometimes translated as "faith."

shunyata "empty" or "void." The illusory quality of all phenomena, of particular importance in the Mahayana tradition.

soka "value creation." A pedagogical theory key to the Nichiren Buddhism of Soka Gakkai International.

son "dhyana," or state of deep mental absorption in the Korean tradition, used to denote a major school of Mahayana Buddhism.

Soto School of Japanese Zen typically associated with an emphasis on sitting meditation.

stupa A Buddhist reliquary mound; often a pilgrimage site.

sunim Korean term for monk.

tanha "craving." The Second Noble Truth.

tariki "other power." In the Japanese tradition, contrasted with *jiriki* or "one's own efforts" and used to refer to the conviction of Pure Land Buddhists that realization comes from the power and grace of Amida.

Tathagatha "truly gone." One of the names of the Buddha.

terma In the Tibetan tradition, a form of teachings thought to be hidden centuries ago by the great sage Padmasambhava, only to be revealed at a later date.

terton In the Tibetan tradition, one who recovers terma or hidden teachings.

Theravada "the way of the elders." The most traditional and orthodox of the three vehicles.

Three Great Secret Laws Key doctrine in the Nichiren Shoshu tradition: the gohonzon (scroll), the kaidan (sanctuary), and the daimoku (chant).

tokudo "attainment of going beyond." Often translated as "monk's or monastic ordination."

tozan Pilgrimage to Taiseki-ji, the temple complex that is the headquarters for Nichiren Shoshu Temple.

Triratna The Triple Gem or Jewel; the Buddha, dharma, and sangha; the essence of the tradition in which Buddhists take refuge.

tulku In the Tibetan tradition, a reincarnation of a prominent, highly evolved teacher.

upasaka Lay male Buddhist.

upasika Lay female Buddhist.

Vajrayana The Diamond Vehicle, the third vehicle or tradition of Buddhism that emerged from Mahayana.

Vesak (var. **Visakha**) A spring celebration commemorating the Buddha's birth, enlightenment, death, and passing into nirvana, the most important Buddhist holiday in Asia.

vihara Temple in the Sri Lankan Theravada tradition.

vinaya "discipline." The rules and regulations for monastic communal life.

vipassana A variety of "insight" meditation technique in the Theravada tradition.

wat Temple in the Thai Theravada tradition.

yana "vehicle" or "raft." Used in reference to the various traditions of teachings in Buddhism thought to carry one from samsara to nirvana.

zazen Sitting meditation in the Zen tradition.

Zen "dhyana" or state of deep mental absorption in the Japanese tradition; used to denote a major school of Mahayana Buddhism.

RESOURCES FOR THE
STUDY OF AMERICAN BUDDHISM

Selected Bibliography

This bibliography includes selected scholarly and secondary texts of interest to students of American Buddhism, but does not list all sources cited in the endnotes.

Badiner, Alan Hunt. *Dharma Gaia: A Harvest of Essays in Buddhism and Ecology* (Berkeley: Parallax Press, 1990). Excerpted essays on the relationship between Buddhism and environmentalism by Asian teachers, American social activists, and proponents of eclectic spiritual philosophy.

Bethel, Dayle M. *Makaguchi the Value Creator: Revolutionary Japanese Educator and Founder of Soka Gakkai* (1973; New York and Tokyo: Weatherhill, 1994). Study of the impact of Makaguchi's ideas on the origins and evolution of Soka Gakkai in Japan, with some attention to the life and work of Josei Toda and Daisaku Ikeda.

Buddhist Churches of America. *Buddhist Churches of America*. 2 vols. (Chicago: Nobart, 1974). Seventy-fifth anniversary publication chronicling the history of the BCA from 1899–1974.

Butterfield, Stephen T. *The Double Mirror: A Skeptical Journey in Buddhist Tantra* (Berkeley: North Atlantic Books, 1994). Memoir of events in the American Tibetan practice community circa 1970 to 1990 by a disaffected student of Chogyam Trungpa.

Coleman, Graham, ed. *Handbook of Tibetan Culture: A Guide to Tibetan Centres and Resources Throughout the World* (Boston: Shambhala Publications, 1994). Brief histories of Tibetan schools, biographies of leading teachers, and an extensive listing, with short notations, of Tibetan and Tibet-related religious and cultural organizations worldwide.

Dresser, Marianne, ed. *Buddhist Women on the Edge: Contemporary Perspectives from the Dharma Frontier* (Berkeley: North Atlantic Books, 1996). More than twenty-five essays written in a variety of styles, dealing with a cross-section of issues encountered by convert Buddhist women in the United States.

Eck, Diana L. and The Harvard Pluralism Project, eds. *On Common Ground: World Religions in America* CD-ROM (New York: Columbia University Press, 1997). Introduction to issues related to American religious pluralism and to a wide range of traditions including Buddhism, with brief accompanying texts, all in a multimedia CD-ROM format.

Ellwood, Robert S. *Alternative Altars: Unconventional and Eastern Spirituality in America* (Chicago: University of Chicago Press, 1979). Dated but useful interpretation in the context of the general interest in Buddhism in and around the 1960s.

Fields, Rick. *How the Swans Came to the Lake: A Narrative History of Buddhism in America*, 3rd rev. ed. (Boston and London: Shambhala International, 1992). Classic chronicle of the development of Buddhism in the United States, told from the perspective of 1960s-era converts.

———. *Taking Refuge in L.A.: Life in a Vietnamese Buddhist Temple* (New York: Aperture Foundation, 1987). Descriptive account with interview material related to daily life at Chua Vietnam, a major immigrant temple in Los Angeles, with photographs by Don Farber.

Furlong, Monica. *Zen Effects: The Life of Alan Watts* (Boston: Houghton Mifflin, 1986). Sympathetic but skeptical account of Watts's life and career, with particular attention to developments in the United States in the 1950s and '60s.

Goldberg, Natalie. *Long Quiet Highway: Waking up in America* (New York: Bantam, 1993). Memoir of years spent in and around San Francisco Zen Center, Minneapolis Zen Meditation Society, and the Santa Fe Buddhist scene, by a well-known convert community writer.

Hurst, Jane D. *Nichiren Shoshu Buddhism and the Soka Gakkai in America: The Ethos of a New Religious Movement* (New York: Garland, 1992). Sociological and historical look at the SGI movement on the eve of its break with Nichiren Shoshu.

Kashima, Tetsuden. *Buddhism in America: The Social Organization of an Ethnic Religious Institution* (Westport, Conn.: Greenwood Press, 1977). Sociological and historical study of the evolution of the Buddhist Churches of America since the late nineteenth century.

Kotler, Arnold, ed. *Engaged Buddhist Reader: Ten Years of Engaged Buddhist Publishing* (Berkeley: Parallax Press, 1996). More than forty excerpts from the writings of Asians and Americans on Buddhist social activism.

Layman, Emma McCloy. *Buddhism in America* (Chicago: Nelson Hall, 1976).

Early journalistic exploration of a wide range of Buddhist traditions in the United States.

Lopez, Donald S. *Prisoners of Shangri-La: Tibetan Buddhism and the West* (Chicago and London: University of Chicago Press, 1998). Discussion and interpretation of the way Tibet has been imaginatively perceived in the West and the impact of this romantic view on contemporary religious, academic, and political issues.

Metraux, Daniel. *The History and Theology of Soka Gakkai: A Japanese New Religion* (Lewiston, N.Y.: Edwin Mellen Press, 1988). In-depth treatment of Nichiren Shoshu and Soka Gakkai philosophy and practice.

Mitchell, Donald W. and James Wiseman, eds. *Gethsemani Encounter: A Dialogue on the Spiritual Life by Buddhist and Christian Monastics* (New York: Continuum, 1998). Papers and presentations, along with some descriptive material, from the Buddhist-Christian dialogue and encounter at Gethsemani monastery in June 1996.

Moore, Dinty W. *The Accidental Buddhist: Mindfulness, Enlightenment, and Sitting Still* (Chapel Hill, N.C.: Algonquin Books, 1997). Popular account of an American searching out Buddhism in the mid-1990s, with occasionally useful vignettes of selected centers.

Morreale, Don, ed. *The Complete Guide to Buddhist America* (Boston and London: Shambhala Publications, 1998). Guide to and descriptions of meditation centers, together with selected vignettes and articles on developments in American Buddhism, as seen from the perspective of the lay convert community.

Nordstrom, Louis, ed. *Namu Dai Bosa: A Transmission of Zen Buddhism to America* (New York: The Zen Studies Society, 1976). Selected texts, including historically useful memoirs, of leading figures in the Rinzai lineage associated with Eido Shimano of the Zen Studies Society.

Numrich, Paul David. *Old Wisdom in the New World: Americanization in Two Immigrant Theravada Buddhist Temples* (Knoxville: University of Tennessee Press, 1996). In-depth look at historical developments, ritual life, and social adaptation in Theravada temples in Los Angeles and Chicago.

Prebish, Charles S. *American Buddhism* (North Scituate, Mass.: Duxbury Press, 1979). Early exploration of American Buddhism as it emerged in the 1970s by an academically trained Buddhologist.

———. *Luminous Passage: The Practice and Study of Buddhism in America* (Berkeley: University of California Press, 1999). Survey of Buddhist communities with in-depth analysis of selected issues in the development of distinctly American forms of Buddhism.

Prebish, Charles S. and Kenneth K. Tanaka, eds. *The Faces of Buddhism in America* (Berkeley: University of California Press, 1998). Collection of essays by academics and practitioners on a range of convert and immigrant traditions.

Preston, David L. *The Social Organization of Zen Practice: Constructing Transcultural Reality* (Cambridge: Cambridge University Press, 1998). Sociological study of Zen Center of Los Angeles in the 1980s.

Prothero, Stephen. *The White Buddhist: The Asian Odyssey of Henry Steel Olcott* (Bloomington: Indiana University Press, 1996). Interpretation of the contributions of an American founder of Theosophy to modern Buddhism in south Asia.

Queen, Christopher, S. and Sallie B. King, eds. *Engaged Buddhism: Buddhist Liberation Movements in Asia* (Albany: State University Press of New York, 1996). Essays dealing with the history, institutional expression, and teachings of contemporary social activists and movements, some bearing closely on socially engaged Buddhism in the United States.

Rapaport, Al, ed. *Buddhism in America: The Official Record of the Landmark Conference on the Future of Meditative Practices in the West* (Boston: Tuttle, 1997). Record of and addresses from a gathering of prominent figures in convert Buddhism held in Boston in 1997.

Seager, Richard Hughes. *The World's Parliament of Religions: The East/West Encounter, Chicago, 1893* (Bloomington: Indiana University Press, 1995). Interpretation of one of the signal events in the history of American Buddhism in the nineteenth century.

Senzaki, Nyogen. *Like a Dream, Like a Fantasy: The Zen Writings and Translations of Nyogen Senzaki*, edited by Eido Shimano (Tokyo and New York: Japan Publications, 1978). Selected writings of one of the early Japanese Zen teachers in this country.

Shainberg, Lawrence. *Ambivalent Zen: A Memoir* (New York: Pantheon, 1995). Memoir reflecting events in the Zen world in New York circa 1970 to 1990.

Storlie, Erik Fraser. *Nothing on My Mind: Berkeley, LSD, Two Zen Masters, and a Life on the Dharma Trail* (Boston: Shambhala Publications, 1996). A 1960s-era memoir of events related to the flowering of Buddhism in the Bay area, the development of the San Francisco Zen Center, and the founding of the Minneapolis Zen Meditation Center under Dainin Katagiri Roshi.

Tamney, Joseph B. *American Society in the Buddhist Mirror* (New York and London: Garland, 1992). Sociological interpretation of four eras during which native-born Americans turned to Buddhism.

Tanaka, Kenneth K. *Ocean: An Introduction to Jodo Shinshu Buddhism in America* (Berkeley: Wisdom Ocean Publications, 1997). Exposition of philosophy and practice in the contemporary Buddhist Churches of America and other Jodo Shinshu groups by an academically trained historian of Asian Buddhism.

Tonkinson, Carole, ed. *Big Sky Mind: Buddhism and the Beat Generation* (New York: Riverhead, 1995). Anthology of Buddhist-related Beat poetry with historical and biographical introductions.

Tsomo, Karma Lekshe, ed. *Buddhism Through American Women's Eyes* (Ithaca: Snow Lion Press, 1995). Thirteen first-person accounts of life in the dharma by some of America's leading Buddhist woman.

———, ed. *Sakyadhita: Daughters of the Buddha* (Ithaca: Snow Lion Publications, 1988). Abridged speeches from the International Conference on Buddhist Nuns in Bodhgaya, India in 1987, including the remarks of a number of prominent American women.

Tuck, Donald. *Buddhist Churches of America: Jodo Shinshu* (Lewiston, N.Y.: Edwin Mellen Press, 1987). Interpretive account with particular attention to Protestantization.

Tweed, Thomas A. *The American Encounter With Buddhism, 1844–1912: Victorian Culture and the Limits of Dissent* (Bloomington: Indiana University Press, 1992). Analysis of the extent and quality of the Buddhist vogue in America in the nineteenth century.

Tweed, Thomas A. and Stephen Prothero, eds. *Asian Religions in America: A Documentary History* (New York and London: Oxford University Press, 1998). Anthology of material on Asian religions in the United States from the antebellum era to the present.

Tworkov, Helen. *Zen in America: Five Teachers and the Search for an American Buddhism* (New York: Kodansha International, 1989). In-depth examination of five prominent American Zen teachers—Robert Aitken, Jakusho Kwong, Bernard Glassman, Maurine Stuart, and Richard Baker.

Williams, Duncan Ryuken and Christopher S. Queen, eds. *American Buddhism: Methods and Findings in Recent Scholarship* (Surrey, U.K.: Curzon Press, 1998). Essays on contemporary developments in selected Asian and convert communities.

Selected Print and Online Journals, Magazines, and Newsletters
URLs are accurate as of May 26, 1999.

Buddhist-Christian Studies. Journal of the Buddhist-Christian Studies Society devoted to historical, philosophical, and theological issues. c/o David Chappell, Department of Religion, University of Hawaii at Manoa, 2530 Dole Street, Honolulu, HI 96822.

Cybersangha: the Buddhist Alternative Journal. Online back issues of articles treating controversial topics in American Buddhism to 1997.
http://www.santavihara.org/CyberSangha/

Fearless Mountain Newsletter. Information related to the Thai Forest tradition in northern California. Abhayagiri Buddhist Monastery, 16201 Tomki Road, Redwood Valley, CA 95470.
http://www.dharmanet.org/Abhayagiri/fmtn.html

Inquiring Mind. National journal of the vipassana meditation movement. P.O. Box 9999, North Berkeley Station, Berkeley, CA 95709.

Insight Magazine Online. Journal published by the Insight Meditation Society. http://www.dharma.org/insight.htm

Jinn, the Online Magazine of the Pacific News Service. Articles related to Asian and Asian-American issues.
http://www.pacificnews.org/jinn/stories/columns/pacific-pulse/950711-normal.html

Journal of Buddhist Ethics. Academic journal devoted to Buddhist ethics, but with attention to related topics. http://jbe.la.psu.edu/

Living Buddhism (formerly *Seikyo Times*). General readership publication of Soka Gakkai International-USA addressing issues in American society. Subscriptions Department, SGI-USA, 525 Wilshire Boulevard, Santa Monica, CA, 90401.

Mandala. News magazine of the Foundation for the Preservation of the Mahayana Tradition. FPMT International Office, P.O. Box 800, Soquel, CA 95073. http://www.fpmt.org/Mandala/

Mindfulness Bell. Journal of the Order of Interbeing and Thich Nhat Hanh's Community of Mindful Living. P.O. Box 7355, Berkeley, CA 94707.

Mountain Record. Quarterly published by Dharma Communications, affiliate of the Mountains and Rivers Order and Zen Mountain Monastery. P.O. Box 156 MR, South Plank Road, Mount Tremper, NY 12457.
http://www.zen-mtn.org/mr/journal.shtml

The Pacific World. Journal of the Institute for Buddhist Studies, primarily devoted to Shin Buddhism. 650 Castro Street, Suite 120–202, Mountain View, CA 94041.

Primary Point. Journal of the Kwan Um school of Zen. 99 Pound Road, Cumberland, RI 02864.
http://www.kwanumzen.com/pzc/pzc-body.shtml#archives

Sakyadhita Newsletter. Information on international issues and events related to Buddhist women. Sakyadhita: International Association of Buddhist Women, 400 Hobron Lane #2615, Honolulu, HI 96815.
http://www2.hawaii.edu/~tsomo/NewsLetters/newsindx.htm

Shambhala Sun. Buddhist-inspired bimonthly magazine historically associated with Shambhala International. 585 Barrington Street, Suite 300, Halifax, Nova Scotia, Canada B3J 1Z8. http://www.shambhalasun.com/

Tricycle: The Buddhist Review. Leading independent quarterly review of American Buddhism. 92 Vandam Street, New York, NY 10013.
http://www.tricycle.com/

Turning Wheel. Journal of the Buddhist Peace Fellowship devoted to national and international news and articles related to BPF and engaged Buddhism.

Buddhist Peace Fellowship National Office, Box 4650, Berkeley, CA 94704.
http://www.igc.apc.org/bpf/tw.html

Western Buddhist Review. Articles and papers with a focus on the tradition within
the Friends of the Western Buddhist Order. http://www.fwbo.org/wbr/

World Tribune. Soka Gakkai International weekly newspaper devoted to organizational and world news. Subscriptions Department, SGI-USA, 525 Wilshire
Boulevard, Santa Monica, CA 90401.

Videotapes

Videos include some titles devoted to Asian American political and social issues.
Distribution information has been included when available. Major dharma centers
offer a wide range of videos related to their teachers and traditions.

Blue Collar and Buddha. Produced by Taggart Siegel and Kati Johnston for
Filmmakers Library, 1989, 57 minutes. Obstacles faced by Laotian
Buddhists in establishing a community and temple in Rockford, Illinois
in the 1980s. National Asian American Telecommunications Association,
346 Ninth Street, 2nd Floor, San Francisco, CA 94103 (hereafter
NAATA).

Becoming the Buddha in L.A. Produced by WGBH Educational Foundation, 1993,
est. 57 minutes. Introduction to Buddhism in Los Angeles, with special
attention to convert, Cambodian Theravada, and Jodo Shinshu Buddhism.
The Pluralism Project at Harvard University, 25 Francis Avenue, 201
Vanserg Hall, Cambridge, MA 02138.

Cambodians in America: Rebuilding the Temple. 1992, 58 minutes. Cambodian
refugees work to establish their religious lives. WGBH Educational Fund,
Boston, MA.

Creating Enlightened Society. Produced by Kapala Recordings, 1997, 75 minutes.
Restored footage of Chogyam Trungpa teaching in Boston in 1982 from
Shambhala International's Vajradhatu archive. Kapala Recordings, 1084
Tower Road, Halifax, Nova Scotia, Canada B3H 2Y5.

Exploring the Mandala. By Pema Losang Chogyen, n.d., 10 minutes. Computer-
simulated three-dimensional mandala created by a monk from Namgyal
monastery and researchers at Cornell University's computer graphics program. Snow Lion Publications, P.O. Box 6483, Ithaca, NY 14851–6483.

Embodying Buddhism. Produced for Thinking Allowed, a series of KCSM-TV,
San Mateo, CA, n.d. Sylvia Boorstein on the Four Noble Truths and mind-
fulness meditation. Thinking Allowed, 2560 9th Street, Suite 123, Berkeley,
CA 94710.

Heart of Tibet. Produced by Martin Wassell and directed by David Cherniak,
1991, 60 minutes. The life and work of the Dalai Lama, with particular

attention to his 1989 United States tour. Mystic Fire Video, P.O. Box 422, New York, NY 10012–0008 (hereafter Mystic Fire).

Human Rights and Moral Practice. Directed by Robin Gathwait and Dan Griffin, n.d., 35 minutes. The Dalai Lama speaks on moral responses to contemporary issues at the University of California at Berkeley. Mystic Fire.

Maceo: Demon Drummer from East L.A. Directed and produced by John Esaki, 1993, 30-minute and 44-minute formats. A Chicano inspired by drumming in L.A. Buddhist temples is recruited by Ondekoza, a world-famous taiko troupe. NAATA.

Meeting at Tule Lake. Directed and produced by Scott T. Tsuchitani, 1994, 33 minutes. Seven internees recall their experiences at the Tule Lake camp. NAATA.

Memorial Video of the Life of Venerable Master Hua and the Cremation Ceremony. Produced by the Dharma Realm Buddhist Association, n.d., est. 60 minutes. The life, work, and death of the founder of DRBA as told by his followers. City of Ten Thousand Buddhas, P.O. Box 21, Talmage, CA 95481.

Now I Know You: A Tribute to Taizan Maezumi Roshi. Produced by Dharma Communications, 1997, 60 minutes. Maezumi Roshi, his death and funeral, and his successors in the White Plum Sangha. Dharma Communications, P.O. Box 156 DC, Mount Tremper, NY 12457.

Ossian. Produced by the Public Broadcasting Service, 1990, 30 minutes. Documentary about a four-year-old American boy recognized as a tulku, shot in a Nepal monastery, with attention to his daily life with his teacher, other monks, and his mother. Mystic Fire.

Oryoki: Formal Monastic Meal, Master Dogen's Instructions for a Miraculous Occasion. 1995. Instructional guide to oryoki, with dharma commentary by John Daido Loori. Dharma Communications, P.O. Box 156 DC, Mount Tremper, NY 12457.

Peace Is Every Step. Directed by Gaetano Kazuo Maida, n.d., 60 minutes. Thich Nhat Hanh's life and work from Plum Village to Washington, D.C. and his work with American veterans. Mystic Fire.

Reflections: Returning to Vietnam. Produced by KCSM-TV60, San Mateo, CA, 1992, 30 minutes. Vietnamese refugees reflect on exile twenty years after the fall of Saigon. NAATA.

Shadow Over Tibet: Stories in Exile. Produced by Rachel Lyon and Valerie Mrak, 1994, 57 minutes. Struggle of Tibetans in exile to preserve their culture, seen through the experiences of a refugee in Chicago and of the Dalai Lama. NAATA.

Sun Rising East: Zen Master Seung Sahn Gives Transmission. 1993, 34 minutes. Record of a dharma transmission made in 1992 and the twentieth-anniversary celebrations of the Kwan Um school. Primary Point Press, 99 Pound Road, Cumberland, RI 02864.

Tibet in Exile. Produced by Barbara Banks and Meg McLagan, n.d., 30 min. The plight of Tibet, focusing on exile communities in Nepal and India. The Video Project, 200 Estates Drive, Ben Lomond, CA 95005.

Timeless Wisdom: Being the Knowing. n.d., 60 minutes. Two western monastics, Thubten Chodron, an American Tibetan nun, and Ajahn Amaro of Abhayagiri Forest monastery, discuss aspects of Buddhist teachings in Seattle. Snow Lion Publications, P.O. Box 6483, Ithaca, NY 14851–6483.

Touching Peace. Directed by Gaetano Kazuo Maida, n.d., 90 minutes. Thich Nhat Hanh teaching before an audience of 3,500 in Berkeley, California. Mystic Fire.

Wataridori: Birds of Passage. Directed by Robert A. Nakamura and produced by Visual Communications, 1976, 37 minutes. Tribute to the Issei with attention to the internment camp experience. NAATA.

World Buddhism in North America: A Documentary. 1989, 120 minutes. Selected presentations and commentary on the Americanization of Buddhism from the Conference of World Buddhism in North America, Ann Arbor, MI, 1987. Zen Buddhist Temple, 1710 W. Cornelia, Chicago, IL 60657.

Zen Center: Portrait of an American Zen Center. Written and produced by Anne Cushman and directed by Lou Hawthorne, 1987, 53 minutes. Life in ZCLA in the mid-1980s, during a period of crisis.

Selected Internet Resources

There is a great deal of information about American Buddhism on the Internet, although Web resources overwhelmingly reflect the interests and concerns of convert Buddhists. The following are only a few of the many sites that can be accessed. URLs are accurate as of May 26, 1999.

Access to Insight. Texts and traditions in Theravada Buddhism, including modern material and directories of temples and centers.
   http://world.std.com/%7Emetta
Asian Classics Input Project. http://www.asianclassics.org
Asian Classics Institute. http://www.world-view.org/
Buddhist Association of the United States. http://www.baus.org/
Buddhist Peace Fellowship. http://www.igc.apc.org/bpf/
Buddhist Studies WWW Virtual Library: The Internet Guide to Buddhism and Buddhist Studies. Wide range of scholarly material, including some related to selected American centers, lineages, and teachers.
   http://www.ciolek.com/WWWVL-Buddhism.html

DharmaNet International. Gateways to a wide range of American centers, resources, and links. http://www.dharmanet.org/journals.html

Dharma Realm Buddhist Association. http://www.drba.org/

Dharma Ring Index. Descriptive index to 200-plus sites linked in the Dharma Ring. http://www.webring.org/cgi-bin/webring?ring=dharma&list

Hsi Lai Temple English Homepage. http://www.hsilai.org/english2/index-e.html

Insight Meditation Society. http://www.dharma.org/ims.htm

International Campaign for Tibet. http://www.savetibet.org/index.html

International Tibet Independence Movement (Rangzen). http://www.rangzen.com/

Jinn: The Online Magazine of the Pacific News Service.
http://www.pacificnews.org/jinn/stories/columns/pacific-pulse/950711-normal.html

Karma Triyana Dharmachakra. http://www.kagyu.org/

Kwan Um School of Zen. http://www.kwanumzen.com/

Links Pitaka World Directory. Shin Buddhist sites in the United States and Buddhist Churches of America.
http://www.ville-ge.ch/musinfo/ethg/ducor/dirshin.htm#usa

Nichiren Shoshu. Unofficial gateway to selected sites.
http://vanbc.wimsey.com/~glenz/nichsite.html

Quiet Mountain Tibetan Buddhist Resource Guide. Comprehensive index to Tibetan Buddhist centers in the United States, organized by major schools.
http://quietmountain.com/

Sakyadhita: The International Association of Buddhist Women.
http://www2.hawaii.edu/~tsomo/

San Francisco Zen Center. http://www.sfzc.com/index.html

Spirit Rock Meditation Center. http://www.spiritrock.org/

Shambhala International. http://www.shambhala.org/

Soka Gakkai International-USA. http://sgi-usa.org/

Tibetan Cultural Center. http://www.tibetancc.com/

White Plum Sangha. http://www.zen-mtn.org/zmm/white-plum.shtml

Women Active in Buddhism. http://members.tripod.com/~Lhamo/

Zen Center of Los Angeles. http://www.zencenter.org/

Zen Mountain Monastery/Mountains and Rivers Order. http://www.zen-mtn.org/

Zen Peacemaker Order.
http://www.peacemakercommunity.org/zpo/index.htm

Zen Studies Society. http://www.daibosatsu.org/

INDEX

Page numbers in *italics* indicate illustrations.